AIR FRYER COOKBOOK

400+ Delicious Simple and Healthy Recipes for Beginners

CLARISSA HEWITT

Sommario - Easy, Healthy Recipes for Beginners (Vol.1)+(Vol.2)

Introduction

We all know it, and you are here because you know it too; eating healthy is not only a fad choice but an entire change to your lifestyle and state of mind.

Each day you must strive to make good decisions and take baby steps towards your fitness goals. Slowly but surely, you seem to create healthy habits that stick. But in the world, we live in today, there is literally temptation around every corner. From the candy bowl at work to the restaurant menu to the fast food joint perfectly stationed on your commute home, it is hard to say no to such delicious enticements. So, how is one supposed to fortify themselves to stay on track?

We will tackle some of the best tips to assist you in achieving your fitness goals, whether you wish to shed some excess fat or are just wanting to look and feel a bit better, there is always a way to shield yourself against unhealthy temptations.

Eat before you go

It is difficult to make healthy decisions when your stomach is growling.

Make sure you eat before you head to work, to the store, or anywhere where you might be led to make a poor choice in food.

Or, take a healthy snack with you. If you are always letting yourself get to the point of "hangry-ness," you are blatantly setting yourself up to feast in the land of junk foods.

It is also important to eat consistent meals throughout the day to help you stay on track as well. Learn to cook in the comfort of your own home instead of wasting your hard-earned money on food that really doesn't suit you well.

Plan ahead

It is in your best interest to be prepared. Start each week by making yourself a meal plan. List what you need and make it a goal to stick as close as you can to this plan. This will help you to reduce the number of times you go to the store, which results in a decrease of impulsive buys.

Plan for dining out too! Many restaurants now post their entire menu online for customers to look at. Know what options they have available, which will make it easier to make healthier decisions.

Trick what triggers you

All of us have a version of kryptonite, those delicious but bad-for-you eats that leave us feeling helpless and unable to fight back.

Keep these sorts of temptations out of sight and out of mind, or better yet, out of your home and office altogether.

To stay the course of becoming a healthier version of yourself, you must learn the importance of making decisions when confronted with healthier alternatives to what you are triggered by to counteract them.

For example, if you are like me, ice cream is always a losing battle. Instead of heading to scoop some mint chocolate chip that is loaded with sugar and countless calories, opt to make a healthier version, such as Banana Ice Cream!

Investigate cravings

When you find yourself in a hankering for something unsavory for your body, take a moment to stop and ask yourself why you are craving a certain item. What is it that you are craving? There are many of us, myself included, that mix up our emotional cravings with food, and sadly, food will never fill this type of void.

If you are always falling for some sort of temptation, look inside yourself and consider what your energy is like and what you are feeling and thinking at that moment. People are more prone to unhealthy and overeating when they are stressed out, tired, anxious, bored, or trying to cope with an uncertain situation. Instead of using food to cope, evaluate your emotional status and see how you can resolve the negativity that is fueling your bad choice making when it comes to what you eat and what you crave.

Create a path to success

Make it a priority to keep up with a food journal. Track what you eat, how you feel when you eat items, what makes you crave certain things, etc. Often, simply jotting down a terrible choice of food can lead you to make much better decisions in the future.

You can also write out mantras in this journal as well. Make up a phrase you can easily remember that will help you to find the motivation to keep moving forward in a healthy pattern.

"I'm worth it."

"I am striving for ultimate health."

"I am in control of the choices I make."

Act on "give-ins" in moderation

It is perfectly fine to give in and succumb to our favorite junk foods that ultimately satisfy our taste buds on occasion. Make sure to write down your cravings in your food journal. I like to tell people to eat for fuel 90% of the time and eat for fun 10%!

Don't stop

Don't let an occasional slip-up detour you from sticking to your goal of becoming a healthier version of yourself. We are all human and make mistakes. Don't get all caught up in eating something unhealthy and ruin your day because of it. You have the control to turn that once unhealthy day into a very healthy one.

Let carbs fight for you

Anti-carb attitudes are wildly outdated. Research has shown how carbohydrates that are packed with resistant starches can help you to feel more satisfied and promote overall satiety. It takes energy to break down these starches and causes a decrease in insulin spikes compared to "bad carbs."

Believe it or not, carbs are essential to the weight loss game. If you eat more healthy carbs and avoid the processed ones, you are giving your body the energy source it needs and prefers, which provides you with the ultimate mental satisfaction you need to keep pushing forward.

Get grateful

When you are famished, and at home alone, it can be very tempting to grab that bag of mini donuts to nom on instead of picking a piece of fruit. Before you decide on s snack, take a moment to pause and appreciate.

Ponder over how hard it is to grow produce to eat, how much you enjoy the natural juiciness of biting into an orange, or walking to the farmers market. Can you say any of these things about that bag of mini donuts you were about to devour?

Gratitude is one of those off-key things that can ultimately help you in your weight loss and fitness journey. You are taking a second to find the foods that bring your nourishment, which is a lot harder to come by with processed eats. This helps in the decision process of making thoughtful choices.

Don't fear these foods

Despite what many people think and what you have read time after time, the following foods at great if you are striving for a finer waistline!

Cereal and milk: While there are many cereals out there that are packed with excess sugars with barely any nutritional value, there are many others that have 2 ½ grams of fiber per serving. Eat these types with 8 ounces of whole milk to feel satisfied in the morning. Opt for cereals that have 10 grams or less of sugar per serving. If you are hankering for additional sweetness, eat a piece of fruit!

Greek yogurt: Opt for whole-milk Greek yogurt, and you will get a healthy source of fat that satiates you! Eating high-fat dairy items can help in lowering the risk of becoming overweight by 8%.

Dried fruits: While many people think that dried fruit is as bad for you as gummy candies are, this is simply not true. While you should never overeat dried fruit, these are not packed with added sugars and is denser in calories than raw fruit. Loaded with vitamins and fiber, it can make a great snack in moderation.

White potatoes: Known for their high carbohydrate content, many people try their best to avoid white potatoes. But it isn't their carb content as much as it is the forms we eat them in. From potato chips to fries drizzled with butter, it is no wonder these below ground veggies have gotten a bad rap. Potatoes, when not covered in processed things, are packed with potassium, full of vitamins and are relatively low in calorie count. They are good carbs and increase overall satiety.

Don't force foods you hate on yourself

Do not feel bad if you are not with your friends and coworkers on hopping on the newest and latest diet fads. This certainly does not mean you are on the wrong track. If there are certain foods you do not like and appreciate, then don't force yourself to eat them.

This will only detour you from sticking to your health goals. It will leave you more unsatisfied than before, and you will feel less nourished.

What is an Air Fryer?

The air fryer is a relatively new kitchen appliance used to fry foods with a little oil. An air fryer is the direct counterpart of the traditional frying pan, oven, and multi-cooker. With an air fryer, you use hot air instead of frying oil to cook dishes. With an air fryer, you can bake, roast, grill, and fry. You only need to use a little oil for baking, frying, roasting, and grilling. The air fryer heats the air to a temperature of around 400 degrees Fahrenheit. The hot air constantly circulates through the pan, enabling you to cook dishes evenly all around. This cooks all sides equally and creates a crispy crust.

Function Keys

Button / Play/Pause Button

This Play/Pause button allows you to pause during the middle of the cooking so you can shake the air fryer basket or flip the food to ensure it cooks evenly.

-/+ Button /Minus/Plus Button

This button is used to change the time or temperature.

Keep Warm

This function keeps your food warm for 30 minutes.

Food Presets

This button gives you the ability to cook food without second-guessing. The time and temperature are already set, so new users find this setting useful.

Roast or Broil

You can roast or broil with this setting. When using a conventional oven, you need to brown the meat before roasting. You can skip this step when cooking with an air fryer.

Dehydrate

This setting cooks and dries food at a low temperature for a few hours. With this option, you can create your own beef jerky or dried fruit.

Features of Your Air Fryer

Portable: The cooking device is portable. The air fryer is designed to be easily transferred from your kitchen storage cabinet to the countertop or elsewhere

Automatic temperature control: You get perfectly cooked food every time with an air fryer.

Digital touch screen: You don't have to learn complicated cooking skills, simplicity is inbuilt with an air fryer. With a few taps on the touch panel's screen, you can cook a variety of foods.

Timer and buzzer: No need to worry about overcooking your food. The timer and buzzer will let you know when your food is cooked.

Benefits of an Air Fryer

Reduces fat content: One-reason air fryers are better than deep fryers is the fact that they help cut down on fat. When you deep-fry your meals, the fat content in your food is very high because it requires immersing your food in oil.

However, air fryers allow you to fry your food with little oil. This helps to reduce the fat content in your meal.

Helps you lose weight: Air fryers are really good for weight loss. Aside from lowering the fat content in your meal, air fryers also help you reduce your calorie intake. The air fryer requires very little oil to make your food crispy and crunchy, thereby reducing your calorie intake. When deep-frying food in oil, we add many calories, so one of the most attractive benefits of an air fryer is the reduction of these extra calories.

Lowers your consumption of harmful compounds: Deep fried foods contain a chemical called acrylamide content. This chemical is hardly ever present in air-fried meals.

Much healthier than deep-fried foods: If you desire to eat healthy meals, join the number of people who have made air-fryer meals their lifestyle.

Reduction in cooking time: With the programming of temperature and time, you can control the constant flow of hot air and accelerate the process of cooking food. It could save up to 40% of the time used in a regular frying process.

Reduction of energy expenditure: If you compare the energy consumption of the air fryer with that of a standard electric oven, you can see consumption varies by a reasonably high percentage. You can save more than 50% of electrical energy when using the fryer. For example, the air fryer consumes about 390Wh to fry a pound of potatoes, 45% less electricity than a conventional oven uses.

Saving money: You use less oil, and you need less energy when cooking with an air fryer. So you save money.

Easy to clean: The cleaning is easier with an air fryer. The container where the food is placed is removable, which makes it easy to wash and clean.

Saves space: You can save kitchen space when using an air fryer.

Air Fryer vs. Deep Fryer

Oil usage: Air fryers use less oil, this means using an air fryer costs you less. You need to use a lot more oil when deep-frying. Although you can reuse the oil, most health experts do not recommend it.

Healthy cooking: Fried foods such as air fried French fries contain up to 80% less fat in comparison to deep-fried French fries.

Cleaning: Compared to a deep fryer, cleaning an air fryer is easy. You need to clean the deep fryer and the oil vapor that settles on the kitchen walls and countertop.

Safety: An air fryer is safe to use. With a deep fryer, there is always a risk of accidents.

Multiple uses: You can only fry in a deep-fryer. On the other hand, you can cook in many different ways in an air fryer.

Air Fryer vs. Convection Oven

Less hazardous: An air fryer gives you a one-stop cooking solution. With ovens, you often must cook food in a pan for a few minutes to bring out the color and aromas before putting it in the oven.

Safe: You can open and close the air fryer without the risk of burning yourself. A traditional oven presents a risk of fire.

Time: You can cook faster in an air fryer.

Cleaning: Cleaning your air fryer is easy. On the other hand, cleaning an oven is time-consuming.

Frequently Asked Questions

Q: Can I cook different foods in the air fryer?

A: Yes, you can cook different foods in your air fryer. You can use it for cooking different types of foods like casseroles and even desserts.

Q: How much food can I put inside?

A: Different air fryers tend to have different capacities. To know how much food you can put in, look for the "max" mark and use it as a guide to filling the basket.

Q: Can I add ingredients during the cooking process?

A: Yes, you can. Just open the air fryer and add ingredients. There is no need to change the internal temperature as it will stabilize once you close the air fryer chamber.

Q: Can I put aluminum or baking paper at the bottom of the air fryer?

A: Yes, you can use both to line the base of the air fryer. However, make sure that you poke holes so that the hot air can pass through the material and allow the food to cook.

Q: Do I need to preheat?

A: Preheating the air fryer can reduce the cooking time. However, if you forgot to preheat, it is still okay. To preheat the air fryer, simply set it to the cooking temperature and set the timer for 5 minutes. Once the timer turns off, place your food in the basket and continue cooking.

Tips for the Perfect Air Fry

Find a place in your kitchen where it will always be easy to access the air fryer, to the point that you simply need to open the cooking container and add your ingredients.

Different recipes require different temperatures to ensure that the food is cooked properly. Follow the recipe as precisely as possible to ensure that your food tastes delicious.

Aluminum foil helps with cleaning and is often used to add even more gradual control to the cooking process for the ingredients.

Add a dash of water when cooking fatty foods. You will notice a small drawer at the bottom of your air fryer. This is where you can add a splash of water when you are cooking foods that are high in fat. If the fat becomes too hot and drips to the bottom for too long, it can sometimes start to smoke. Adding vegetables prevents smoke. But if you are only cooking meat, then it is a good idea to add water to prevent the unpleasant smoke from rising.

Do not overcrowd the air fryer's cooking basket with too many ingredients. Make sure that the ingredients are all at one level, especially if you are preparing meat.

Flip foods halfway through the cooking time if you want both sides of your food to have a crispy coating.

Do not worry about opening the air fryer mid-cycle. Unlike other cooking methods, the air fryer doesn't lose heat intensity if you open it in the middle of cooking. Once you close the top again, the device will go back to cooking temperature and continue to cook the food.

There is a basket at the bottom of the air fryer to collect grease. If you take out both the cooking basket and the bottom basket at the same time and you tip them over, the grease from the bottom will be transferred onto your plate along with food. So, remove the bottom basket before serving the food.

Clean the air fryer after every use. Leftover food particles can turn into mold, develop bacteria, and cause unpleasant after-effects. To avoid this, clean the air fryer after every use.

Once you clean the air fryer, assemble everything. The air fryer will dry itself within a few minutes.

Here are some of the cooking techniques that you can use with this appliance:

Fry: You can avoid oil when cooking, but a small amount adds crunch and flavor to your food.

Roast: You can produce high quality roasted food in the air fryer

Bake: You can bake bread, cookies, and pastries.

Grill: You can effectively grill your food, no mess.

To start cooking, you just need to spray the fryer basket with some cooking spray or put in a little cooking oil, add the ingredients, and adjust the temperature and time.

Step-By-Step Air Frying

Air fryers work on Rapid Air Technology. The cooking chamber of the air fryer emits heat from a heating element that is close to the food. The exhaust fan that is present above the cooking chamber aids in the necessary airflow from the underside. For cooking using an air fryer, here are some steps that you need to follow:

Prepare Fried Foods:

Place the air fryer on a level and heatproof kitchen top.

Prepare the foods.

Grease the basket with a little oil and add a bit more to the food to avoid sticking.

If the food is marinated, pat it dry lightly to prevent splattering and excess smoke.

Use aluminum foil for easy cleaning.

Before Cooking:

Preheat the air fryer for 3 minutes before cooking.

Avoid overcrowding and leave sufficient space for air circulation.

During Cooking time:

Add water into the air fryer drawer to prevent excessive smoke and heat

Shake the basket or flip the food for even cooking at the halfway mark.

After Cooking:

Remove the basket from the drawer before taking out the food.

The juices in the air fryer drawer can be used to make delicious marinades and sauces

Unplug, cool, and then clean both the basket and drawer after use

Troubleshooting

Food not cooking perfectly: Follow the recipe exactly. Check whether or not you have overcrowded the ingredients. This is the main reason why food might not cook evenly in an air fryer.

White smoke: White smoke is usually the result of grease, so make sure that you have added some water to the bottom drawer to prevent the grease from overheating.

Black smoke: Black smoke is usually due to burnt food. You need to clean the air fryer after every use. If you do not, then the remaining food particles are burned when you use the appliance again. Turn the machine off and cool it completely. Then check it for burned food.

The appliance won't stop: The fan of the air fryer operates at high speed and needs some time to stop. Do not worry, it will stop soon.

Cleaning Your Air Fryer

Unplug the appliance and let it cool down.

Wipe the outside with a damp cloth.

Wash the basket, tray, and pan with hot water and soap. You can also use a dishwasher to wash these parts.

Clean the inside of the air fryer with a damp cloth or sponge.

Clean any food that is stuck to the heating element.

Dry the parts and assemble the air fryer.

Tips:

Use damp cloths to remove stuck-on food. Do not use utensils to avoid scratching the non-stick coating.

If the stuck-on food has hardened onto the basket or pan, then soak them in hot soapy water before trying to remove them.

Safety Tips

Do not buy a cheap, low-quality air fryer.

Do not place it on an uneven surface.

Do not overcrowd the basket.

Do not leave the appliance unattended.

Read the air fryer manual before using it.

Clean the appliance after every use.

Do not wash the electrical components.

Use the right amount of oil. Your air fryer needs only a little oil, so do not use extra.

Grease the air fryer basket. It will prevent food from getting stuck and prevent potential burning and smoking.

Dry your hands before touching the air fryer.

Make sure accessories are air fryer safe.

Shake the basket or flip the food during the middle of the cooking to ensure even cooking.

If your air fryer needs repairing, seek professional support.

Breakfast Recipes

1. Fluffy Cheesy Omelet

Preparation Time: 10 minutes
Cooking time: 15 minutes
Servings: 2
Ingredients:
4 eggs
1 large onion, sliced
1/8 cup cheddar cheese, grated
1/8 cup mozzarella cheese, grated
Cooking spray
¼ teaspoon soy sauce
Freshly ground black pepper, to taste
Directions:
Preheat the Air fryer to 360 o F and grease a pan with cooking spray.
Whisk together eggs, soy sauce and black pepper in a bowl.
Place onions in the pan and cook for about 10 minutes.
Pour the egg mixture over onion slices and top evenly with cheese.
Cook for about 5 more minutes and serve.
Nutrition:
Calories: 216, Fat: 13.8g, Carbohydrates: 7.9g, Sugar: 3.9g, Protein: 15.5g,
Sodium: 251mg

2. Crust-Less Quiche

Preparation Time: 5 minutes
Cooking time: 30 minutes
Servings: 2
Ingredients:
4 eggs
¼ cup onion, chopped
½ cup tomatoes, chopped
½ cup milk
1 cup Gouda cheese, shredded
Salt, to taste
Directions:
Preheat the Air fryer to 340 o F and grease 2 ramekins lightly.
Mix together all the ingredients in a ramekin until well combined.
Place in the Air fryer and cook for about 30 minutes.
Dish out and serve.
Nutrition:

Calories: 348, Fat: 23.8g, Carbohydrates: 7.9g, Sugar: 6.3g, Protein: 26.1g, Sodium: 642mg

3. Milky Scrambled Eggs

Preparation Time: 10 minutes
Cooking time: 9 minutes
Servings: 2
Ingredients:
¾ cup milk
4 eggs
8 grape tomatoes, halved
½ cup Parmesan cheese, grated
1 tablespoon butter
Salt and black pepper, to taste
Directions:
Preheat the Air fryer to 360 o F and grease an Air fryer pan with butter.
Whisk together eggs with milk, salt and black pepper in a bowl.
Transfer the egg mixture into the prepared pan and place in the Air fryer.
Cook for about 6 minutes and stir in the grape tomatoes and cheese.
Cook for about 3 minutes and serve warm.
Nutrition:
Calories: 351, Fat: 22g, Carbohydrates: 25.2g, Sugar: 17.7g, Protein: 26.4g, Sodium: 422mg

4. Toasties and Sausage in Egg Pond

Preparation Time: 10 minutes
Cooking time: 22 minutes
Servings: 2
Ingredients:
3 eggs
2 cooked sausages, sliced
1 bread slice, cut into sticks
1/8 cup mozzarella cheese, grated
1/8 cup Parmesan cheese, grated
¼ cup cream
Directions:
Preheat the Air fryer to 365 o F and grease 2 ramekins lightly.
Whisk together eggs with cream in a bowl and place in the ramekins.
Stir in the bread and sausage slices in the egg mixture and top with cheese.
Transfer the ramekins in the Air fryer basket and cook for about 22 minutes.
Dish out and serve warm.
Nutrition:

Calories: 261, Fat: 18.8g, Carbohydrates: 4.2g, Sugar: 1.3g, Protein: 18.3g, Sodium: 428mg

5. Banana Bread

Preparation Time: 10 minutes
Cooking time: 20 minutes
Servings: 8
Ingredients:
1 1/3 cups flour
1 teaspoon baking soda
1 teaspoon baking powder
½ cup milk
3 bananas, peeled and sliced
2/3 cup sugar
1 teaspoon ground cinnamon
1 teaspoon salt
½ cup olive oil
Directions:
Preheat the Air fryer to 330 o F and grease a loaf pan.
Mix together all the dry ingredients with the wet ingredients to form a dough.
Place the dough into the prepared loaf pan and transfer into an air fryer basket.
Cook for about 20 minutes and remove from air fryer.
Cut the bread into desired size slices and serve warm.
Nutrition:
Calories: 295, Fat: 13.3g, Carbohydrates: 44g, Sugar: 22.8g, Protein: 3.1g, Sodium: 458mg

6. Flavorful Bacon Cups

Preparation Time: 10 minutes
Cooking time: 15 minutes
Servings: 6
Ingredients:
6 bacon slices
6 bread slices
1 scallion, chopped
3 tablespoons green bell pepper, seeded and chopped
6 eggs
2 tablespoons low-fat mayonnaise
Directions:
Preheat the Air fryer to 375 o F and grease 6 cups muffin tin with cooking spray.
Place each bacon slice in a prepared muffin cup.
Cut the bread slices with round cookie cutter and place over the bacon slices.

Top with bell pepper, scallion and mayonnaise evenly and crack 1 egg in each muffin cup.

Place in the Air fryer and cook for about 15 minutes.

Dish out and serve warm.

Nutrition:

Calories: 260, Fat: 18g, Carbohydrates: 6.9g, Sugar: 1.03g, Protein: 16.7g, Sodium: 805mg

7. Crispy Potato Rosti

Preparation Time: 10 minutes

Cooking time: 15 minutes

Servings: 2

Ingredients:

½ pound russet potatoes, peeled and grated roughly

1 tablespoon chives, chopped finely

2 tablespoons shallots, minced

1/8 cup cheddar cheese

3.5 ounces smoked salmon, cut into slices

2 tablespoons sour cream

1 tablespoon olive oil

Salt and black pepper, to taste

Directions:

Preheat the Air fryer to 365 o F and grease a pizza pan with the olive oil.

Mix together potatoes, shallots, chives, cheese, salt and black pepper in a large bowl until well combined.

Transfer the potato mixture into the prepared pizza pan and place in the Air fryer basket.

Cook for about 15 minutes and dish out in a platter.

Cut the potato rosti into wedges and top with smoked salmon slices and sour cream to serve.

Nutrition:

Calories: 327, Fat: 20.2g, Carbohydrates: 23.3g, Sugar: 2.8g, Protein: 15.3g, Sodium: 316mg

8. Stylish Ham Omelet

Preparation Time: 10 minutes

Cooking time: 30 minutes

Servings: 2

Ingredients:

4 small tomatoes, chopped

4 eggs

2 ham slices

1 onion, chopped

2 tablespoons cheddar cheese

Salt and black pepper, to taste

Directions:

Preheat the Air fryer to 390 o F and grease an Air fryer pan.

Place the tomatoes in the Air fryer pan and cook for about 10 minutes.

Heat a nonstick skillet on medium heat and add onion and ham.

Stir fry for about 5 minutes and transfer into the Air fryer pan.

Whisk together eggs, salt and black pepper in a bowl and pour in the Air fryer pan.

Set the Air fryer to 335 o F and cook for about 15 minutes.

Dish out and serve warm.

Nutrition:

Calories: 255, Fat: 13.9g, Carbohydrates: 14.1g, Sugar: 7.8g, Protein: 19.7g, Sodium: 543mg

9. Healthy Tofu Omelet

Preparation Time: 10 minutes

Cooking time: 29 minutes

Servings: 2

Ingredients:

¼ of onion, chopped

12-ounce silken tofu, pressed and sliced

3 eggs, beaten

1 tablespoon chives, chopped

1 garlic clove, minced

2 teaspoons olive oil

Salt and black pepper, to taste

Directions:

Preheat the Air fryer to 355 o F and grease an Air fryer pan with olive oil.

Add onion and garlic to the greased pan and cook for about 4 minutes.

Add tofu, mushrooms and chives and season with salt and black pepper.

Beat the eggs and pour over the tofu mixture.

Cook for about 25 minutes, poking the eggs twice in between.

Dish out and serve warm.

Nutrition:

Calories: 248, Fat: 15.9g, Carbohydrates: 6.5g, Sugar: 3.3g, Protein: 20.4g, Sodium: 155mg

10. Peanut Butter Banana Bread

Preparation Time: 15 minutes

Cooking time: 40 minutes

Servings: 6

Ingredients:

1 cup plus 1 tablespoon all-purpose flour
1¼ teaspoons baking powder
1 large egg
2 medium ripe bananas, peeled and mashed
¾ cup walnuts, roughly chopped
¼ teaspoon salt
1/3 cup granulated sugar
¼ cup canola oil
2 tablespoons creamy peanut butter
2 tablespoons sour cream
1 teaspoon vanilla extract
Directions:
Preheat the Air fryer to 330 o F and grease a non-stick baking dish.
Mix together the flour, baking powder and salt in a bowl.
Whisk together egg with sugar, canola oil, sour cream, peanut butter and vanilla extract in a bowl.
Stir in the bananas and beat until well combined.
Now, add the flour mixture and fold in the walnuts gently.
Mix until combined and transfer the mixture evenly into the prepared baking dish.
Arrange the baking dish in an Air fryer basket and cook for about 40 minutes.
Remove from the Air fryer and place onto a wire rack to cool.
Cut the bread into desired size slices and serve.
Nutrition:
Calories: 384, Fat: 2.6g, Carbohydrates: 39.3g, Sugar: 16.6g, Protein: 8.9g, Sodium: 189mg

11. Yummy Savory French Toasts

Preparation Time: 10 minutes
Cooking time: 4 minutes
Servings: 2
Ingredients:
¼ cup chickpea flour
3 tablespoons onion, chopped finely
2 teaspoons green chili, seeded and chopped finely
Water, as required
4 bread slices
½ teaspoon red chili powder
¼ teaspoon ground turmeric
¼ teaspoon ground cumin
Salt, to taste
Directions:
Preheat the Air fryer to 375 o F and line an Air fryer pan with a foil paper.

Mix together all the ingredients in a large bowl except the bread slices.
Spread the mixture over both sides of the bread slices and transfer into the Air fryer pan.
Cook for about 4 minutes and remove from the Air fryer to serve.
Nutrition:
Calories: 151, Fat: 2.3g, Carbohydrates: 26.7g, Sugar: 4.3g, Protein: 6.5g, Sodium: 234mg

12. Aromatic Potato Hash

Preparation Time: 10 minutes
Cooking time: 42 minutes
Servings: 4
Ingredients:
2 teaspoons butter, melted
1 medium onion, chopped
½ of green bell pepper, seeded and chopped
1½ pound russet potatoes, peeled and cubed
5 eggs, beaten
½ teaspoon dried thyme, crushed
½ teaspoon dried savory, crushed
Salt and black pepper, to taste
Directions:
Preheat the Air fryer to 390 o F and grease an Air fryer pan with melted butter.
Put onion and bell pepper in the Air fryer pan and cook for about 5 minutes.
Add the potatoes, thyme, savory, salt and black pepper and cook for about 30 minutes.
Meanwhile, heat a greased skillet on medium heat and stir in the beaten eggs.
Cook for about 1 minute on each side and remove from the skillet.
Cut it into small pieces and transfer the egg pieces into the Air fryer pan.
Cook for about 5 more minutes and serve warm.
Nutrition:
Calories: 229, Fat: 7.6g, Carbohydrates: 30.8g, Sugar: 4.2g, Protein: 10.3g, Sodium: 103mg

13. Pumpkin and Yogurt Bread

Preparation Time: 10 minutes
Cooking time: 15 minutes
Servings: 4
Ingredients:
2 large eggs
8 tablespoons pumpkin puree
6 tablespoons banana flour
4 tablespoons plain Greek yogurt

6 tablespoons oats
4 tablespoons honey
2 tablespoons vanilla essence
Pinch of ground nutmeg
Directions:
Preheat the Air fryer to 360 o F and grease a loaf pan.
Mix together all the ingredients except oats in a bowl and beat with the hand mixer until smooth.
Add oats and mix until well combined.
Transfer the mixture into the prepared loaf pan and place in the Air fryer.
Cook for about 15 minutes and remove from the Air fryer.
Place onto a wire rack to cool and cut the bread into desired size slices to serve.
Nutrition:
Calories: 212, Fat: 3.4g, Carbohydrates: 36g, Sugar: 20.5g, Protein: 6.6g, Sodium: 49mg

14. Zucchini Fritters

Preparation Time: 15 minutes
Cooking time: 7 minutes
Servings: 4
Ingredients:
10½ ounces zucchini, grated and squeezed
7 ounces Halloumi cheese
¼ cup all-purpose flour
2 eggs
1 teaspoon fresh dill, minced
Salt and black pepper, to taste
Directions:
Preheat the Air fryer to 360 o F and grease a baking dish.
Mix together all the ingredients in a large bowl.
Make small fritters from this mixture and place them on the prepared baking dish.
Transfer the dish in the Air Fryer basket and cook for about 7 minutes.
Dish out and serve warm.
Nutrition:
Calories: 250, Fat: 17.2g, Carbohydrates: 10g, Sugar: 2.7g, Protein: 15.2g, Sodium: 330mg

15. Chicken Omelet

Preparation Time: 15 minutes
Cooking time: 16 minutes
Servings: 8

Ingredients:
1 teaspoon butter
1 onion, chopped
½ jalapeño pepper, seeded and chopped
3 eggs
¼ cup chicken, cooked and shredded
Salt and black pepper, to taste
Directions:
Preheat the Air fryer to 355 o F and grease an Air Fryer pan.
Heat butter in a frying pan over medium heat and add onions.
Sauté for about 5 minutes and add jalapeño pepper.
Sauté for about 1 minute and stir in the chicken.
Remove from the heat and keep aside.
Meanwhile, whisk together the eggs, salt, and black pepper in a bowl.
Place the chicken mixture into the prepared pan and top with the egg mixture.
Cook for about 10 minutes until completely done and serve hot.
Nutrition:
Calories: 161, Fat: 3.4g, Carbohydrates: 5.9g, Sugar: 3g, Protein: 14.1g, Sodium: 197mg
Breakfast Egg Bowls Preparation time: 10 minutes
Cooking time: 20 minutes
Servings: 4
Ingredients:
4 dinner rolls, tops cut off and insides scooped out
4 tablespoons heavy cream
4 eggs
4 tablespoons mixed chives and parsley
Salt and black pepper to the taste
4 tablespoons parmesan, grated
Directions:
Arrange dinner rolls on a baking sheet and crack an egg in each.
Divide heavy cream, mixed herbs in each roll and season with salt and pepper.
Sprinkle parmesan on top of your rolls, place them in your air fryer and cook at 350 degrees F for 20 minutes.
Divide your bread bowls on plates and serve for breakfast.
Enjoy! Nutrition: calories 238, fat 4, fiber 7, carbs 14, protein 7Delicious
Breakfast Soufflé Preparation time: 10 minutes
Cooking time: 8 minutes
Servings: 4Ingredients:
4 eggs, whisk
4 tablespoons heavy cream
A pinch of crushed red pepper
2 tablespoons parsley, chopped

2 tablespoons chives, minced

Salt and black pepper taste to taste

Directions:

In a cup, combine the eggs with the oil, the vinegar, the heavy cream, the chili pepper, the parsley and the chives, mix well and split into 4 soufflé bowls.

Organize the dishes in the air fryer and boil the soufflés at 350 degrees F to 8 minutes.

Serve when hot, Enjoy! Nutrition: calories 300, fat 7, fiber 9, carbs 15, protein 6Air Fried Sandwich Preparation time: 10 minutes

Cooking time: 6 minutes

Servings: 2

Ingredients:

2 English muffins, halved

2 eggs

2 bacon strips

Salt and black pepper to the tasteDirections:

Crack eggs in your air fryer, add bacon on top, cover and cook at 392 degrees F for 6 minutes.

Heat up your English muffin halves in your microwave for a few seconds, divide eggs on 2 halves, add bacon on top, season with salt and pepper, cover with the other 2 English muffins and serve for breakfast.

Enjoy! Nutrition: calories 261, fat 5, fiber 8, carbs 12, protein 4

16. Rustic Breakfast

Preparation time: 10 minutes

Cooking time: 13 minutes

Servings: 4Ingredients:

7 ounces baby spinach

8 chestnuts mushrooms, halved

8 tomatoes, halved

1 garlic clove, minced

4 chipolatas

4 bacon slices, chopped

Salt and black pepper to the taste

4 eggs

Cooking spray Directions:

Grease a cooking pan with the oil and add tomatoes, garlic and mushrooms.

Add bacon and chipolatas, also add spinach and crack eggs at the end.

Season with salt and pepper, place pan in the cooking basket of your air fryer and cook for 13 minutes at 350 degrees F.

Divide among plates and serve for breakfast.

Enjoy! Nutrition: calories 312, fat 6, fiber 8, carbs 15, protein 5

17. Egg Muffins

Preparation time: 10 minutes

Cooking time: 15 minutes

Servings: 4Ingredients:

1 egg

2 tablespoons olive oil

3 tablespoons milk

3.5 ounces white flour

1 tablespoon baking powder

2 ounces parmesan, grated

A splash of Worcestershire sauce Directions:

In a bowl, mix egg with flour, oil, baking powder, milk, Worcestershire and parmesan, whisk well and divide into 4 silicon muffin cups.

Arrange cups in your air fryer's cooking basket, cover and cook at 392, degrees F for 15 minutes.

Serve warm for breakfast.

Enjoy! Nutrition: calories 251, fat 6, fiber 8, carbs 9, protein 3

Lunch Recipes

18. Yogurt Garlic Chicken

Preparation Time: 30 min

Cooking time: 60 min

Servings: 6

Ingredients:

Pita bread rounds, halved (6 pieces)

English cucumber, sliced thinly, w/ each slice halved (1 cup)

Olive oil (3 tablespoons)

Black pepper, freshly ground (1/2 teaspoon)

Chicken thighs, skinless, boneless (20 ounces)

Bell pepper, red, sliced into half-inch portions (1 piece)

Garlic cloves, chopped finely (4 pieces)

Cumin, ground (1/2 teaspoon)

Red onion, medium, sliced into half-inch wedges (1 piece)

Yogurt, plain, fat free (1/2 cup)

Lemon juice (2 tablespoons)

Salt (1 ½ teaspoons)

Red pepper flakes, crushed (1/2 teaspoon)

Allspice, ground (1/2 teaspoon)

Bell pepper, yellow, sliced into half-inch portions (1 piece)

Yogurt sauce

Olive oil (2 tablespoons)

Salt (1/4 teaspoon)

Parsley, flat leaf, chopped finely (1 tablespoon)

Yogurt, plain, fat free (1 cup)

Lemon juice, fresh (1 tablespoon)

Garlic clove, chopped finely (1 piece)

Directions:

Mix the yogurt (1/2 cup), garlic cloves (4 pieces), olive oil (1 tablespoon), salt (1 teaspoon), lemon juice (2 tablespoons), pepper (1/4 teaspoon), allspice, cumin, and pepper flakes. Stir in the chicken and coat well. Cover and marinate in the fridge for two hours.

Preheat the air fryer at 400 degrees Fahrenheit.

Grease a rimmed baking sheet (18x13-inch) with cooking spray.

Toss the bell peppers and onion with remaining olive oil (2 tablespoons), pepper (1/4 teaspoon), and salt (1/2 teaspoon).

Arrange veggies on the baking sheet's left side and the marinated chicken thighs (drain first) on the right side. Cook in the air fryer for twenty-five to thirty minutes.

Mix the yogurt sauce ingredients.

Slice air-fried chicken into half-inch strips.

Top each pita round with chicken strips, roasted veggies, cucumbers, and yogurt sauce.

Nutrition: Calories 380 Fat 15.0 g Protein 26.0 g Carbohydrates 34.0 g

19. Lemony Parmesan Salmon

Preparation Time: 10 min

Cooking time: 25 min

Servings: 4

Ingredients:

Butter, melted (2 tablespoons)

Green onions, sliced thinly (2 tablespoons)

Breadcrumbs, white, fresh (3/4 cup)

Thyme leaves, dried (1/4 teaspoon)

Salmon fillet, 1 ¼-pound (1 piece)

Salt (1/4 teaspoon)

Parmesan cheese, grated (1/4 cup)

Lemon peel, grated (2 teaspoons)

Directions:

Preheat the air fryer at 350 degrees Fahrenheit.

Mist cooking spray onto a baking pan (shallow). Fill with pat-dried salmon.

Brush salmon with butter (1 tablespoon) before sprinkling with salt.

Combine the breadcrumbs with onions, thyme, lemon peel, cheese, and remaining butter (1 tablespoon).

Cover salmon with the breadcrumb mixture. Air-fry for fifteen to twenty-five minutes.

Nutrition: Calories 290 Fat 16.0 g Protein 33.0 g Carbohydrates 4.0 g

20. Easiest Tuna Cobbler Ever

Preparation time: 15 min Cooking time: 25 min

Servings: 4

Ingredients:

Water, cold (1/3 cup)

Tuna, canned, drained (10 ounces)

Sweet pickle relish (2 tablespoons)

Mixed vegetables, frozen (1 ½ cups)

Soup, cream of chicken, condensed (10 ¾ ounces)

Pimientos, sliced, drained (2 ounces)

Lemon juice (1 teaspoon)

Paprika

Directions:

Preheat the air fryer at 375 degrees Fahrenheit.

Mist cooking spray into a round casserole (1 ½ quarts).

Mix the frozen vegetables with milk, soup, lemon juice, relish, pimientos, and tuna in a saucepan. Cook for six to eight minutes over medium heat.

Fill the casserole with the tuna mixture.

Mix the biscuit mix with cold water to form a soft dough. Beat for half a minute before dropping by four spoonfuls into the casserole.

Dust the dish with paprika before air-frying for twenty to twenty-five minutes.

Nutrition: Calories 320 Fat 11.0 g Protein 28.0 g Carbohydrates 31.0 g

21. Deliciously Homemade Pork Buns

Preparation time: 20 min

Cooking time: 25 min

Servings: 8

Ingredients:

Green onions, sliced thinly (3 pieces)

Egg, beaten (1 piece)

Pulled pork, diced, w/ barbecue sauce (1 cup)

Buttermilk biscuits, refrigerated (16 1/3 ounces)

Soy sauce (1 teaspoon)

Directions:

Preheat the air fryer at 325 degrees Fahrenheit.

Use parchment paper to line your baking sheet.

Combine pork with green onions.

Separate and press the dough to form 8 four-inch rounds.

Fill each biscuit round's center with two tablespoons of pork mixture. Cover with the dough edges and seal by pinching. Arrange the buns on the sheet and brush with a mixture of soy sauce and egg.

Cook in the air fryer for twenty to twenty-five minutes.

Nutrition: Calories 240 Fat 9.0 g Protein 8.0 g Carbohydrates 29.0 g

22. Mouthwatering Tuna Melts

Preparation time: 15 min

Cooking time: 20 min

Servings: 8

Ingredients:

Salt (1/8 teaspoon)

Onion, chopped (1/3 cup)

Biscuits, refrigerated, flaky layers (16 1/3 ounces)

Tuna, water packed, drained (10 ounces)

Mayonnaise (1/3 cup)

Pepper (1/8 teaspoon)

Cheddar cheese, shredded (4 ounces)

Tomato, chopped

Sour cream

Lettuce, shredded

Directions:

Preheat the air fryer at 325 degrees Fahrenheit.

Mist cooking spray onto a cookie sheet.

Mix tuna with mayonnaise, pepper, salt, and onion.

Separate dough so you have 8 biscuits; press each into 5-inch rounds.

Arrange 4 biscuit rounds on the sheet. Fill at the center with tuna mixture before topping with cheese. Cover with the remaining biscuit rounds and press to seal.

Air-fry for fifteen to twenty minutes. Slice each sandwich into halves. Serve each piece topped with lettuce, tomato, and sour cream.

23. Nutrition: Calories 320 Fat 18.0 g Protein 14.0 g Carbohydrates 27.0 g Bacon Wings

Preparation time: 15 min

Cooking time: 1 hr 15 min

Servings: 12

Ingredients:

Bacon strips (12 pieces)

Paprika (1 teaspoon)

Black pepper (1 tablespoon)

Oregano (1 teaspoon)

Chicken wings (12 pieces)

Kosher salt (1 tablespoon)

Brown sugar (1 tablespoon)

Chili powder (1 teaspoon)

Celery sticks

Blue cheese dressing

Directions:

Preheat the air fryer at 325 degrees Fahrenheit.

Mix sugar, salt, chili powder, oregano, pepper, and paprika. Coat chicken wings with this dry rub.

Wrap a bacon strip around each wing. Arrange wrapped wings in the air fryer basket.

Cook for thirty minutes on each side in the air fryer. Let cool for five minutes. Serve and enjoy with celery and blue cheese.

Nutrition: Calories 100 Fat 5.0 g Protein 10.0 g Carbohydrates 2.0 g

24. Pepper Pesto Lamb

Preparation time: 15 min

Cooking time: 1 hr 15 min

Servings: 12

Ingredients:

Pesto

Rosemary leaves, fresh (1/4 cup)
Garlic cloves (3 pieces)
Parsley, fresh, packed firmly (3/4 cup)
Mint leaves, fresh (1/4 cup)
Olive oil (2 tablespoons)
Lamb
Red bell peppers, roasted, drained (7 ½ ounces)
Leg of lamb, boneless, rolled (5 pounds)
Seasoning, lemon pepper (2 teaspoons)
Directions:
Preheat the oven at 325 degrees Fahrenheit.
Mix the pesto ingredients in the food processor.
Unroll the lamb and cover the cut side with pesto. Top with roasted peppers before rolling up the lamb and tying with kitchen twine.
Coat lamb with seasoning (lemon pepper) and air-fry for one hour.
Nutrition: Calories 310 Fat 15.0 g Protein 40.0 g Carbohydrates 1.0 g

25. Tuna Spinach Casserole

Preparation time: 30 min
Cooking time: 25 min
Servings: 8
Ingredients:
Mushroom soup, creamy (18 ounces)
Milk (1/2 cup)
White tuna, solid, in-water, drained (12 ounces)
Crescent dinner rolls, refrigerated (8 ounces)
Egg noodles, wide, uncooked (8 ounces)
Cheddar cheese, shredded (8 ounces)
Spinach, chopped, frozen, thawed, drained (9 ounces)
Lemon peel grated (2 teaspoons)
Directions:
Preheat the oven at 350 degrees Fahrenheit.
Mist cooking spray onto a glass baking dish (11x7-inch).
Follow package directions in cooking and draining the noodles.
Stir the cheese (1 ½ cups) and soup together in a skillet heated on medium. Once cheese melts, stir in your noodles, milk, spinach, tuna, and lemon peel. Once bubbling, pour into the prepped dish.
Unroll the dough and sprinkle with remaining cheese (1/2 cup). Roll up dough and pinch at the seams to seal. Slice into 8 portions and place over the tuna mixture.
Air-fry for twenty to twenty-five minutes.
Nutrition: Calories 400 Fat 19.0 g Protein 21.0 g Carbohydrates 35.0 g

26. Greek Style Mini Burger Pies

Preparation time: 15 min

Cooking time: 40 min

Servings: 6

Ingredients:

Burger mixture:

Onion, large, chopped (1 piece)

Red bell peppers, roasted, diced (1/2 cup)

Ground lamb, 80% lean (1 pound)

Red pepper flakes (1/4 teaspoon)

Feta cheese, crumbled (2 ounces)

Baking mixture

Milk (1/2 cup)

Biscuit mix, classic (1/2 cup)

Eggs (2 pieces)

Directions:

Preheat the air fryer at 350 degrees Fahrenheit.

Grease 12 muffin cups using cooking spray.

Cook the onion and beef in a skillet heated on medium-high. Once beef is browned and cooked through, drain and let cool for five minutes. Stir together with feta cheese, roasted red peppers, and red pepper flakes.

Whisk the baking mixture ingredients together. Fill each muffin cup with baking mixture (1 tablespoon).

Air-fry for twenty-five to thirty minutes. Let cool before serving.

Nutrition: Calories 270 Fat 15.0 g Protein 19.0 g Carbohydrates 13.0 g

27. Family Fun Pizza

Preparation time: 30 min

Cooking time: 25 min

Servings: 16

Ingredients:

Pizza crust

Water, warm (1 cup)

Salt (1/2 teaspoon)

Flour, whole wheat (1 cup)

Olive oil (2 tablespoons)

Dry yeast, quick active (1 package)

Flour, all purpose (1 ½ cups)

Cornmeal

Olive oil

Filling:

Onion, chopped (1 cup)

Mushrooms, sliced, drained (4 ounces)

Garlic cloves, chopped finely (2 pieces)
Parmesan cheese, grated (1/4 cup)
Ground lamb, 80% lean (1 pound)
Italian seasoning (1 teaspoon)
Pizza sauce (8 ounces)
Mozzarella cheese, shredded (2 cups)
Directions:
Mix yeast with warm water. Combine with flours, oil (2 tablespoons), and salt by stirring and then beating vigorously for half a minute. Let the dough sit for twenty minutes.
Preheat the air fryer at 350 degrees Fahrenheit.
Prep 2 square pans (8-inch) by greasing with oil before sprinkling with cornmeal.
Cut the rested dough in half; place each half inside each pan. Set aside, covered, for thirty to forty-five minutes. Cook in the air fryer for twenty to twenty-two minutes.
Sauté the onion, beef, garlic, and Italian seasoning until beef is completely cooked. Drain and set aside.
Cover the air-fried crusts with pizza sauce before topping with beef mixture, cheeses, and mushrooms.
Return to the air fryer and cook for twenty minutes.
Nutrition: Calories 215 Fat 10.0 g Protein 13.0 g Carbohydrates 20.0 g

28. Tso's Cauliflower

Preparation Time: 5 minutes
Cooking Time: 25 minutes
Servings: 2
Ingredients:
1 head cauliflower, cut in florets
¾ cup all-purpose flour, divided
3 eggs
1 cup panko breadcrumbs
Tso sauce
Canola or peanut oil
2 tbsp oyster sauce
¼ cup soy sauce
2 tsp chili paste
2 tbsp rice wine vinegar
2 tbsp sugar
¼ cup water
Directions:
Add cauliflower to a large bowl and sprinkle ¼ cup flour over it.

Whisk eggs in one bowl, spread panko crumbs in another, and put remaining flour in a third bowl.

Dredge the cauliflower florets through the flour then dip in the eggs.

Coat them with breadcrumbs.

Place the coated cauliflower florets in the air fryer basket and spray them with cooking oil.

Return the fryer basket to the air fryer and cook on air fry mode for 15 minutes at 400 degrees F.

Prepare the Tso sauce by mixing all its ingredients in a saucepan.

Stir and cook this mixture for 10 minutes until it thickens.

Pour this sauce over the air fried cauliflower florets.

Enjoy.

Nutrition:

Calories 301

Total Fat 12.2 g

Saturated Fat 2.4 g

Cholesterol 110 mg

Sodium 276 mg

Total Carbs 12.5 g

Fiber 0.9 g

Sugar 1.4 g

Protein 8.8 g

29. Crispy Hot Sauce Chicken

Preparation Time: 5 minutes

Cooking Time: 30 minutes

Total Time: 35 minutes

Servings: 4

Ingredients:

2 cups buttermilk

1 tbsp hot sauce

1 whole chicken, cut up

1 cup Kentucky Kernel flour

Oil for spraying

Directions:

Whisk hot sauce with buttermilk in a large bowl.

Add chicken pieces to the buttermilk mixture and marinate for 1 hour in the refrigerator.

Dredge the chicken through seasoned flour and shake off the excess.

Place the coated chicken in the air fryer basket and spray them with cooking oil.

Return the fryer basket to the air fryer and cook on air fry mode for 30 minutes at 380 degrees F.

Flip the chicken pieces once cooked half way through.

Enjoy right away.
Nutrition:
Calories 695
Total Fat 17.5 g
Saturated Fat 4.8 g
Cholesterol 283 mg
Sodium 355 mg
Total Carbs 6.4 g
Fiber 1.8 g
Sugar 0.8 g
Protein 117.4 g

30. Teriyaki Chicken Meatballs

Preparation Time: 5 minutes
Cooking Time: 10 minutes
Total Time: 15 minutes
Servings: 4
Ingredients:
For Chicken Meatballs
1 lb ground chicken
½ cup gluten-free oat flour
1 small onion, chopped
¾ tsp garlic powder
¾ tsp crushed chili flakes
1 tsp dried cilantro leaves
Salt, to taste
Scallions, for garnish
Sesame seeds, for garnish
For Spicy Teriyaki Sauce
¼ cup sweet and sour sauce
2 tbsp rice vinegar
2 tbsp soy sauce (light)
2 tbsp honey
½ tsp hot sauce (optional)
1 tsp crushed chili flakes
¾ tsp garlic powder
¾ tsp ginger powder
Directions:
Add the ingredients for the meatballs in a suitable bowl.
Mix well and knead the dough.
Make small meatballs out of this dough and place them in the air fryer basket.
Spray them with cooking oil.

Return the fryer basket to the air fryer and cook on air fry mode for 10 minutes at 350 degrees F.

Meanwhile, mix all the ingredients for the teriyaki sauce in a saucepan.

Stir and cook this sauce until it thickens,

Add the air fried balls to the sauce.

Garnish with scallions and sesame seeds.

Enjoy.

Nutrition:

Calories 401

Total Fat 8.9 g

Saturated Fat 4.5 g

Cholesterol 57 mg

Sodium 340 mg

Total Carbs 24.7 g

Fiber 1.2 g

Sugar 1.3 g

Protein 55.3 g

31. Orange Tofu

Preparation Time: 5 minutes

Cooking Time: 20 minutes

Total Time: 25 minutes

Servings: 2

Ingredients:

1 lb extra-firm tofu, drained and pressed

1 tbsp tamari

1 tbsp cornstarch

For Sauce:

1 tsp orange zest

1/3 cup orange juice

½ cup water

2 tsp cornstarch

¼ tsp crushed red pepper flakes

1 tsp fresh ginger, minced

1 tsp fresh garlic, minced

1 tbsp pure maple syrup

How to Prepare:

Dice the squeezed tofu into cubes then place them in a Ziploc bag.

Add tamari and 1 tablespoon of cornstarch to the tofu.

Seal the tofu bag and shake well to coat.

Spread this tofu in the air fryer basket and spray them with cooking oil.

Return the fryer basket to the air fryer and cook on air fry mode for 15 minutes at 350 degrees F.

Air fry the tofu cubes in two batches.
Mix all the ingredients for the sauce in a saucepan and stir cook until it thickens.
Toss in fried tofu and mix well.
Enjoy.
Nutrition:
Calories 427
Total Fat 31.1 g
Saturated Fat 4.2 g
Cholesterol 123 mg
Sodium 86 mg
Total Carbs 9 g
Sugar 12.4 g
Fiber 19.8 g
Protein 23.5 g

32. Madagascan Stew

Preparation Time: 5 minutes
Cooking Time: 19 minutes
Total Time: 24 minutes
Servings: 4

Ingredients:
7 oz baby new potatoes
1 tbsp oil
½ onion, finely diced
1 ¼ cups canned black beans, drained
1 ¼ cups canned kidney beans, drained
3 cloves garlic, minced
1 tbsp pureed ginger
2 large tomatoes, chopped
1 tbsp tomato puree
Salt
Black pepper
1 cup vegetable stock
½ tbsp cornstarch
1 tbsp water
1 large handful arugula
Cooked rice, to serve (optional)
Directions:
Cut the potatoes into quarters and toss them with cooking oil.
Place the potatoes in the air fryer basket.
Add onion to the basket and continue air frying for another 4 minutes.
Transfer them to a saucepan and place over medium heat.

Add garlic, ginger, beans, tomatoes, seasoning, vegetable stock, and tomato puree.

Mix cornstarch with water in a bowl and pour into the pan.

Simmer this mixture for 15 minutes.

Add arugula and cook for another 4 minutes.

Serve with rice.

Nutrition:

Calories 398

Total Fat 13.8 g

Saturated Fat 5.1 g

Cholesterol 200 mg

Sodium 272 mg

Total Carbs 53.6 g

Fiber 1 g

Sugar 1.3 g

Protein 11.8 g

33. Tofu Sushi Burrito

Preparation Time: 5 minutes

Cooking Time: 15 minutes

Total Time: 20 minutes

Servings: 2

Ingredients:

¼ block extra firm tofu, pressed and sliced

1 tbsp low-sodium soy sauce

¼ tsp ground ginger

¼ tsp garlic powder

Sriracha sauce, to taste

2 cups cooked sushi rice

2 sheets nori

Filling:

¼ avocado, sliced

3 tbsp mango, sliced

1 green onion, finely chopped

2 tbsp pickled ginger

2 tbsp panko breadcrumbs

Directions:

Whisk ginger, garlic, soy sauce, sriracha sauce, and tofu in a large bowl.

Let them marinate for 10 minutes then transfer them to the air fryer basket.

Return the fryer basket to the air fryer and cook on air fry mode for 15 minutes at 370 degrees F.

Toss the tofu cubes after 8 minutes then resume cooking.

Spread a nori sheet on a work surface and top it with a layer of sushi rice.

Place tofu and half of the other filling ingredients over the rice.
Roll the sheet tightly to secure the filling inside.
Repeat the same steps to make another sushi roll.
Enjoy.
Nutrition:
Calories 372
Total Fat 11.8 g
Saturated Fat 4.4 g
Cholesterol 62 mg
Sodium 871 mg
Total Carbs 45.8 g
Fiber 0.6 g
Sugar 27.3 g
Protein 34 g

34. Rosemary Brussels Sprouts

Preparation Time: 5 minutes
Cooking Time: 13 minutes
Total Time: 18 minutes
Servings: 2
Ingredients:
3 tbsp olive oil
2 garlic cloves, minced
½ tsp salt
¼ tsp pepper
1 lb Brussels sprouts, trimmed and halved
½ cup panko breadcrumbs
1 ½ tsp fresh rosemary, minced
Directions:
Let your air fryer preheat at 350 degrees F.
Mix oil, garlic, salt, and pepper in a bowl and heat for 30 seconds in the microwave.
Add 2 tablespoons of this mixture to the Brussel sprouts in a bowl and mix well to coat.
Spread the sprouts in the air fryer basket.
Return the fryer basket to the air fryer and cook on air fry mode for 5 minutes at 220 degrees F.
Toss the sprouts well and continue air frying for 8 minutes more.
Mix the remaining oil mixture with rosemary and breadcrumbs in a bowl.
Spread this mixture over the Brussel sprouts and return the basket to the fryer.
Air fry them for 5 minutes.
Enjoy.
Nutrition:

Calories 246
Total Fat 7.4 g
Saturated Fat 4.6 g
Cholesterol 105 mg
Sodium 353 mg
Total Carbs 9.4 g
Sugar 6.5 g
Fiber 2.7 g
Protein 37.2 g

35. Peach-Bourbon Wings

Preparation Time: 5 minutes
Cooking Time: 14 minutes
Total Time: 19 minutes
Servings: 8
Ingredients:
½ cup peach preserves
1 tbsp brown sugar
1 garlic cloves, minced
¼ tsp salt
2 tbsp white vinegar
2 tbsp bourbon
1 tsp cornstarch
1½ tsp water
2 lbs chicken wings
Directions:
Let your air fryer preheat at 400 degrees F.
Add salt, garlic, and brown sugar to a food processor and blend well until smooth.
Transfer this mixture to a saucepan and add bourbon, peach preserves, and vinegar.
Stir cook this mixture to a boil then reduce heat to a simmer.
Cook for 6 minutes until the mixture thickens.
Mix cornstarch with water and pour this mixture in the saucepan.
Stir cook for 2 minutes until it thickens. Keep ¼ cup of this sauce aside.
Place the wings in the air fryer basket and brush them with prepared sauce.
Return the fryer basket to the air fryer and cook on air fry mode for 6 minutes at 350 degrees F.
Flip the wings and brush them again with the sauce.
Air fry the wings for another 8 minutes.
Serve with reserved sauce.
Nutrition:
Calories 293

Total Fat 16 g
Saturated Fat 2.3 g
Cholesterol 75 mg
Sodium 386 mg
Total Carbs 5.2 g
Sugar 2.6 g
Fiber 1.9 g
Protein 34.2 g

36. Reuben Calzones

Preparation Time: 5 minutes
Cooking Time: 12 minutes
Total Time: 17 minutes
Servings: 4
Ingredients:
1 tube (13.8 ounces) refrigerated pizza crust
4 slices Swiss cheese
1 cup sauerkraut, rinsed and well drained
½ lb corned beef, sliced & cooked
Directions:
Let your air fryer preheat at 400 degrees F. Grease the air fryer basket with cooking oil.
Spread the pizza crust on a lightly floured surface into a 12-inch square.
Slice the crust into four smaller squares.
Place one slice of cheese, ¼ of the sauerkraut, and 1 slice corned beef over each square diagonally.
Fold the squares in half diagonally to form a triangle and pinch the edges together.
Place 2 triangles in the air fryer basket at a time and spray them with cooking oil.
Return the fryer basket to the air fryer and cook on air fry mode for 12 minutes at 350 degrees F.
Air fry the remaining calazone triangles.
Enjoy with fresh salad.
Nutrition:
Calories 604
Total Fat 30.6 g
Saturated Fat 13.1 g
Cholesterol 131 mg
Sodium 834 mg
Total Carbs 31.4 g
Fiber 0.2 g
Sugar 20.3 g

Protein 54.6 g

37. Mushroom Maple Rice

Preparation Time: 5 minutes
Cooking Time: 15 minutes
Total Time: 20 minutes
Servings: 4
Ingredients:
16 oz jasmine rice, cooked
½ cup soy sauce
4 tbsp maple syrup
4 cloves garlic, finely chopped
2 tsp Chinese five spice
½ tsp ground ginger
4 tbsp white wine
16 oz cremini mushrooms, cut in half
½ cup frozen peas
Directions:
Mix soy sauce with maple syrup, garlic, Chinese five spice, ginger, and white wine in a bowl.
Spread the mushrooms in the air fryer basket and spray them with cooking oil.
Return the fryer basket to the air fryer and cook on air fry mode for 10 minutes at 350 degrees F.
Add peas and prepared sauce over the mushrooms and mix well.
Return the fryer basket to the air fryer and cook on air fry mode for 5 minutes at 350 degrees F.
Mix the mushrooms with the rice in a pot.
Enjoy.
Nutrition:
Calories 311
Total Fat 25.5 g
Saturated Fat 12.4 g
Cholesterol 69 mg
Sodium 58 mg
Total Carbs 32.4 g
Fiber 0.7 g
Sugar 0.3 g
Protein 18.4 g

Poultry Recipes

Creamy Coconut Chicken Preparation time: 2 hours

Cooking time: 25 minutes

Servings: 4Ingredients:

4 big chicken legs

5 teaspoons turmeric powder

2 tablespoons ginger, grated

Salt and black pepper to the taste

4 tablespoons coconut cream Directions:

In a bowl, mix cream with turmeric, ginger, salt and pepper, whisk, add chicken pieces, toss them well and leave aside for 2 hours.

Transfer chicken to your preheated air fryer, cook at 370 degrees F for 25 minutes, divide among plates and serve with a side salad.

Enjoy! Nutrition: calories 300, fat 4, fiber 12, carbs 22, protein 20

Chinese Chicken Wings Preparation time: 2 hours

Cooking time: 15 minutes

Servings: 6Ingredients:

16 chicken wings

2 tablespoons honey

2 tablespoons soy sauce

Salt and black pepper to the taste

¼ teaspoon white pepper

3 tablespoons lime juice Directions:

In a bowl, mix honey with soy sauce, salt, black and white pepper and lime juice, whisk well, add chicken pieces, toss to coat and keep in the fridge for 2 hours.

Transfer chicken to your air fryer, cook at 370 degrees F for 6 minutes on each side, increase heat to 400 degrees F and cook for 3 minutes more.

Serve hot.

Enjoy! Nutrition: calories 372, fat 9, fiber 10, carbs 37, protein 24

Herbed Chicken Preparation time: 30 minutes

Cooking time: 40 minutes

Servings: 4Ingredients:

1 whole chicken

Salt and black pepper to the taste

1 teaspoon garlic powder

1 teaspoon onion powder

½ teaspoon thyme, dried

1 teaspoon rosemary, dried

1 tablespoon lemon juice

2 tablespoons olive oil Directions:

Use pepper and salt to season the chicken, mix with thyme, rosemary, garlic powder and onion powder, rub with lemon juice and olive oil and leave aside for 30 minutes.

Put chicken in your air fryer and cook at 360 degrees F for 20 minutes on each side.

Leave chicken aside to cool down, carve and serve.

Enjoy! Nutrition: calories 390, fat 10, fiber 5, carbs 22, protein 20 Chicken Parmesan Preparation time: 10 minutes

Cooking time: 15 minutes

Servings: 4Ingredients:

2 cups panko bread crumbs

¼ cup parmesan, grated

½ teaspoon garlic powder

2 cups white flour

1 egg, whisked

1 and ½ pounds chicken cutlets, skinless and boneless

Salt and black pepper to the taste

1 cup mozzarella, grated

2 cups tomato sauce

3 tablespoons basil, chopped Directions:

In a bowl, mix panko with parmesan and garlic powder and stir.

Put flour in a second bowl and the egg in a third.

Season chicken with salt and pepper, dip in flour, then in egg mix and in panko. Put chicken pieces in your air fryer and cook them at 360 degrees F for 3 minutes on each side.

Transfer chicken to a baking dish that fits your air fryer, add tomato sauce and top with mozzarella, introduce in your air fryer and cook at 375 degrees F for 7 minutes.

Divide among plates, sprinkle basil on top and serve.

Enjoy! Nutrition: calories 304, fat 12, fiber 11, carbs 22, protein 15

Mexican Chicken Preparation time: 10 minutes

Cooking time: 20 minutes

Servings: 4Ingredients:

16 ounces salsa verde

1 tablespoon olive oil

Salt and black pepper to the taste

1 pound chicken breast, boneless and skinless

1 and ½ cup Monterey Jack cheese, grated

¼ cup cilantro, chopped

1 teaspoon garlic powder

Directions:

Pour salsa verde in a baking dish that fits your air fryer, season chicken with salt, pepper, garlic powder, brush with olive oil and place it over your salsa verde.

put in your air fryer and boil at 380 degrees F for 20 minutes.

Sprinkle cheese on top and cook for 2 minutes more.

Divide among plates and serve hot.

Enjoy! Nutrition: calories 340, fat 18, fiber 14, carbs 32, protein 18

Creamy Chicken, Rice and Peas Preparation time: 10 minutes

Cooking time: 30 minutes

Servings: 4Ingredients:

1 pound chicken breasts, skinless, boneless and cut into quarters

1 cup white rice, already cooked

Salt and black pepper to the taste

1 tablespoon olive oil

3 garlic cloves, minced

1 yellow onion, chopped

½ cup white wine

¼ cup heavy cream

1 cup chicken stock

¼ cup parsley, chopped

2 cups peas, frozen

1 and ½ cups parmesan, grated Directions:

Season chicken breasts with salt and pepper, drizzle half of the oil over them, rub well, put in your air fryer's basket and cook them at 360 degrees F for 6 minutes.

Warm the pot with the remaining oil over medium high heat, add garlic, onion, wine, stock, salt, pepper and heavy cream, stir, bring to a simmer and cook for 9 minutes.

Transfer chicken breasts to a heat proof dish that fits your air fryer, add peas, rice and cream mix over them, toss, sprinkle parmesan and parsley all over, place in your air fryer and cook at 420 degrees F for 10 minutes.

Divide among plates and serve hot.

Enjoy! Nutrition: calories 313, fat 12, fiber 14, carbs 27, protein 44

Italian Chicken Preparation time: 10 minutes

Cooking time: 16 minutes

Servings: 4Ingredients:

5 chicken thighs

1 tablespoon olive oil

2 garlic cloves, minced

1 tablespoon thyme, chopped

½ cup heavy cream

¾ cup chicken stock

1 teaspoon red pepper flakes, crushed

¼ cup parmesan, grated

½ cup sun dried tomatoes

2 tablespoons basil, chopped

Salt and black pepper to the taste

Directions:

Season the chicken with salt and hu season, rub with half of the oil and cook in a 350 ° F preheated air fryer for 4 minutes.

Meanwhile, heat the pot with the remaining oil over medium high heat, add thyme garlic, pepper flakes, sun dried tomatoes, heavy cream, stock, parmesan, salt and pepper, stir, bring to a simmer, take off heat and transfer to a dish that fits your air fryer.

Add chicken thighs on top, introduce in your air fryer and cook at 320 degrees F for 12 minutes.

Divide among plates and serve with basil sprinkled on top.

Enjoy! Nutrition: calories 272, fat 9, fiber 12, carbs 37, protein 23

Honey Duck Breast Preparation time: 10 minutes

Cooking time: 22 minutes

Servings: 2Ingredients:

1 smoked duck breast, halved

1 teaspoon honey

1 teaspoon tomato paste

1 tablespoon mustard

½ teaspoon apple vinegar Directions:

In a bowl, mix honey with tomato paste, mustard and vinegar, whisk well, add duck breast pieces, toss to coat well, transfer to your air fryer and cook at 370 degrees F for 15 minutes.

Take duck breast out of the fryer, add to honey mix, toss again, return to air fryer and for a duration of 6 minutes boil at 370 degrees.

Divide among plates and serve with a side salad.

Enjoy! Nutrition: calories 274, fat 11, fiber 13, carbs 22, protein 13

Chinese Duck Legs Preparation time: 10 minutes

Cooking time: 36 minutes

Servings: 2Ingredients:

2 duck legs

2 dried chilies, chopped

1 tablespoon olive oil

2 star anise

1 bunch spring onions, chopped

4 ginger slices

1 tablespoon oyster sauce

1 tablespoon soy sauce

1 teaspoon sesame oil

14 ounces water

1 tablespoon rice wine

Directions:

Over an average heat, add heat to the oven and add chili, star anise, sesame oil, rice wine, ginger, oyster sauce, soy sauce and water, stir and cook for 6 minutes. Add spring onions and duck legs, toss to coat, transfer to a pan that fits your air fryer, put in your air fryer and cook at 370 degrees F for 30 minutes.

Divide among plates and serve.

Enjoy! Nutrition: calories 300, fat 12, fiber 12, carbs 26, protein 18

Chinese Stuffed Chicken Preparation time: 10 minutes

Cooking time: 35 minutes

Servings: 8Ingredients:

1 whole chicken

10 wolfberries

2 red chilies, chopped

4 ginger slices

1 yam, cubed

1 teaspoon soy sauce

Salt and white pepper to the taste

3 teaspoons sesame oil

Directions:

Season chicken with salt, pepper, rub with soy sauce and sesame oil and stuff with wolfberries, yam cubes, chilies and ginger.

Place in your air fryer, cook at 400 degrees F for 20 minutes and then at 360 degrees F for 15 minutes.

Carve chicken, divide among plates and serve.

Enjoy! Nutrition: calories 320, fat 12, fiber 17, carbs 22, protein 12

38. Chicken Parmesan Cutlets

Preparation time: 10 minutes

Cooking time: 15 minutes

Servings: 2

Ingredients:

1 cup Panko bread crumbs

2 tablespoons parmesan cheese, grated

¼ teaspoon garlic powder

1 cup white flour

1 egg, whisked

¾ pound skinless, boneless chicken cutlets

Salt and pepper, to taste

½ cup mozzarella, grated

1 cup tomato sauce

1 ½ tablespoons basil, chopped

Directions:

In a bowl, mix garlic powder and parmesan and stir.

Put flour in a second bowl. Put the egg in a third and beat.

Season chicken with salt and pepper.
Dip in flour, then in the egg mix. Finally, coat in panko.
Cook chicken pieces in the air fryer at 360F for 3 minutes on each side.
Transfer chicken to a baking dish.
Add tomato sauce and top with mozzarella.
Cook in the air fryer at 375F for 7 minutes.
Divide among plates, sprinkle basil on top and serve.
Nutrition:
Calories: 304
Fat: 12g
Carb: 22g
Protein: 15g

39. Mexican Chicken Breast

Preparation time: 10 minutes
Cooking time: 20 minutes
Servings: 2
Ingredients:
8 ounces salsa verde
½ tablespoon olive oil
Salt and black pepper, to taste
½ pound boneless, skinless chicken breast
¾ cup Monetary Jack cheese, grated
2 tablespoons cilantro, chopped
½ teaspoon garlic powder
Directions:
Pour salsa verde into a baking dish.
Season chicken with salt, pepper, garlic powder, and brush with olive oil. Place over the salsa verde.
Place baking dish in the air fryer and cook at 380F for 20 minutes.
Sprinkle cheese over the top and cook 2 more minutes.
Serve.
Nutrition:
Calories: 340
Fat: 18g
Carb: 32g
Protein: 18g

40. Turkey and Cream Cheese Breast Pillows

Preparation time: 5 minutes
Cooking time: 10 minutes
Servings: 45
Ingredients:

1 cup of milk with 1 egg inside (put the egg in the cup and then fill with milk)
1/3 cup of water
¼ cup olive oil or oil
1 and ¾ teaspoon of salt
2 tbsp sugar
2 and ½ tbsp dried granular yeast
4 cups of flour
1 egg yolk to brush
2 jars of cream cheese
15 slices of turkey breast cut in 4
Directions:
Mix all the dough ingredients with your hands until it is very smooth. After the ready dough, make small balls and place on a floured surface. Reserve
Open each dough ball with a roller trying to make it square. Cut squares of approximately 10 X 10 cm. Fill with a piece of turkey breast and 1 teaspoon of cream cheese coffee. Close the union of the masses joining the 4 points. Brush with the egg yolk and set aside.
Preheat the air fryer. Set the timer of 5 minutes and the temperature to 200C. Place 6 units in the basket of the air fryer and bake for 4 or 5 minutes at 180C. Repeat until all the pillows have finished cooking.
Nutrition:
Calories: 538
Fat: 29.97g
Carbohydrates: 22.69g
Protein: 43.64g
Sugar: 0.56g
Cholesterol: 137mg

41. Chicken Wings

Preparation time: 10 minutes
Cooking time: 25 minutes
Servings: 2
Ingredients:
10 chicken wings (about 700g)
Oil in spay
1 tbsp soy sauce
½ tbsp cornstarch
2 tbsp honey
1 tbsp ground fresh chili paste
1 tbsp minced garlic
½ tsp chopped fresh ginger
1 tbsp lime sumo
½ tbsp salt

2 tbsp chives

Directions:

Dry the chicken with a tea towel. Cover the chicken with the oil spray.

Place the chicken inside the hot air electric fryer, separating the wings towards the edge so that it is not on top of each other. Cook at 200°C until the skin is crispy for about 25 min. Turn them around half the time.

Mix the soy sauce with cornstarch in a small pan. Add honey, chili paste, garlic, ginger, and lime sumo. Simmer until it boils and thickens. Place the chicken in a bowl, add the sauce and cover all the chicken. Sprinkle with chives.

Nutrition:

Calories: 81

Fat: 5.4g

Carbohydrates: 0g

Protein: 7.46g

Sugar: 0g

Cholesterol: 23mg

42. Pickled Poultry

Preparation time: 10 minutes

Cooking time: 25 minutes

Servings: 4

Ingredients:

600g of poultry, without bones or skin

3 white onions, peeled and cut into thin slices

5 garlic cloves, peeled and sliced

3 dl olive oil

1 dl apple cider vinegar

½ l white wine

2 bay leaves

5 g peppercorns

Flour

Pepper

Salt

Directions:

Rub the bird in dice that we will pepper and flour

Put a pan with oil on the fire. When the oil is hot, fry the floured meat dice in it until golden brown. Take them out and reserve, placing them in a clay or oven dish. Strain the oil in which you have fried the meat

Preheat the oven to 170° C

Put the already cast oil in another pan over the fire. Sauté the garlic and onions in it. Add the white wine and let cook about 3 minutes. Remove the pan from the heat, add the vinegar to the oil and wine. Remove, rectify salt, and pour this mixture into the source where you had left the bird dice. Introduce the source in the oven, lower the temperature to 140°C and bake for 1 and ½ hours. Remove the source from the oven and let it stand at room temperature

When the source is cold, put it in the fridge and let it rest a few hours before serving.

Nutrition:
Calories: 232
Fat: 15g
Carbohydrates: 5.89g
Protein: 18.2g
Sugar: 1.72g
Cholesterol: 141mg

43. Cordon Bleu Chicken Breast

Preparation time: 10 minutes
Cooking time: 40 minutes
Servings: 6
Ingredients:
4 flattened chicken breasts
8 slices of ham
16 slices of Swiss cheese
2 tsp fresh thyme
¼ cup flour
1 cup of ground bread
2 tsp melted butter
2 eggs
1 clove garlic finely chopped
pam cooking spray
Directions:
Preheat the air fryer to 350 degrees Fahrenheit (180 °C), set timer to 5 minutes. Then, flatten chicken breasts.

Fill the chicken breasts with two slices of cheese, then 2 slices of ham and finally 2 slices of cheese and roll up. Use a stick if necessary, to save the shape. Mix the ground bread with the thyme, the garlic finely chopped, with the melted butter and with salt and pepper. Beat the eggs. Season the flour with salt and pepper.

Pass the chicken rolls first through the flour, then through the egg and finally through the breadcrumbs.

Bake until the breasts are cooked, about 20 minutes.

Alternatively, before putting the chicken breasts in the air fryer you can fry them in a little butter and then finish cooking in the air fryer for 13-15 minutes.

Nutrition:
Calories: 387
Fat: 20g

Carbohydrates: 18g
Protein: 33g
Sugar: 0g
Cholesterol: 42mg

44. Fried Chicken

Preparation time: 15 minutes
Cooking time: 25 minutes
Servings: 4
Ingredients:
1kg of chicken chopped into small pieces
Garlic powder
Salt
Ground pepper
1 little grated ginger
1 lemon
Extra virgin olive oil
Directions:
Put the chicken in a large bowl.
Add the lemon juice and pepper.
Add some grated ginger and mix well.
Leave 15 minutes in the refrigerator.
Add now a jet of extra virgin olive oil and mix.
Put the chicken in the air fryer, if it does not fit in a batch, it is put in two.
Select 180 degrees, 25 minutes.
Shake the baskets a few times so that the chicken rotates and is made on all sides.
If you want to pass the chicken for flour, before putting it in the basket and frying, you can do it.
Nutrition:
Calories: 4
Fat: 3.3g
Carbohydrates: 2.3g
Protein: 2.5g
Sugar: 0.1g
Cholesterol: 8.8mg

45. Rolls Stuffed with Broccoli and Carrots with Chicken

Preparation time: 15 minutes
Cooking time: 25 minutes
Servings: 4
Ingredients:
8 sheets of rice pasta

1 chicken breast
1 onion
1 carrot
150g broccolis
1 can of sweet corn
Extra virgin olive oil
Salt
Ground pepper
Soy sauce
1 bag of rice three delicacies
Directions:
Start with the vegetable that you have to cook previously, stop them, peel the carrot.
Cut the carrot and broccoli as small as you can. Add the broccolis and the carrot to a pot with boiling water and let cook a few minutes, they have to be tender, but not too much, that crunch a little.
Drain well and reserve.
Cut the onion into julienne.
Cut the breast into strips.
In the Wok, put some extra virgin olive oil.
Add to the wok when it is hot, the onion and the chicken breast.
Sauté well until the chicken is cooked.
Drain the corn and add to the wok along with the broccolis and the carrot.
Sauté so that the ingredients are mixed.
Add salt, ground pepper and a little soy sauce.
Mix well and let the filling cool.
Hydrate the rice pasta sheets.
Spread on the worktable and distribute the filling between the sheets of rice paste.
Assemble the rolls and paint with a little oil.
Put in the air fryer, those who enter do not pile up.
Select 10 minutes 200 degrees.
When you have all the rolls made, the first ones will have cooled, because to solve it, you now place all the rolls already cooked inside the air fryer, now it does not matter that they are piled up.
Select 180 degrees, 5 minutes.
Make while the rice as indicated by the manufacturer in its bag.
Serve the rice with the rolls.
Nutrition:
Calories: 125
Fat: 4.58g
Carbohydrates: 16.83g
Protein: 4.69g

Sugar: 4.43g
Cholesterol: 0mg

46. Chicken Flutes with Sour Sauce and Guacamole

Preparation time: 15 minutes
Cooking time: 25 minutes
Servings: 4
Ingredients:
8 wheat cakes
1 large roasted breast
Grated cheese
Sour sauce
Guacamole
Extra virgin olive oil
Directions:
Extend the wheat cakes.
Stuffed with grated cheese and well-roasted chicken breast.
Form the flues and paint with extra virgin olive oil.
Place in batches in the air fryer and select 180 degrees, 5 minutes on each side or until you see the flutes golden.
Serve with sour sauce and guacamole.
Nutrition:
Calories: 325
Fat: 7g
Carbohydrates: 45g
Protein: 13g
Sugar: 7g
Cholesterol: 0mg

47. Spicy Chicken Strips

Preparation time: 5 minutes
Cooking time: 12 minutes
Servings: 5
Ingredients:
1 cup buttermilk
1½ tbsp hot pepper sauce
1 tsp salt
½ tsp black pepper, divided
1 pound boneless and skinless chicken breasts, cut into ¾ inch strips
¾ cup panko breadcrumbs
½ tsp salt
¼ tsp hot pepper, or to taste
1 tbsp olive oil

Directions:
Put the buttermilk, hot sauce, salt and ¼ teaspoon of black pepper in shallow bowl. Add chicken strips and refrigerate for at least two hours. Put breadcrumbs, salt, and the remaining black pepper and hot pepper in another bowl; Add and stir the oil.

Remove the chicken strips from the marinade and discard the marinade. Put the strips, few at the same time, to the crumb mixture. Press the crumbs to the strips to achieve a uniform and firm cover.

Put half of the strips in single layer inside the basket. Cook at a temperature of 350°F for 12 minutes. Cook the rest when the first batch is cooked.

Nutrition:
Calories: 207
Fat: 9g
Carbohydrates: 5g
Protein: 25g
Sugar: 0g
Cholesterol: 0mg

48. Spinach Stuffed Chicken Breasts

Servings: 2
Preparation Time: 15 minutes
Cooking Time: 30 minutes
Ingredients
1 tablespoon olive oil
1¾ ounces fresh spinach
¼ cup ricotta cheese, shredded
2, 4-ouncesskinless, boneless chicken breasts
Salt and ground black pepper, as required
2 tablespoons cheddar cheese, grated
¼ teaspoon paprika
Instructions
In a medium skillet, add the oil over medium heat and cook until heated.
Add the spinach and cook for about 3-4 minutes.
Stir in the ricotta and cook for about 40-60 seconds.
Remove the skillet from heat and set aside to cool.
Cut slits into the chicken breasts about ¼-inch apart but not all the way through.
Stuff each chicken breast with the spinach mixture.
Sprinkle each chicken breast evenly with salt and black pepper and then with cheddar cheese and paprika.
Set the temperature of Air Fryer to 390 degrees F. Grease an Air Fryer basket.
Arrange chicken breasts into the prepared basket in a single layer.
Air Fry for about 20-25 minutes.

Remove from Air Fryer and transfer the chicken breasts onto a serving platter. Serve hot.
Nutrition:
Calories: 279
Carbohydrate: 2.7g
Protein: 31.4g
Fat: 16g
Sugar: 0.3g
Sodium: 220mg

49. Cheese Stuffed Chicken Breasts
Servings: 4
Preparation Time: 15 minutes
Cooking Time: 15 minutes
Ingredients
2, 8-ouncesskinless, boneless chicken breast fillets
Salt and ground black pepper, as required
4 Brie cheese slices
1 tablespoon fresh chive, minced
4 cured ham slices
Instructions
Cut each chicken fillet in 2 equal-sized pieces.
Carefully, make a slit in each chicken piece horizontally about ¼-inch from the edge.
Open each chicken piece and season with the salt and black pepper.
Place 1 cheese slice in the open area of each chicken piece and sprinkle with chives.
Close the chicken pieces and wrap each one with a ham slice.
Set the temperature of Air Fryer to 355 degrees F. Grease an Air Fryer basket.
Arrange the wrapped chicken pieces into the prepared Air Fryer basket.
Air Fry for about 15 minutes.
Remove from Air Fryer and transfer the chicken fillets onto a serving platter. Serve hot.
Nutrition:
Calories: 376
Carbohydrate: 1.5g
Protein: 44.5g
Fat: 20.2g
Sugar: 0g
Sodium: 639mg

50. Bacon Wrapped Chicken Breasts

Servings: 4
Preparation Time: 20 minutes
Cooking Time: 23 minutes
Ingredients
1 tablespoon palm sugar
6-7 Fresh basil leaves
2 tablespoons fish sauce
2 tablespoons water
2, 8-ounceschicken breasts, cut each breast in half horizontally
Salt and ground black pepper, as required
12 bacon strips
1½ teaspoon honey
Instructions
In a small heavy-bottomed pan, add palm sugar over medium-low heat and cook for about 2-3 minutes or until caramelized, stirring continuously.
Add the basil, fish sauce and water and stir to combine.
Remove from heat and transfer the sugar mixture into a large bowl.
Sprinkle each chicken breast with salt and black pepper.
Add the chicken pieces in sugar mixture and coat generously.
Refrigerate to marinate for about 4-6 hours.
Set the temperature of Air Fryer to 365 degrees F. Grease an Air Fryer basket.
Wrap each chicken piece with 3 bacon strips.
Coat each piece slightly with honey.
Arrange chicken pieces into the prepared Air Fryer basket.
Air Fry for about 20 minutes, flipping once halfway through.
Remove from Air Fryer and transfer the chicken pieces onto a serving platter.
Serve hot.
Nutrition:
Calories: 365
Carbohydrate: 2.7g
Protein: 30.2g
Fat: 24.8g
Sugar: 2.1g
Sodium: 1300mg

51. Buffalo Chicken Tenders

Servings: 3
Preparation Time: 20 minutes
Cooking Time: 12 minutes
Ingredients
1 tablespoon water
1 large egg

16 ounces boneless, skinless chicken breasts, sliced into tenders
½ cup pork rinds, crushed
½ cup unflavored whey protein powder
½ teaspoon garlic powder
Salt and ground black pepper, as required
2 tablespoons butter, melted
¼ cup buffalo wing sauce
Instructions
In a large bowl, add the water, and egg. Beat until well combined.
Add the chicken and generously coat with egg mixture.
Place the chicken in a colander to drain completely.
In a shallow bowl, mix together the pork rinds, protein powder, garlic powder, salt, and black pepper.
Coat chicken tenders with the pork rinds mixture.
Set the temperature of Air Fryer to 400 degrees F. Grease an Air Fryer basket.
Arrange chicken tenders into the prepared Air Fryer basket and drizzle with the melted butter.
Air Fry for about 10-12 minutes.
Remove from Air Fryer and transfer the chicken tenders into a bowl.
Place with the buffalo sauce and toss to coat well.
Serve immediately.
Nutrition:
Calories: 292
Carbohydrate: 0.9g
Protein: 43.6g
Fat: 12.9g
Sugar: 0.2g
Sodium: 261mg

52. Crispy Chicken Tenders
Servings: 3
Preparation Time: 20 minutes
Cooking Time: 30 minutes
Ingredients
2, 6-ouncesboneless, skinless chicken breasts, pounded into ½-inch thickness and cut into tenders
¾ cup buttermilk
1½ teaspoons Worcestershire sauce, divided
½ teaspoon smoked paprika, divided
Salt and ground black pepper, as required
½ cup all-purpose flour
1½ cups panko breadcrumbs
¼ cup Parmesan cheese, finely grated

2 tablespoons butter, melted

2 large eggs

Instructions

In a large bowl, mix together buttermilk, ¾ teaspoon of Worcestershire sauce, ¼ teaspoon of paprika, salt, and black pepper.

Add in the chicken tenders and refrigerate overnight.

In another bowl, mix together the flour, remaining paprika, salt, and black pepper.

Place the remaining Worcestershire sauce and eggs in a third bowl and beat until well combined.

Mix well the panko, Parmesan, and butter in a fourth bowl.

Remove the chicken tenders from bowl and discard the buttermilk.

Coat the chicken tenders with flour mixture, then dip into egg mixture and finally coat with the panko mixture.

Set the temperature of air fryer to 400 degrees F. Grease an air fryer basket.

Arrange chicken tenders into the prepared air fryer basket in 2 batches in a single layer.

Air fry for about 13-15 minutes, flipping once halfway through.

Remove from air fryer and transfer the chicken tenders onto a serving platter. Serve hot.

Nutrition

Calories: 654

Carbohydrate: 28g

Protein: 454g

Fat: 25.5g

Sugar: 3.9g

Sodium: 399mg

53. Simple Chicken Wings

Servings: 2

Preparation Time: 10 minutes

Cooking Time: 25 minutes

Ingredients

1 pound chicken wings

Salt and ground black pepper, as required

Instructions

Set the temperature of Air Fryer to 380 degrees F. Generously, grease an Air Fryer basket.

Sprinkle the chicken wings evenly with salt and black pepper.

Arrange chicken wings into the prepared Air Fryer basket in a single layer.

Air Fry for about 25 minutes, flip the wings once halfway through.

Remove from Air Fryer and transfer the chicken wings onto a serving platter.

Serve hot.
Nutrition
Calories: 431
Carbohydrate: 0g
Protein: 65.6g
Fat: 16.8g
Sugar: 0g
Sodium: 273mg

54. Crispy Chicken Wings

Servings: 2
Preparation Time: 20 minutes
Cooking Time: 25 minutes
Ingredients
2 lemongrass stalk, white portion, minced
1 onion, finely chopped
1 tablespoon soy sauce
1½ tablespoons honey
Salt and ground white pepper, as required
1 pound chicken wings, rinsed and trimmed
½ cup cornstarch
Instructions
In a bowl, mix together the lemongrass, onion, soy sauce, honey, salt, and white pepper.
Add the wings and generously coat with marinade.
Cover and refrigerate to marinate overnight.
Set the temperature of Air Fryer to 355 degrees F. Grease an Air Fryer basket.
Remove the chicken wings from marinade and coat with the cornstarch.
Arrange chicken wings into the prepared Air Fryer basket in a single layer.
Air Fry for about 25 minutes, flipping once halfway through.
Remove from Air Fryer and transfer the chicken wings onto a serving platter.
Serve hot.
Nutrition:
Calories: 724
Carbohydrate: 56.9g
Protein: 43.5g
Fat: 36.2g
Sugar: 15.4g
Sodium: 702mg

55. BBQ Chicken Wings

Servings: 4
Preparation Time: 10 minutes
Cooking Time: 30 minutes
Ingredients
2 pounds chicken wings, cut into drumettes and flats
½ cup BBQ sauce
Instructions
Set the temperature of Air Fryer to 380 degrees F. Grease an Air Fryer basket.
Arrange chicken wings into the prepared Air Fryer basket in a single layer.
Air Fry for about 24 minutes, flipping once halfway through.
Now, set the temperature of Air Fryer to 400 degrees F.
Air Fry for about 6 minutes.
Remove from Air Fryer and transfer the chicken wings into a bowl.
Drizzle with the BBQ sauce and toss to coat well.
Serve immediately.
Nutrition
Calories: 478
Carbohydrate: 11.3g
Protein: 65.6g
Fat: 16.9g
Sugar: 8.1g
Sodium: 545mg

56. Buffalo Chicken Wings

Servings: 6
Preparation Time: 20 minutes
Cooking Time: 22 minutes
Ingredients
2 pounds chicken wings, cut into drumettes and flats
1 teaspoon chicken seasoning
1 teaspoon garlic powder
Ground black pepper, to taste
1 tablespoon olive oil
¼ cup red hot sauce
2 tablespoons low-sodium soy sauce
Instructions
Set the temperature of Air Fryer to 400 degrees F. Grease an Air Fryer basket.
Sprinkle each chicken wing evenly with chicken seasoning, garlic powder, and black pepper.
Arrange chicken wings into the prepared Air Fryer basket in a single layer and drizzle with oil.
Air Fry for about 10 minutes, shaking the basket once halfway through.

Remove from Air Fryer and transfer the chicken wings into a bowl.

Drizzle with the red hot sauce, oil, and soy sauce. Toss to coat well.

Place chicken wings for the second time into the Air Fryer basket in a single layer.

Air Fry for about 7-12 minutes at the same temperature.

Remove from Air Fryer and transfer the chicken wings onto a serving platter.

Serve hot.

Nutrition:

Calories: 311

Carbohydrate: 0.6g

Protein: 44g

Fat: 13.6g

Sugar: 0.3g

Sodium: 491mg

>-Note: Buffalo Chicken Wings – When red hot sauce is used with chicken wings, it's called Buffalo Chicken Wings.

57. Sweet Chicken Kabobs

Servings: 3

Preparation Time: 20 minutes

Cooking Time: 14 minutes

Ingredients

4 scallions, chopped

1 tablespoon fresh ginger, finely grated

4 garlic cloves, minced

½ cup pineapple juice

½ cup soy sauce

¼ cup sesame oil

2 teaspoons sesame seeds, toasted

A pinch of black pepper

1 pound chicken tenders

Instructions

In a large baking dish, mix together the scallion, ginger, garlic, pineapple juice, soy sauce, oil, sesame seeds, and black pepper.

Thread chicken tenders onto the pre-soaked wooden skewers.

Add the skewers into the baking dish and evenly coat with marinade.

Cover and refrigerate for about 2 hours or overnight.

Set the temperature of Air Fryer to 390 degrees F. Grease an Air Fryer basket.

Place chicken skewers into the prepared Air Fryer basket in 2 batches.

Air Fry for about 5-7 minutes.

Remove from Air Fryer and transfer the chicken skewers onto a serving platter.

Serve hot.

Nutrition:

Calories: 392
Carbohydrate: 9.9g
Protein: 35.8g
Fat: 23g
Sugar: 4.1g
Sodium: 1800mg

58. Chicken & Scallion Kabobs
Servings: 4
Preparation Time: 20 minutes
Cooking Time: 24 minutes
Ingredients
¼ cup light soy sauce
1 tablespoon mirin
1 teaspoon garlic salt
1 teaspoon sugar
4, 4-ouncesskinless, boneless chicken thighs, cubed into 1-inch size
5 scallions, cut into 1-inch pieces lengthwise
Instructions
In a baking dish, mix together the soy sauce, mirin, garlic salt, and sugar.
Thread chicken and scallions onto pre-soaked wooden skewers.
Place skewers into the baking dish and generously coat with marinade.
Cover and refrigerate for about 3 hours.
Set the temperature of Air Fryer to 355 degrees F. Grease an Air Fryer basket.
Arrange skewers into the prepared Air Fryer basket in 2 batches in a single layer.
Air Fry for about 10-12 minutes.
Once done, remove from Air Fryer and transfer the chicken skewers onto a serving platter.
Serve hot.
Nutrition
Calories: 161
Carbohydrate: 6.9g
Protein: 26.2g
Fat: 4.1g
Sugar: 4g
Sodium: 781mg

59. Chicken & Veggie Kabobs
Servings: 3
Preparation Time: 20 minutes
Cooking Time: 30 minutes
Ingredients
1 lb. skinless, boneless chicken thighs, cut into cubes

½ cup plain Greek yogurt

1 tablespoon olive oil

2 teaspoons curry powder

½ teaspoon smoked paprika

¼ teaspoon cayenne pepper

Salt, to taste

2 small bell peppers, seeded and cut into large chunks

1 large red onion, cut into large chunks

Instructions

In a bowl, add the chicken, oil, yogurt, and spices and mix until well combined

Refrigerate to marinate for about 2 hours.

Thread the chicken cubes, bell pepper and onion onto pre-soaked wooden skewers.

Set the temperature of Air Fryer to 360 degrees F. Grease an Air Fryer basket.

Arrange chicken skewers into the prepared Air Fryer basket in 2 batches.

Air Fry for about 15 minutes.

Remove from Air Fryer and transfer the chicken skewers onto a serving platter. Serve hot.

Nutrition

Calories: 222

Carbohydrate: 8.7g

Protein: 27.9g

Fat: 8.2g

Sugar: 5.3g

Sodium: 104mg

60.   Jerk Chicken, Pineapple & Veggie Kabobs

Servings: 8

Preparation Time: 20 minutes

Cooking Time: 18 minutes

Ingredients

8, 4-ouncesboneless, skinless chicken thigh fillets, trimmed and cut into cubes

1 tablespoon jerk seasoning

2 large zucchini, sliced

8 ounces white mushrooms, stems removed

Salt and ground black pepper, as required

1, 20-ouncescan pineapple chunks, drained

1 tablespoon jerk sauce

Instructions

In a bowl, mix together the chicken cubes and jerk seasoning.

Cover the bowl and refrigerate overnight.

Sprinkle the zucchini slices, and mushrooms evenly with salt and black pepper.

Thread the chicken, vegetables and pineapple onto greased metal skewers.

Set the temperature of Air Fryer to 370 degrees F. Grease an Air Fryer basket.

Arrange skewers into the prepared Air Fryer basket in 2 batches.

Air Fry for about 8-9 minutes, flipping and coating with jerk sauce once halfway through.

Remove from Air Fryer and transfer the chicken skewers onto a serving platter.

Serve hot.

Nutrition

Calories: 274

Carbohydrate: 14.1g

Protein: 35.1g

Fat: 8.7g

Sugar: 9.9g

Sodium: 150mg

61.   Curried Chicken

Servings: 3

Preparation Time: 15 minutes

Cooking Time: 18 minutes

Ingredients

1-pound boneless chicken, cubed

1 tablespoon light soy sauce

½ tablespoon cornstarch

1 egg

2 tablespoons olive oil

1 medium yellow onion, thinly sliced

1 green chili, chopped

3 teaspoons garlic, minced

1 teaspoon fresh ginger, grated

5 curry leaves

1 teaspoon curry powder

1 tablespoon chili sauce

1 teaspoon sugar

Salt and ground black pepper, as required

½ cup evaporated milk

Instructions

In a bowl, add the chicken cubes, soy sauce, cornstarch, and egg and mix until well combined.

Cover the bowl and place at room temperature for about 1 hour.

Remove chicken cubes from the bowl and with paper towels, pat them dry.

Set the temperature of Air Fryer to 390 degrees F. Grease an Air Fryer basket.

Arrange chicken cubes into the prepared Air Fryer basket.

Air Fry for about 10 minutes.

Remove chicken cubes from the Air fryer and set aside.

In a medium skillet, add the oil over medium heat and cook until heated.

Add the onion, green chili, garlic, ginger, and curry leaves. Sauté for about 3-4 minutes.

Add the chicken cubes, curry powder, chili sauce, sugar, salt, and black pepper and mix until well combined.

Stir in the evaporated milk and cook for about 3-4 minutes.

Remove from heat and transfer the chicken mixture into a serving bowl.

Serve hot.

Nutrition:

Calories: 363

Carbohydrate: 10g

Protein: 37.1g

Fat: 19g

Sugar: 0.8g

Sodium: 789mg

62. Chicken with Apple

Servings: 2

Preparation Time: 20 minutes

Cooking Time: 20 minutes

Ingredients

1 shallot, thinly sliced

1 tablespoon fresh ginger, finely grated

1 teaspoon fresh thyme, minced

½ cup apple cider

2 tablespoons maple syrup

Salt and ground black pepper, as required

2, 4-ouncesboneless, skinless chicken thighs, sliced into chunks

1 large apple, cored and cubed

Instructions

In a bowl, mix together the shallot, ginger, thyme, apple cider, maple syrup, salt, and black pepper.

Add the chicken pieces and generously mix with the marinade.

Refrigerate to marinate for about 6-8 hours.

Set the temperature of Air Fryer to 390 degrees F. Grease an Air Fryer basket.

Place the chicken pieces and cubed apple into the prepared Air Fryer basket.

Air Fry for about 20 minutes, flipping once halfway.

Remove from Air Fryer and transfer the chicken mixture onto a serving platter.

Serve hot.

Nutrition:

Calories: 299

Carbohydrate: 39.9g

Protein: 26.2g
Fat: 4.6g
Sugar: 30.4g
Sodium: 125mg

63. Chicken with Carrots

Servings: 2
Preparation Time: 15 minutes
Cooking Time: 25 minutes
Ingredients
1 carrot, peeled and thinly sliced
Salt and ground black pepper, as required
2 tablespoons butter
2, 4-ounceschicken breast halves
1 tablespoon fresh rosemary, chopped
2 tablespoons fresh lemon juice
Instructions
Arrange 2 square-shaped parchment papers onto a smooth surface.
Place carrot slices evenly in the center of each parchment paper.
Place ½ tablespoon of butter over carrot slices and sprinkle with salt and black pepper.
Arrange 1 chicken breast over carrot slices in each parcel.
Top each chicken breast evenly with rosemary and drizzle with lemon juice.
Top with the remaining butter.
Seal each parchment paper by folding all four corners.
Set the temperature of Air Fryer to 375 degrees F.
Arrange the chicken parcels into an Air Fryer basket.
Air Fry for about 20-25 minutes.
Remove from Air Fryer and transfer the chicken mixture onto a serving platter.
Serve hot.
Nutrition:
Calories: 339
Carbohydrate: 4.4g
Protein: 33.4g
Fat: 20.3g
Sugar: 18g
Sodium: 282mg

64. Chicken with Veggies

Servings: 2
Preparation Time: 20 minutes
Cooking Time: 45 minutes

Ingredients

2 garlic cloves, minced

2 tablespoons chicken broth

2 tablespoons red wine vinegar

2 tablespoons olive oil

1 tablespoon Dijon mustard

1/8 teaspoon dried thyme

1/8 teaspoon dried basil

4 small artichoke hearts, quartered

4 fresh large button mushrooms, quartered

½ small onion, cut in large chunks

Salt and ground black pepper, as required

2 skinless, boneless chicken breasts

2 tablespoons fresh parsley, chopped

Instructions

Grease a small baking dish that will fit in the cooking basket of Air Fryer.

In a small bowl, mix together the garlic, broth, vinegar, olive oil, mustard, thyme, and basil.

In the prepared baking dish, add the artichokes, mushrooms, onions, salt, and black pepper and mix well

Now, place the chicken breasts on top of veggie mixture in a single layer.

Spread half of the mustard mixture evenly over chicken breasts.

Set the temperature of Air Fryer to 350 degrees F.

Arrange the baking dish into an Air Fryer cooking basket.

Air Fry for about 23 minutes.

Coat the chicken breasts with the remaining mustard mixture and flip the side.

Air Fry for about 22 minutes.

Remove from Air Fryer and transfer the chicken mixture onto a serving platter.

Garnish with parsley and serve hot.

Nutrition:

Calories: 448

Carbohydrate: 39.1g

Protein: 38.5g

Fat: 19.1g

Sugar: 5g

Sodium: 566mg

>-Note: If you want your chicken to be crispy, then set the temperature of air fryer to 375 degrees F.

65.   Chicken Chilaquiles

Servings: 3

Preparation Time: 20 minutes

Cooking Time: 50 minutes

Ingredients

1, 8-ouncesskinless, boneless chicken breast

2 bay leaves

1 small yellow onion, chopped

3 garlic cloves, chopped

½ of poblano pepper

1, 14½-ouncecan diced tomatoes

1, 10-ouncescan Rotel tomatoes

Salt, to taste

10 corn tortillas, cut into diamond slices

1 tablespoon olive oil

4 tablespoons feta cheese, crumbled

¼ cup sour cream

2 red onions, sliced

Instructions

In a pan of water, add the chicken, and bay leaves and cook for about 20 minutes.

With a slotted spoon, transfer chicken breasts into a bowl and set aside to cool. Shred the chicken using 2 forks.

In a food processor, add the onion, garlic, poblano pepper, and both cans of tomatoes and pulse until smooth.

Transfer the sauce into a skillet over medium-high heat and bring to a boil.

Reduce the heat to medium-low and cook for about 10 minutes.

Season with salt and remove from the heat.

Set the temperature of Air Fryer to 400 degrees F. Grease an Air Fryer basket.

In a bowl, add the tortilla slices, oil and salt and toss to coat well.

Arrange tortilla slices into the prepared Air Fryer basket in 2 batches in a single layer.

Air Fry for about 10 minutes.

Transfer the tortilla slices into the serving bowl.

Add the sauce, cheese, and sour cream and mix well.

Top with the chicken, and red onions and serve.

Nutrition

Calories: 375

Carbohydrate: 42.8g

Protein: 25.9g

Fat: 12.7g

Sugar: 7g

Sodium: 536mg

66.   Chicken with Broccoli & Rice

Servings: 6
Preparation Time: 20 minutes
Cooking Time: 15 minutes
Ingredients
3 tablespoons dried parsley, crushed
1 tablespoon onion powder
1 tablespoon garlic powder
½ teaspoon red chili powder
½ teaspoon paprika
2 pounds boneless, skinless chicken breasts, sliced
3 cups instant white rice
¾ cup cream soup
3 cups small broccoli florets
1/3 cup butter
3 cups water
Instructions
Mix together the parsley and spices in a large bowl.
Add the chicken slices and generously coat with spice mixture.
Arrange 6 large pieces of foil onto a smooth surface.
Place ½ cup of rice over each foil piece, followed by 1/6 of chicken, 2
tablespoons of cream soup, ½ cup of broccoli, 1 tablespoon of butter, and ½
cup of water.
Fold the foil tightly to seal the rice mixture.
Set the temperature of Air Fryer to 390 degrees F.
Arrange the foil packets into an Air Fryer basket.
Air Fry for about 15 minutes.
Remove from Air Fryer and carefully, transfer the rice mixture onto serving
plates.
Serve hot.
Nutrition
Calories: 583
Carbohydrate: 65.6g
Protein: 42.7g
Fat: 23.1g
Sugar: 1.6g
Sodium: 374mg

67.   Chicken with Veggies & Rice

Servings: 3
Preparation Time: 15 minutes
Cooking Time: 20 minutes
Ingredients

3 cups cold boiled white rice
6 tablespoons soy sauce
1 tablespoon vegetable oil
1 cup cooked chicken, diced
½ cup frozen carrots
½ cup frozen peas
½ cup onion, chopped
Instructions
In a large bowl, add the rice, soy sauce, and oil and mix thoroughly.
Add the remaining ingredients and mix until well combined.
Transfer the rice mixture into a 7" nonstick pan.
Arrange the pan into an Air Fryer basket.
Set the temperature of Air Fryer to 360 degrees F.
Air Fry for about 20 minutes.
Remove the pan from Air Fryer and transfer the rice mixture onto serving plates.
Serve immediately.
Nutrition:
Calories: 405
Carbohydrate: 63g
Protein: 21.7g
Fat: 6.4g
Sugar: 3.5g
Sodium: 1500mg

Fish and Seafood Recipes

68. Cajun Style Shrimp

Preparation time: 3 minutes
Cooking time: 10 minutes
Servings: 2
Ingredients:
6g of salt
2g smoked paprika
2g garlic powder
2g Italian seasoning
2g chili powder
1g onion powder
1g cayenne pepper
1g black pepper
1g dried thyme
454g large shrimp, peeled and unveiled
30 ml of olive oil
Lime wedges, to serve
Directions:
Select Preheat, in the air fryer, set the temperature to 190°C and press Start/Pause.
Combine all seasonings in a large bowl. Set aside
Mix the shrimp with olive oil until they are evenly coated.
Sprinkle the dressing mixture over the shrimp and stir until well coated.
Place the shrimp in the preheated air fryer.
Select Shrimp set the time to 5 minutes and press Start/Pause.
Shake the baskets in the middle of cooking.
Serve with pieces of lime.
Nutrition:
Calories: 126
Fat: 6g
Carbohydrates: 2g
Proteins: 33g
Cholesterol: 199mg
Sodium: 231mg

69. Crab Cakes

Preparation time: 10 minutes
Cooking time: 40 minutes
Servings: 2
Ingredients:
For crab cakes:
1 large egg, beaten

17g of mayonnaise
11g Dijon mustard
5 ml Worcestershire sauce
2g Old Bay seasoning
2g of salt
A pinch of white pepper
A pinch of cayenne
26g celery, finely diced
45g red pepper, finely diced
8g fresh parsley, finely chopped
227g of crab meat
28g breadcrumbs
Nonstick Spray Oil
Remodeled:
55g of mayonnaise
15g capers, washed and drained
5g sweet pickles, chopped
5g red onion, finely chopped
8 ml of lemon juice
8g Dijon mustard
Salt and pepper to taste
Directions:
Mix the ingredients of remodeled until everything is well incorporated. Set aside
Beat the egg, mayonnaise, mustard, Worcestershire sauce, Old Bay seasoning, salt, white pepper, cayenne pepper, celery, pepper, and parsley.
Gently stir the crab meat in the egg mixture and stir it until well mixed.
Sprinkle the breadcrumbs over the crab mixture and fold them gently until the breadcrumbs cover every corner.
Shape the crab mixture into 4 cakes and chill in the fridge for 30 minutes.
Select Preheat in the air fryer and press Start/Pause.
Place a sheet of baking paper in the basket of the preheated air fryer. Sprinkle the crab cakes with cooking spray and place them gently on the paper.
Cook the crab cakes at 205°C for 8 minutes until golden brown.
Flip crab cakes during cooking.
Serve with remodeled.
Nutrition:
Calories: 110
Fat: 6.5g
Carbohydrates: 5.5g
Protein: 7g
Sugar: 2g

70. Tuna Pie

Preparation time: 10 minutes
Cooking time: 30 minutes
Servings: 4
Ingredients:
2 hard-boiled eggs
2 tuna cans
200 ml fried tomato
1 sheet of broken dough.
Directions:
Cut the eggs into small pieces and mix with the tuna and tomato.
Spread the sheet of broken dough and cut into two equal squares.
Put the mixture of tuna, eggs, and tomato on one of the squares.
Cover with the other, join at the ends and decorate with leftover little pieces.
Preheat the air fryer a few minutes at 1800C.
Enter in the air fryer basket and set the timer for 15 minutes at 1800C
Nutrition:
Calories: 244
Fat: 13.67g
Carbohydrates: 21.06g
Protein: 8.72g
Sugar: 0.22g
Cholesterol: 59mg

71. Tuna Puff Pastry

Preparation time: 5 minutes
Cooking time: 15 minutes
Servings: 2
Ingredients:
2 square puff pastry dough, bought ready
1 egg (white and yolk separated)
½ cup tuna tea
½ cup chopped parsley tea
½ cup chopped tea olives
Salt and pepper to taste
Directions:
Preheat the air fryer. Set the timer of 5 minutes and the temperature to 200C.
Mix the tuna with olives and parsley. Season to taste and set aside. Place half of the filling in each dough and fold in half. Brush with egg white and close gently. After closing, make two small cuts at the top of the air outlet. Brush with the egg yolk.
Place in the basket of the air fryer. Set the time to 10 minutes and press the power button.
Nutrition:

Calories: 291
Fat: 16g
Carbohydrates: 26g
Protein: 8g
Sugar: 0g
Cholesterol: 0

72. Cajun Style Catfish

Preparation time: 3 minutes
Cooking time: 7 minutes
Servings: 2
Ingredients:
5g of paprika
3g garlic powder
2g onion powder
2g ground dried thyme
1g ground black pepper
1g cayenne pepper
1g dried basil
1g dried oregano
2 catfish fillets (6 oz)
Nonstick Spray Oil
Direction:
Preheat the air fryer for a few minutes. Set the temperature to 175°C.
Mix all seasonings in a bowl.
Cover the fish generously on each side with the dressing mixture.
Spray each side of the fish with oil spray and place it in the preheated air fryer.
Select Marine Food and press Start /Pause.
Remove carefully when you finish cooking and serve on semolina.
Nutrition:
Calories: 228
Fat; 13g
Carbohydrates: 0g
Protein: 20g
Sugar: 0g
Cholesterol: 71mg

73. Tuna Chipotle

Preparation time: 5 minutes
Cooking time: 8 minutes
Servings: 2
Ingredients:
142g tuna

45g chipotle sauce
4 slices of white bread
2 slices of pepper jack cheese
Directions:
Preheat the air fryer set the temperature to 160°C.
Mix the tuna and chipotle until combined.
Spread half of the chipotle tuna mixture on each of the 2 slices of bread.
Add a slice of pepper jack cheese on each and close with the remaining 2 slices of bread, making 2 sandwiches.
Place the sandwiches in the preheated air fryer. Set the timer to 8 minutes.
Cut diagonally and serve.
Nutrition:
Calories: 121
Fat: 4g
Carbohydrates: 2g
Protein: 16g
Sugar: 0g
Cholesterol: 36mg

74. Fish Tacos

Preparation time: 10 minutes
Cooking time: 7 minutes
Servings: 4-5
Ingredients:
454g of tilapia, cut into strips of
38 mm thick
52g yellow cornmeal
1g ground cumin
1g chili powder
2g garlic powder
1g onion powder
3g of salt
1g black pepper
Nonstick Spray Oil
Corn tortillas, to serve
Tartar sauce, to serve
Lime wedges, to serve
Directions:
Cut the tilapia into strips 38 mm thick.
Mix cornmeal and seasonings in a shallow dish.
Cover the fish strips with seasoned cornmeal. Set aside in the fridge.
Preheat the air fryer for 5 minutes. Set the temperature to 170°C.
Sprinkle the fish coated with oil spray and place it in the preheated air fryer.

Put the fish in the air fryer, set the timer to 7 minutes.

Turn the fish halfway through cooking.

Serve the fish in corn tortillas with tartar sauce and a splash of lemon.

Nutrition:

Calories: 108

Fat: 26g

Carbohydrates: 11g

Protein: 9g

Sugar: 0g

Cholesterol: 56mg

75. Delicious Prawns and Sweet Potatoes

Preparation time: 20 minutes

Cooking time: 20 minutes

Servings: 4

Ingredients:

1 shallot, chopped

1 red chili pepper, seeded and chopped finely

12 king prawns, peeled and deveined

5 large sweet potatoes, peeled and cut into slices

4 lemongrass stalks

2 tablespoons dried rosemary

1/3 cup olive oil, divided

4 garlic cloves, minced

Smoked paprika, to taste

1 tablespoon honey

Directions:

Preheat the Air fryer to 355 o F and grease an Air fryer basket.

Mix ¼ cup of the olive oil, shallot, red chili pepper, garlic and paprika in a bowl.
Add prawns and coat evenly with the mixture.

Thread the prawns onto lemongrass stalks and refrigerate to marinate for about 3 hours.

Mix sweet potatoes, honey and rosemary in a bowl and toss to coat well.

Arrange the potatoes in the Air fryer basket and cook for about 15 minutes.

Remove the sweet potatoes from the Air fryer and set the Air fryer to 390 degrees F.

Place the prawns in the Air fryer basket and cook for about 5 minutes.

Dish out in a bowl and serve with sweet potatoes.

Nutrition:

Calories: 285, Fats: 3.8g, Carbohydrates: 51.6g, Sugar: 5.8g, Proteins: 10.5g, Sodium: 235mg

76. Nutritious Salmon and Veggie Patties

Preparation time: 15 minutes
Cooking time: 7 minutes
Servings: 6
Ingredients:
3 large russet potatoes, boiled and mashed
1 (6-ounce) salmon fillet
1 egg
¾ cup frozen vegetables, parboiled and drained
1 cup breadcrumbs
2 tablespoons dried parsley, chopped
1 teaspoon dried dill, chopped
Salt and freshly ground pepper, to taste
¼ cup olive oil
Directions:
Preheat the Air fryer to 355 o F and line a pan with foil paper.
Place salmon in the Air fryer basket and cook for about 5 minutes.
Dish out the salmon in a large bowl and flake with a fork.
Mix potatoes, egg, parboiled vegetables, parsley, dill, salt and black pepper until well combined.
Make 6 equal sized patties from the mixture and coat the patties evenly with breadcrumbs.
Drizzle with the olive oil and arrange the patties in the pan.
Transfer into the Air fryer basket and cook for about 12 minutes, flipping once in between.
Nutrition:
Calories: 334, Fat: 12.1g, Carbohydrates: 45.1g, Sugar: 4g, Protein: 12.6g, Sodium: 175mg

77. Cod Cakes
Preparation time: 15 minutes
Cooking time: 14 minutes
Servings 4
Ingredients:
1 pound cod fillets
1 egg
1/3 cup coconut, grated and divided
1 scallion, chopped finely
2 tablespoons fresh parsley, chopped
1 teaspoon fresh lime zest, grated finely
1 teaspoon red chili paste
Salt, to taste
1 tablespoon fresh lime juice
Directions:

Preheat the Air fryer to 375 o F and grease an Air fryer basket.

Put cod filets, lime zest, egg, chili paste, salt and lime juice in a food processor and pulse until smooth.

Transfer the cod mixture to a bowl and add 2 tablespoons coconut, scallion and parsley.

Make 12 equal sized round cakes from the mixture.

Put the remaining coconut in a shallow dish and coat the cod cakes in it.

Arrange 6 cakes in the Air fryer basket and cook for about 7 minutes.

Repeat with the remaining cod cakes and serve warm.

Nutrition:

Calories: 171, Fat: 3.3g, Carbohydrates: 16.1g, Sugar: 13.2g, Protein: 19g, Sodium: 115mg

78. Ham-Wrapped Prawns with Roasted Pepper Chutney

Preparation time: 15 minutes

Cooking time: 13 minutes

Servings: 4

Ingredients:

1 large red bell pepper

8 king prawns, peeled and deveined

4 ham slices, halved

1 garlic clove, minced

1 tablespoon olive oil

½ tablespoon paprika

Salt and freshly ground black pepper, to taste

Directions:

Preheat the Air fryer to 375 o F and grease an Air fryer basket.

Place the bell pepper in the Air fryer basket and cook for about 10 minutes.

Dish out the bell pepper into a bowl and keep aside, covered for about 15 minutes.

Now, peel the bell pepper and remove the stems and seeds and chop it.

Put the chopped bell pepper, garlic, paprika and olive oil in a blender and pulse until a puree is formed.

Wrap each ham slice around each prawn and transfer to the Air fryer basket.

Cook for about 3 minutes and serve with roasted pepper chutney.

Nutrition:

Calories: 353, Fat: 9.9g, Carbohydrates: 7.6g, Sugar: 1.8g, Protein: 55.4g, Sodium: 904mg

79. Juicy Salmon and Asparagus Parcels

Preparation time: 5 minutes

Cooking time: 13 minutes

Servings: 2

Ingredients:

2 salmon fillets

4 asparagus stalks

¼ cup champagne

Salt and black pepper, to taste

¼ cup white sauce

1 teaspoon olive oil

Directions:

Preheat the Air fryer to 355 o F and grease an Air fryer basket.

Mix all the ingredients in a bowl and divide this mixture evenly over 2 foil papers.

Arrange the foil papers in the Air fryer basket and cook for about 13 minutes.

Dish out in a platter and serve hot.

Nutrition:

Calories: 328, Fat: 16.6g, Carbohydrates: 4.1g, Sugar: 1.8g, Protein: 36.6g, Sodium: 190mg

80. Appetizing Tuna Patties

Preparation time: 15 minutes

Cooking time: 10 minutes

Servings: 6

Ingredients:

2 (6-ounce) cans tuna, drained

½ cup panko bread crumbs

1 egg

2 tablespoons fresh parsley, chopped

2 teaspoons Dijon mustard

Dash of Tabasco sauce

Salt and black pepper, to taste

1 tablespoon fresh lemon juice

1 tablespoon olive oil

Directions:

Preheat the Air fryer to 355 o F and line a baking tray with foil paper.

Mix all the ingredients in a large bowl until well combined.

Make equal sized patties from the mixture and refrigerate overnight.

Arrange the patties on the baking tray and transfer to an Air fryer basket.

Cook for about 10 minutes and dish out to serve warm.

Nutrition:

Calories: 130, Fat: 6.2g, Carbohydrates: 5.1g, Sugar: 0.5g, Protein: 13g, Sodium: 94mg

81. Quick and Easy Shrimp

Preparation time: 10 minutes

Cooking time: 5 minutes
Servings: 2
Ingredients:
½ pound tiger shrimp
1 tablespoon olive oil
½ teaspoon old bay seasoning
¼ teaspoon smoked paprika
¼ teaspoon cayenne pepper
Salt, to taste
Directions:
Preheat the Air fryer to 390 o F and grease an Air fryer basket.
Mix all the ingredients in a large bowl until well combined.
Place the shrimps in the Air fryer basket and cook for about 5 minutes.
Dish out and serve warm.
Nutrition:
Calories: 174, Fat: 8.3g, Carbohydrates: 0.3g, Sugar: 0g, Protein: 23.8g, Sodium: 492mg

82. Crispy Shrimp with Orange Marmalade Dip

Preparation time: 25 minutes
Cooking time: 20 minutes
Servings: 4
Ingredients:
8 large shrimp, peeled and deveined
8 ounces coconut milk
½ cup panko breadcrumbs
Salt and black pepper, to taste
½ teaspoon cayenne pepper
For Dip
½ cup orange marmalade
1 teaspoon mustard
¼ teaspoon hot sauce
1 tablespoon honey
Directions:
Preheat the Air fryer to 350 o F and grease an Air fryer basket.
Mix coconut milk, salt and black pepper in a shallow dish.
Combine breadcrumbs, cayenne pepper, salt and black pepper in another shallow dish.
Coat the shrimps in coconut milk mixture and then roll into the breadcrumb mixture.
Arrange the shrimps in the Air fryer basket and cook for about 20 minutes.
Meanwhile, mix all the dip ingredients and serve with shrimp.
Nutrition:

Calories: 316, Fat: 14.7g, Carbohydrates: 44.3g, Sugar: 31.1g, Protein: 6g, Sodium: 165mg

83. Tuna-Stuffed Potato Boats

Preparation time: 10 minutes
Cooking time: 16 minutes
Servings: 4
Ingredients:
4 starchy potatoes, soaked for about 30 minutes and drain
1 (6-ounce) can tuna, drained
2 tablespoons plain Greek yogurt
1 scallion, chopped and divided
1 tablespoon capers
½ tablespoon olive oil
1 teaspoon red chili powder
Salt and black pepper, to taste
Directions:
Preheat the Air fryer to 355 o F and grease an Air fryer basket.
Arrange the potatoes in the Air fryer basket and cook for about 30 minutes.
Meanwhile, mix tuna, yogurt, red chili powder, salt, black pepper and half of scallion in a bowl and mash the mixture well.
Remove the potatoes from the Air fryer and halve the potatoes lengthwise carefully.
Stuff in the tuna mixture in the potatoes and top with capers and remaining scallion.
Dish out in a platter and serve immediately.
Nutrition:
Calories: 281, Fat: 13g, Carbohydrates: 15.4g, Sugar: 1.8g, Protein: 26.2g, Sodium: 249mg

84. Super-Simple Scallops

Preparation time: 10 minutes
Cooking time: 4 minutes
Servings: 2
Ingredients:
¾ pound sea scallops
1 tablespoon butter, melted
½ tablespoon fresh thyme, minced
Salt and black pepper, to taste
Directions:
Preheat the Air fryer to 390 o F and grease an Air fryer basket.
Mix all the ingredients in a bowl and toss to coat well.
Arrange the scallops in the Air fryer basket and cook for about 4 minutes.

Dish out and serve warm.
Nutrition:
Calories: 202, Fat: 7.1g, Carbohydrates: 4.4g, Sugar: 0g, Protein: 28.7g, Sodium: 315mg

85. Amazing Salmon Fillets
Preparation time: 5 minutes
Cooking time: 7 minutes
Servings: 2
Ingredients:
2 (7-ounce) (¾-inch thick) salmon fillets
1 tablespoon Italian seasoning
1 tablespoon fresh lemon juice
Directions:
Preheat the Air fryer to 355 o F and grease an Air fryer grill pan.
Rub the salmon evenly with Italian seasoning and transfer into the Air fryer grill pan, skin-side up.
Cook for about 7 minutes and squeeze lemon juice on it to serve.
Nutrition:
Calories: 88, Fat: 4.1g, Carbohydrates: 0.1g, Sugar: 0g, Protein: 12.9g, Sodium: 55mg

86. Glazed Halibut Steak
Preparation time: 30 minutes
Cooking time: 11 minutes
Servings: 4
Ingredients:
1 pound haddock steak
1 garlic clove, minced
¼ teaspoon fresh ginger, grated finely
½ cup low-sodium soy sauce
¼ cup fresh orange juice
2 tablespoons lime juice
½ cup cooking wine
¼ cup sugar
¼ teaspoon red pepper flakes, crushed
Directions:
Preheat the Air fryer to 390 o F and grease an Air fryer basket.
Put all the ingredients except haddock steak in a pan and bring to a boil.
Cook for about 4 minutes, stirring continuously and remove from the heat.
Put the haddock steak and half of the marinade in a resealable bag and shake well.

Refrigerate for about 1 hour and reserve the remaining marinade.
Place the haddock steak in the Air fryer basket and cook for about 11 minutes.
Coat with the remaining glaze and serve hot.
Nutrition:
Calories: 219, Fats: 1.1g, Carbohydrates: 17.9g, Sugar: 16.2g, Proteins: 29.7g, Sodium: 1861mg

87. Steamed Salmon with Dill Sauce

Preparation time: 15 minutes
Cooking time: 11 minutes
Servings 2
Ingredients:
1 cup water
2 (6-ounce) salmon fillets
½ cup Greek yogurt
2 tablespoons fresh dill, chopped and divided
2 teaspoons olive oil
Salt, to taste
½ cup sour cream
Directions:
Preheat the Air fryer to 285 o F and grease an Air fryer basket.
Place water the bottom of the Air fryer pan.
Coat salmon with olive oil and season with a pinch of salt.
Arrange the salmon in the Air fryer and cook for about 11 minutes.
Meanwhile, mix remaining ingredients in a bowl to make dill sauce.
Serve the salmon with dill sauce.
Nutrition:
Calories: 224, Fat: 14.4g, Carbohydrates: 3.6g, Sugar: 1.5g, Protein: 21.2g, Sodium: 108mg

Meat Recipes

88. Lime Lamb Mix

Preparation time: 5 minutes

Cooking time: 30 minutes

Servings: 4

Ingredients

2pounds lamb chops

Juice of 1 lime

Zest of 1 lime, grated

A pinch of salt and black pepper

1tablespoon olive oil

1teaspoon sweet paprika

1teaspoon cumin, ground

1tablespoon cumin, ground

Directions

In the air fryer's basket, mix the lamb chops with the lime juice and the other ingredients, rub and cook at 380 degrees F for 15 minutes on each side.

Serve with a side salad.

Nutrition: Calories 284, Fat 13, Fiber 3, Carbs 5, Protein 15

89. Lamb and Corn

Preparation time: 5 minutes

Cooking time: 30 minutes

Servings: 4

Ingredients

2pounds lamb stew meat, cubed

1cup corn

1cup spring onions, chopped

¼ cup beef stock

1tablespoon olive oil

A pinch of salt and black pepper

2tablespoons rosemary, chopped

Directions

In the air fryer's pan, mix the lamb with the corn, spring onions and the other ingredients, toss and cook at 380 degrees F for 30 minutes.

Divide the mix between plates and serve.

Nutrition: Calories 274, Fat 12, Fiber 3, Carbs 5, Protein 15

90. Herbed Beef and Squash

Preparation time: 10 minutes

Cooking time: 30 minutes

Servings: 4

Ingredients

2pounds beef stew meat, cubed
1cup butternut squash, peeled and cubed
1tablespoon basil, chopped
1tablespoon oregano, chopped
A pinch of salt and black pepper
A drizzle of olive oil
2garlic cloves, minced
Directions
In the air fryer's pan, mix the beef with the squash and the other ingredients, toss and cook at 380 degrees F for 30 minutes.
Divide between plates and serve.
Nutrition: Calories 284, Fat 13, Fiber 3, Carbs 6, Protein 14

91. Smoked Beef Mix

Preparation time: 5 minutes
Cooking time: 20 minutes
Servings: 4
Ingredients
1pound beef stew meat, roughly cubed
1tablespoon smoked paprika
½ cup beef stock
½ teaspoon garam masala
2tablespoons olive oil
A pinch of salt and black pepper
Directions
In the air fryer's basket, mix the beef with the smoked paprika and the other ingredients, toss and cook at 390 degrees F for 20 minutes on each side.
Divide between plates and serve.
Nutrition: Calories 274, Fat 12, Fiber 4, Carbs 6, Protein 17

92. Marjoram Pork Mix

Preparation time: 5 minutes
Cooking time: 25 minutes
Servings: 4
INGREDIENTS
2pounds pork stew meat, roughly cubed
1tablespoon marjoram, chopped
1cup heavy cream
2tablespoons olive oil
Salt and black pepper to the taste
2garlic cloves, minced
Directions

Heat up a pan that fits the air fryer with the oil over medium-high heat, add the meat and brown for 5 minutes

Add the rest of the ingredients, toss, put the pan in the fryer and cook at 400 degrees F for 20 minutes more.

Divide between plates and serve.

Nutrition: Calories 274, Fat 14, Fiber 3, Carbs 6, Protein 14

93. Nutmeg Lamb

Preparation time: 5 minutes

Cooking time: 30 minutes

Servings: 4

Ingredients

1pound lamb stew meat, cubed

2teaspoons nutmeg, ground

1teaspoon coriander, ground

1cup heavy cream

2tablespoons olive oil

2tablespoons chives, chopped

Salt and black pepper to the taste

DIRECTIONS

In the air fryer's pan, mix the lamb with the nutmeg and the other ingredients, put the pan in the air fryer and cook at 380 degrees F for 30 minutes.

Divide everything into bowls and serve.

Nutrition: Calories 287, Fat 13, Fiber 2, Carbs 6, Protein 12

94. Greek Beef Mix

Preparation time: 5 minutes

Cooking time: 30 minutes

Servings: 4

Ingredients:

2pounds beef stew meat, roughly cubed

1teaspoon coriander, ground

1teaspoon garam masala

1teaspoon cumin, ground

A pinch of salt and black pepper

1cup Greek yogurt

½ teaspoon turmeric powder

DIRECTIONS

In the air fryer's pan, mix the beef with the coriander and the other ingredients, toss and cook at 380 degrees F for 30 minutes.

Divide between plates and serve.

Nutrition: Calories 283, Fat 13, Fiber 3, Carbs 6, Protein 15

95. Beef and Fennel

Preparation time: 5 minutes
Cooking time: 30 minutes
Servings: 4
Ingredients
2pounds beef stew meat, cut into strips
2fennel bulbs, sliced
2tablespoons mustard
A pinch of salt and black pepper
1tablespoon black peppercorns, ground
2tablespoons balsamic vinegar
2tablespoons olive oil
Directions
In the air fryer's pan, mix the beef with the fennel and the other ingredients.
Put the pan in the fryer and cook at 380 degrees for 30 minutes.
Divide everything into bowls and serve.
Nutrition: Calories 283, Fat 13, Fiber 2, Carbs 6, Protein 17

96. Lamb and Eggplant Meatloaf

Preparation time: 5 minutes
Cooking time: 35 minutes
Servings: 4
Ingredients
2pounds lamb stew meat, ground
2eggplants, chopped
1yellow onion, chopped
A pinch of salt and black pepper
½ teaspoon coriander, ground
Cooking spray
2tablespoons cilantro, chopped
1egg
2tablespoons tomato paste
Directions
In a bowl, mix the lamb with the eggplants of the ingredients except the cooking spray and stir.
Grease a loaf pan that fits the air fryer with the cooking spray, add the mix and shape the meatloaf.
Put the pan in the air fryer and cook at 380 degrees F for 35 minutes.
Slice and serve with a side salad.
Nutrition: Calories 263, Fat 12, Fiber 3, Carbs 6, Protein 15

97. Pork Chops with Olives and Corn

Preparation time: 10 minutes

Cooking time: 25 minutes
Servings: 4
Ingredients
2pounds pork chops
1cup kalamata olives, pitted and halved
1cup black olives, pitted and halved
1cup corn
Salt and black pepper to the taste
1tablespoons avocado oil
2tablespoons garlic powder
2tablespoons oregano, dried
Directions
In the air fryer's pan, mix the pork chops with the olives and the other ingredients, toss, cook at 400 degrees F for 25 minutes, divide between plates and serve.
Nutrition: Calories 281, Fat 8, Fiber 7, Carbs 17, Protein 19

98. Beef and Broccoli Mix

Preparation time: 10 minutes
Cooking time: 30 minutes
Servings: 4
Ingredients
1pound beef stew meat, cubed
2cups broccoli florets
½ cup tomato sauce
1teaspoon sweet paprika
2teaspoons olive oil
1tablespoon cilantro, chopped
Directions
In your air fryer, mix the beef with the broccoli and the other ingredients, toss, cook at 390 degrees F for 30 minutes, divide into bowls and serve.
Nutrition: Calories 281, Fat 12, Fiber 7, Carbs 19, Protein 20

99. Cajun Beef Mix

Preparation time: 10 minutes
Cooking time: 30 minutes
Servings: 4
Ingredients
2pounds beef stew meat, cubed
1tablespoon Cajun seasoning
1teaspoon sweet paprika
1teaspoon chili powder
Salt and black pepper to the taste

1tablespoon olive oil
Directions
In a baking dish that fits your air fryer, mix the beef with the seasoning and the
other ingredients, toss, introduce the pan in the fryer and cook at 400 degrees F
for 30 minutes.
Divide the mix into bowls and serve.
Nutrition: Calories 291, Fat 8, Fiber 7, Carbs 19, Protein 20

100. Pork with Sprouts and Mushroom Mix

Preparation time: 10 minutes
Cooking time: 30 minutes
Servings: 4
Ingredients
2pounds pork stew meat, cubed
1cup Brussels sprouts, trimmed and halved
1cup mushrooms, sliced
Salt and black pepper to the taste
1tablespoon balsamic vinegar
1yellow onion, chopped
2teaspoons olive oil
Directions
In a baking dish that fits your air fryer, mix the pork with the sprouts and the
other ingredients, introduce the pan in the fryer and cook at 390 degrees F for
30 minutes.
Divide everything between plates and serve.
Nutrition: Calories 285, Fat 8, Fiber 2, Carbs 18, Protein 20

101. Pork Chops and Yogurt Sauce

Preparation time: 10 minutes
Cooking time: 30 minutes
Servings: 4
Ingredients
2tablespoons avocado oil
2pounds pork chops
1cup yogurt
2garlic cloves, minced
1teaspoon turmeric powder
Salt and black pepper to the taste
2tablespoon oregano, chopped
Directions
In the air fryer's pan, mix the pork chops with the yogurt and the other
ingredients, toss and cook at 400 degrees F for 30 minutes.
Divide the mix between plates and serve.

Nutrition: Calories 301, Fat 7, Fiber 5, Carbs 19, Protein 22

102. Lamb and Macadamia Nuts Mix

Preparation time: 10 minutes
Cooking time: 20 minutes
Servings: 4
Ingredients
2pounds lamb stew meat, cubed
2tablespoons macadamia nuts, peeled
1cup baby spinach
½ cup beef stock
2garlic cloves, minced
Salt and black pepper to the taste
1tablespoon oregano, chopped
Directions
In the air fryer's pan, mix the lamb with the nuts and the other ingredients, cook at 380 degrees F for 20 minutes, divide between plates and serve.
Nutrition: Calories 280, Fat 12, Fiber 8, Carbs 20, Protein 19

103. Beef Rolls

Preparation time: 10 minutes
Cooking time: 14 minutes
Servings: 4
Ingredients:
2 pounds beef steak, opened and flattened with a meat tenderizer
Salt and black pepper to the taste
1 cup baby spinach
3 ounces red bell pepper, roasted and chopped
6 slices provolone cheese
3 tablespoons pesto
Directions:
Arrange flattened beef steak on a cutting board, spread pesto all over, add cheese in a single layer, add bell peppers, spinach, salt and pepper to the taste. Roll your steak, secure with toothpicks, season again with salt and pepper, place roll in your air fryer's basket and cook at 400 degrees F for 14 minutes, rotating roll halfway.
Leave aside to cool down, cut into 2 inch smaller rolls, arrange on a platter and serve them as an appetizer.
Enjoy! Nutrition:
calories 230, fat 1, fiber 3, carbs 12, protein 10

104. Greek Beef Meatballs Salad

Preparation time: 10 minutes

Cooking time: 10 minutes
Servings: 6
Ingredients:
¼ cup milk
17 ounces beef, ground
1 yellow onion, grated
5 bread slices, cubed
1 egg, whisked
¼ cup parsley, chopped
Salt and black pepper to the taste
2 garlic cloves, minced
¼ cup mint, chopped
2 and ½ teaspoons oregano, dried
1 tablespoon olive oil
Cooking spray
7 ounces cherry tomatoes, halved
1 cup baby spinach
1 and ½ tablespoons lemon juice
7 ounces Greek yogurt Directions:
Put torn bread in a bowl, add milk, soak for a few minutes, squeeze and transfer to another bowl.
Add beef, egg, salt, pepper, oregano, mint, parsley, garlic and onion, stir and shape medium meatballs out of this mix.
Spray them with cooking spray, place them in your air fryer and cook at 370 degrees F for 10 minutes.
In a salad bowl, mix spinach with cucumber and tomato.
Add meatballs, the oil, some salt, pepper, lemon juice and yogurt, toss and serve.
Enjoy!Nutrition:
calories 200, fat 4, fiber 8, carbs 13, protein 27

105. Beef Patties and Mushroom Sauce

Preparation time: 10 minutes
Cooking time: 25 minutes
Servings: 6
Ingredients:
2 pounds beef, ground
Salt and black pepper to the taste
½ teaspoon garlic powder
1 tablespoon soy sauce
¼ cup beef stock
¾ cup flour
1 tablespoon parsley, chopped

1 tablespoon onion flakes
For the sauce:
1 cup yellow onion, chopped
2 cups mushrooms, sliced
2 tablespoons bacon fat
2 tablespoons butter
½ teaspoon soy sauce
¼ cup sour cream
½ cup beef stock
Salt and black pepper to the taste Directions:
In a bowl, mix beef with salt, pepper, garlic powder, 1 tablespoon soy sauce, ¼
cup beef stock, flour, parsley and onion flakes, stir well, shape 6 patties, place
them in your air fryer and cook at 350 degrees F for 14 minutes.
Meanwhile, heat up a pan with the butter and the bacon fat over medium heat,
add mushrooms, stir and cook for 4 minutes.
Add onions, stir and cook for 4 minutes more.
Add ½ teaspoon soy sauce, sour cream and ½ cup stock, stir well, bring to a
simmer and take off heat.
Divide beef patties on plates and serve with mushroom sauce on top.
Enjoy!
Nutrition:
calories 435, fat 23, fiber 4, carbs 6, protein 32

106. Beef Casserole

Preparation time: 30 minutes
Cooking time: 35 minutes
Servings: 12
Ingredients:
1 tablespoon olive oil
2 pounds beef, ground
2 cups eggplant, chopped
Salt and black pepper to the taste
2 teaspoons mustard
2 teaspoons gluten free Worcestershire sauce
28 ounces canned tomatoes, chopped
2 cups mozzarella, grated
16 ounces tomato sauce
2 tablespoons parsley, chopped
1 teaspoon oregano, dried Directions:
In a bowl, mix eggplant with salt, pepper and oil and toss to coat.
In another bowl, mix beef with salt, pepper, mustard and Worcestershire sauce,
stir well and spread on the bottom of a pan that fits your air fryer.

Add eggplant mix, tomatoes, tomato sauce, parsley, oregano and sprinkle mozzarella at the end.

Introduce in your air fryer and cook at 360 degrees F for 35 minutes

Divide among plates and serve hot.

Enjoy!

Nutrition:

calories 200, fat 12, fiber 2, carbs 16, protein 15

107. Lamb and Spinach Mix

Preparation time: 10 minutes

Cooking time: 35 minutes

Servings: 6

Ingredients:

2 tablespoons ginger, grated

2 garlic cloves, minced

2 teaspoons cardamom, ground

1 red onion, chopped

1 pound lamb meat, cubed

2 teaspoons cumin powder

1 teaspoon garam masala

½ teaspoon chili powder

1 teaspoon turmeric

2 teaspoons coriander, ground

1 pound spinach

14 ounces canned tomatoes, chopped Directions:

In a heat proof dish that fits your air fryer, mix lamb with spinach, tomatoes, ginger, garlic, onion, cardamom, cloves, cumin, garam masala, chili, turmeric and coriander, stir, introduce in preheated air fryer and cook at 360 degrees F for 35 minutes

Divide into bowls and serve.

Enjoy! Nutrition:

calories 160, fat 6, fiber 3, carbs 17, protein 20

Side Dish Recipes

108. Easy Polenta Pie

Preparation time: 10 min
Cooking time: 55 min
Servings: 6
Ingredients:
Egg, slightly beaten (1 piece)
Water (2 cups)
Monterey Jack cheese, w/ jalapeno peppers, shredded (3/4 cup)
Cornmeal (3/4 cup)
Salt (1/4 teaspoon)
Chili beans, drained (15 ounces)
Tortilla chips/crushed corn (1/3 cup)
Directions:
Preheat air fryer at 350 degrees Fahrenheit.
Mist cooking spray onto a pie plate.
In saucepan heated on medium-high, combine water, salt, and cornmeal. Let mixture boil, then cook on medium heat for six minutes. Stir in egg and let sit for five minutes.
Pour cornmeal mixture into pie plate and spread evenly. Air-fry for fifteen minutes and top with beans, corn chips, and cheese. Air-fry for another twenty minutes.
Nutrition: Calories 195 Fat 7.0 g Protein 10.0 g Carbohydrates 27.0 g

109. Bean and Rice Dish

Preparation time: 10 min
Cooking time: 1 hr 5 min
Servings: 4
Ingredients:
Boiling water (1 ½ cups)
Kidney beans, dark red, undrained (15 ounces)
Marjoram leaves, dried (1/2 teaspoon)
Cheddar cheese, shredded (1/2 cup)
White rice, long grain, uncooked (1 cup)
Bouillon, chicken/vegetable, granulated (1 tablespoon)
Onion, medium, chopped (1 piece)
Baby lima beans, frozen, thawed, drained (9 ounces)
Directions:
Preheat air fryer at 325 degrees Fahrenheit.
Combine all ingredients, save for cheese, in casserole.
Cover and air-fry for one hour and fifteen minutes. Give dish a stir before topping with cheese.
Nutrition: Calories 440 Fat 6.0 g Protein 20.0 g Carbohydrates 77.0 g

110. Cheesy Potato Mash Casserole

Preparation time: 25 min

Cooking time: 1 hr 10 min

Servings: 24

Ingredients:

Chives, fresh, chopped (1 teaspoon)

Cream cheese, reduced fat, softened (3 ounces)

Yogurt, plain, fat free (1 cup)

Cheddar cheese, reduced fat, shredded (1 cup)

Paprika (1/4 teaspoon)

White potatoes, peeled, cubed (5 pounds)

Blue cheese, crumbled (1/4 cup)

Parmesan cheese, shredded (1/4 cup)

Garlic salt (1 teaspoon)

Directions:

Place potatoes in saucepan filled with water. Heat to boiling, then cook on simmer for fifteen to eighteen minutes.

Beat together parmesan cheese, cheddar cheese, cream cheese, and blue cheese until smooth. Beat in garlic salt and yogurt.

Preheat air fryer t o 325 degrees Fahrenheit.

Mash cooked potatoes until smooth. Stir in cheese mixture. Add to a baking dish and air-fry for thirty-five to forty minutes.

Nutrition: Calories 110 Fat 2.5 g Protein 4.0 g Carbohydrates 18.0 g

111. Simple Squash Casserole

Preparation time: 20 min

Cooking time: 40 min

Servings: 6

Ingredients:

Yellow summer squash, medium, sliced thinly (1 piece)

Thyme leaves, fresh, chopped (1 tablespoon)

Salt (1/2 teaspoon)

Italian cheese blend, gluten free, shredded (1/2 cup)

Olive oil, extra virgin (1 tablespoon)

Zucchini, medium, sliced thinly (1 piece)

Onion, diced (1/2 cup)

Brown rice, cooked (1 cup)

Plum tomato, diced (1 piece)

Pepper (1/8 teaspoon)

Directions:

Preheat air fryer to 375 degrees Fahrenheit.

Mist cooking spray onto a gratin dish.

Combine rice, onion, tomato, pepper, salt (1/4 teaspoon), oil, and ½ thyme leaves. Spread evenly into gratin dish and layer on top with squash and zucchini. Sprinkle with remaining salt (1/4 teaspoon) and thyme.

Cover and air-fry for twenty minutes. Top with cheese and air-fry for another ten to twelve minutes.

Nutrition: Calories 110 Fat 5.0 g Protein 4.0 g Carbohydrates 12.0 g

112. Delicious Ginger Pork Lasagna

Preparation time: 45 min

Cooking time: 45 min

Servings: 8

Ingredients:

Thai basil leaves, fresh, sliced thinly (2 tablespoons)

Butter (1 tablespoon)

Garlic cloves, minced (2 pieces)

Ricotta cheese, part skim (15 ounces)

Wonton wrappers, square (48 pieces)

Green onion greens & whites, separated, sliced thinly (4 pieces)

Fish sauce (1 tablespoon)

Parmesan cheese, shredded (1 tablespoon)

Sesame oil, toasted (1 tablespoon)

Ground pork (1 pound)

Gingerroot, fresh, minced (1 tablespoon)

Tomato sauce (15 ounces)

Chili garlic sauce (1 tablespoon)

Coconut milk (1/2 cup)

Directions:

Preheat air fryer at 325 degrees Fahrenheit.

Mist cooking spray onto a baking dish.

In skillet heated on medium, cook pork in butter and sesame oil for eight to ten minutes. Stir in garlic, green onion whites, and gingerroot and cook for one to two minutes. Stir in fish sauce, chili garlic sauce, and tomato sauce. Cook on gentle simmer.

Combine coconut milk, ricotta cheese, and parmesan cheese (1 cup).

Arrange 8 overlapping wonton wrappers in baking dish to line bottom, then top with a second layer of eight wrappers. Spread on top 1/3 of cheese mixture, and layer with 1/3 of pork mixture. Repeat layering twice and finish by topping with parmesan cheese.

Cover dish with foil and air-fry for thirty minutes. Remove foil and air-fry for another ten to fifteen minutes.

Serve topped with basil and green onion greens.

Nutrition: Calories 480 Fat 24.0 g Protein 28.0 g Carbohydrates 37.0 g

113. Baked Sweet Potatoes

Preparation time: 10 minutes
Cooking time: 10 minutes
Servings: 2
Ingredients:
2 big sweet potatoes, scrubbed
1 cup water
A pinch of salt and black pepper
½ teaspoon smoked paprika
½ teaspoon cumin, ground
Directions:
Put the water in your pressure cooker, add the steamer basket, add sweet potatoes inside, cover and cook on High for 10 minutes.
Split potatoes, add salt, pepper, paprika and cumin, divide them between plates and serve as a side dish.
Nutrition: calories 152, fat 2, fiber 3, carbs 4, protein 4

114. Broccoli Pasta

Preparation time: 10 minutes
Cooking time: 4 minutes
Servings: 2
 Ingredients:
2 cups water
½ pound pasta
8 ounces cheddar cheese, grated
½ cup broccoli
½ cup half and half
Directions:
Put the water and the pasta in your pressure cooker.
Add the steamer basket, add the broccoli, cover the cooker and cook on High for 4 minutes.
Drain pasta, transfer it as well as the broccoli, and clean the pot.
Set it on sauté mode, add pasta and broccoli, cheese and half and half, stir well, cook for 2 minutes, divide between plates and serve as a side dish for chicken.
Nutrition: calories 211, fat 4, fiber 2, carbs 6, protein 7

115. Cauliflower Rice

Preparation time: 10 minutes
Cooking time: 12 minutes
Servings: 2
 Ingredients:
1 tablespoon olive oil
½ cauliflower head, florets separated

A pinch of salt and black pepper
A pinch of parsley flakes
¼ teaspoon cumin, ground
¼ teaspoon turmeric powder
¼ teaspoon paprika
1 cup water
½ tablespoon cilantro, chopped
Juice from 1/3 lime
Directions:
Put the water in your pressure cooker, add the steamer basket, add cauliflower florets, cover and cook on High for 2 minutes.
Discard water, transfer cauliflower to a plate and leave aside.
Clean your pressure cooker, add the oil, set on sauté mode and heat it up.
Add cauliflower, mash using a potato masher, add salt, pepper, parsley, cumin, turmeric, paprika, cilantro and lime juice, stir well, cook for 10 minutes more, divide between 2 plates and serve as a side dish.
Nutrition: calories 191, fat 1, fiber 2, carbs 4, protein 5

116. Refried Beans

Preparation time: 10 minutes
Cooking time: 35 minutes
Servings: 2
Ingredients:
1 pound pinto beans, soaked for 20 minutes and drained
1 cup onion, chopped
2 garlic cloves, minced
1 teaspoon oregano, dried
½ jalapeno, chopped
1 teaspoon cumin, ground
A pinch of salt and black pepper
1 and ½ tablespoon olive oil
2 cups chicken stock
Directions:
In your pressure cooker, mix oil with onion, jalapeno, garlic, oregano, cumin, salt, pepper, stock and beans, stir, cover and cook on Manual for 30 minutes.
Stir beans one more time, divide them between 2 plates and serve as a side dish.
Nutrition: calories 200, fat 1, fiber 3, carbs 7, protein 7

117. Sweet Brussels Sprouts

Preparation time: 10 minutes
Cooking time: 4 minutes
Servings: 2
Ingredients:

½ pounds Brussels sprouts
2 teaspoon buttery spread
½ teaspoon orange zest, grated
1 tablespoon orange juice
½ tablespoon maple syrup
A pinch of salt and black pepper
Directions:
In your pressure cooker, mix Brussels sprouts with buttery spread, orange zest, orange juice, maple syrup, salt and pepper, stir, cover and cook on High for 4 minutes.
Divide between 2 plates and serve as a side dish.
Nutrition: calories 65, fat 2, fiber 3, carbs 10, protein 3

118. Roasted Potatoes

Preparation time: 10 minutes
Cooking time: 15 minutes
Servings: 2
Ingredients:
½pound potatoes, cut into wedges
¼ teaspoon onion powder
½ teaspoon garlic powder
2 tablespoons avocado oil
A pinch of salt and black pepper
½ cup chicken stock
Directions:
Set your pressure cooker on sauté mode, add the oil and heat it up.
Add potatoes, onion powder, garlic powder, salt and pepper, stir and sauté for 8 minutes.
Add stock, cover and cook on High for 7 minutes more.
Divide between 2 plates and serve as a side dish.
Nutrition: calories 192, fat 1, fiber 4, carbs 8, protein 8

119. Squash Risotto

Preparation time: 10 minutes
Cooking time: 13 minutes
Servings: 2
Ingredients:
1 small yellow onion, chopped
A drizzle of olive oil
1 garlic clove, minced
½ red bell pepper, chopped
1 cup butternut squash, chopped
1 cup Arborio rice

1 and ½ cups veggie stock
3 tablespoons dry white wine
4 ounces mushrooms, chopped
A pinch of salt and black pepper
A pinch of oregano, dried
¼ teaspoon coriander, ground
1 and ½ cups mixed kale and spinach
1 tablespoon nutritional yeast
Directions:
Set your pressure cooker on sauté mode, add the oil and heat it up.
Add onion, bell pepper, squash and garlic, stir and cook for 5 minutes.
Add rice, stock, wine, salt, pepper, mushrooms, oregano and coriander, stir, cover and cook on High for 5 minutes.
Add mixed kale and spinach, parsley and yeast, stir and leave aside for 5 minutes.
Divide between 2 plates and serve as a side dish.
Nutrition: calories 163, fat 1, fiber 2, carbs 3, protein 6

120. Cabbage Side Dish

Preparation time: 10 minutes
Cooking time: 10 minutes
Servings: 2
Ingredients:
½ pound turkey sausage, sliced
½ cabbage head, shredded
2 garlic cloves, minced
½ yellow onion, chopped
1 teaspoon sugar
1 teaspoon balsamic vinegar
1 teaspoon mustard
A drizzle of olive oil
A pinch of salt and black pepper
Directions:
Set your pressure cooker on sauté mode, add the oil and heat it up.
Add onion, sausage and garlic, stir and sauté for 5 minutes.
Add cabbage, sugar, vinegar, mustard, salt and pepper, stir, cover and cook on High for 5 minutes more.
Divide between 2 plates and serve.
Nutrition: calories 200, fat 3, fiber 1, carbs 8, protein 3

121. Beans and Chorizo

Preparation time: 10 minutes
Cooking time: 42 minutes

Servings: 2
Ingredients:
½ tablespoon vegetable oil
3 ounces chorizo, chopped
½ pound black beans
½ yellow onion, chopped
3 garlic cloves, minced
½ orange
1 bay leaf
1 quart chicken stock
A pinch of salt and black pepper
1 tablespoon cilantro, chopped
Directions:
Set your pressure cooker on sauté mode, add the oil and heat it up.
Add chorizo, stir and cook for 2 minutes.
Add garlic, onion, beans, orange, bay leaf, salt, pepper and stock, stir, cover and cook on High for 40 minutes.
Discard bay leaf and orange, add cilantro, stir, divide between plates and serve as a side dish.
Nutrition: calories 224, fat 1, fiber 2, carbs 7, protein 10

122. Spanish Rice

Preparation time: 10 minutes
Cooking time: 12 minutes
Servings: 2
Ingredients:
½ tablespoon olive oil
½ tablespoon butter
½ cup rice
½ cup chicken stock
½ cup tomato sauce
1 teaspoon chili powder
½ teaspoon cumin, ground
¼ teaspoon oregano, dried
A pinch of salt and black pepper
2 tablespoons tomatoes, chopped
Directions:
Put the oil in your pressure cooker, set on sauté mode and heat it up.
Add rice, stir and cook for 4 minutes.
Add stock, tomato sauce, chili powder, cumin, oregano, tomatoes, salt and pepper, stir, cover and cook on High for 8 minutes.
Stir rice one more time, divide between 2 plates and serve as a side dish.

Nutrition: calories 174, fat 1, fiber 2, carbs 6, protein 8

123.Spaghetti Squash Delight

Preparation time: 10 minutes
Cooking time: 33 minutes
Servings: 2
Ingredients:
1 cup water
1 small spaghetti squash
½ cup apple juice
1 tablespoon duck fat
A pinch of salt and black pepper
Directions:
Put the water in your pressure cooker, add the steamer basket, add the squash inside, cover and cook on High for 30 minutes.
Cut squash in half, scoop seeds and take out squash spaghetti.
Clean the pressure cooker, set it on sauté mode, add duck fat and heat it up.
Add apple juice, salt and pepper, stir and simmer for 3 minutes.
Divide squash spaghetti between 2 plates, drizzle the sauce all over, toss a bit and serve as a side dish.
Nutrition: calories 183, fat 3, fiber 3, carbs 7, protein 8

124.Artichokes Side Dish

Preparation time: 10 minutes
Cooking time: 20 minutes
Servings: 2
Ingredients:
2 artichokes, trimmed and tops cut off
1 cup water
1 lemon wedges
Directions:
Rub artichokes with the lemon wedge.
Add the water to your pressure cooker, add the steamer basket, place artichokes inside, cover and cook on High for 20 minutes.
Divide between 2 plates and serve as a side dish.
Nutrition: calories 100, fat 1, fiber 1, carbs 1, protein 3

125.Cabbage and Cream

Preparation time: 10 minutes
Cooking time: 10 minutes
Servings: 2
Ingredients:
½ cup bacon, chopped

½ yellow onion, chopped
1 cup beef stock
1 pound Savoy cabbage, chopped
A pinch of nutmeg, ground
½ cup coconut milk
1 small bay leaf
1 tablespoon parsley flakes
A pinch of salt
Directions:
Set your pressure cooker on sauté mode, add bacon and onion, stir and cook for 3 minutes.
Add stock, bay leaf and cabbage, cover the cooker and cook on Manual for 4 minutes.
Set the cooker on sauté mode again, add coconut milk, nutmeg and a pinch of salt, discard bay leaf, stir cabbage and simmer for 4 minutes.
Sprinkle parsley flakes at the end, divide between 2 plates and serve.
Nutrition: calories 229, fat 2, fiber 4, carbs 9, protein 6

126. Carrots and Kale

Preparation time: 10 minutes
Cooking time: 11 minutes
Servings: 2
Ingredients:
10 ounces kale, roughly chopped
1 tablespoon butter
3 carrots, sliced
1 yellow onion, chopped
4 garlic cloves, minced
½ cup chicken stock
A pinch of salt and black pepper
A splash of balsamic vinegar
¼ teaspoon red pepper flakes
Directions:
Set your pressure cooker on sauté mode, add butter and melt it.
Add onion and carrots, stir and cook for 3 minutes.
Add garlic, stir and cook for 1 minute more.
Add kale and stock, cover and cook on High for 7 minutes.
Add vinegar and pepper flakes, stir, divide between 2 plates and serve.
Nutrition: calories 183, fat 2, fiber 3, carbs 6, protein 8

127. Beets Side Dish

Preparation time: 10 minutes
Cooking time: 25 minutes

Servings: 2
Ingredients:
2 beets
1 tablespoon balsamic vinegar
½ bunch parsley, chopped
A pinch of salt and black pepper
1 small garlic clove, minced
½ tablespoon olive oil
1 tablespoon capers
1 cup water
Directions:
Put the water in your pressure cooker, add the steamer basket, add beets inside, cover and cook on High for 25 minutes.
Transfer beets to a cutting board, leave aside to cool down, peel, slice and transfer to a bowl.
In another bowl, mix parsley with salt, pepper, garlic, oil and capers and whisk really well.
Divide beets on plates, drizzle vinegar all over, add parsley dressing and serve as a side dish.
Nutrition: calories 76, fat 2, fiber 1, carbs 4, protein 1

Dessert Recipes

128. Fiesta Pastries

Preparation time: 15 minutes

Cooking time: 20 minutes

Servings: 8

Ingredients:

½ of apple, peeled, cored and chopped

1 teaspoon fresh orange zest, grated finely

7.05-ounce prepared frozen puff pastry, cut into 16 squares

½ tablespoon white sugar

½ teaspoon ground cinnamon

Directions:

Preheat the Air fryer to 390 o F and grease an Air fryer basket.

Mix all ingredients in a bowl except puff pastry.

Arrange about 1 teaspoon of this mixture in the center of each square.

Fold each square into a triangle and slightly press the edges with a fork.

Arrange the pastries in the Air fryer basket and cook for about 10 minutes.

Dish out and serve immediately.

Nutrition:

Calories: 147, Fat: 9.5g, Carbohydrates: 13.8g, Sugar: 2.1g, Protein: 1.9g, Sodium: 62mg

129. Classic Buttermilk Biscuits

Preparation time: 15 minutes

Cooking time: 8 minutes

Servings: 4

Ingredients:

½ cup cake flour

1¼ cups all-purpose flour

¾ teaspoon baking powder

¼ cup + 2 tablespoons butter, cut into cubes

¾ cup buttermilk

1 teaspoon granulated sugar

Salt, to taste

Directions:

Preheat the Air fryer to 400 o F and grease a pie pan lightly.

Sift together flours, baking soda, baking powder, sugar and salt in a large bowl.

Add cold butter and mix until a coarse crumb is formed.

Stir in the buttermilk slowly and mix until a dough is formed.

Press the dough into ½ inch thickness onto a floured surface and cut out circles with a 1¾-inch round cookie cutter.

Arrange the biscuits in a pie pan in a single layer and brush butter on them. Transfer into the Air fryer and cook for about 8 minutes until golden brown.
Nutrition:
Calories: 374, Fat: 18.2g, Carbohydrates: 45.2g, Sugar: 3.4g, Protein: 7.3g, Sodium: 291mg

130. Blueberry bowls
Preparation time: 10 minutes
Cooking time: 12 minutes
Servings: 4
Ingredients:
2 cups blueberries
1 cup coconut water
2 tablespoons sugar
2 teaspoons vanilla extract
Juice of ½ lime
Directions:
In your air fryer's pan, combine the blueberries with the water and the other ingredients, toss and cook at 320 degrees f for 12 minutes.
Serve cold.
Nutrition: calories 230, fat 2, fiber 2, carbs 14, protein 7

131. Carrot brownies
Preparation time: 10 minutes
Cooking time: 25 minutes
Servings: 8
Ingredients:
1 teaspoon almond extract
2 eggs, whisked
½ cup butter, melted
4 tablespoons sugar
2 cups almond flour
½ cup carrot, peeled and grated
Directions:
In a bowl, combine the eggs with the butter and the other ingredients, whisk, spread this into a pan that fits your air fryer, introduce in the fryer and cook at 340 degrees f for 25 minutes.
Cool down, slice and serve.
Nutrition: calories 230, fat 12, fiber 2, carbs 12, protein 5

132. Yogurt cake
Preparation time: 10 minutes
Cooking time: 30 minutes

Servings: 8
Ingredients:
6 eggs, whisked
1 teaspoon vanilla extract
1 teaspoon baking soda
9 ounces almond flour
4 tablespoons sugar
2 cups yogurt
Directions:
In a blender, combine the eggs with the vanilla and the other ingredients, pulse, spread into a cake pan lined with parchment paper, put it in the air fryer and cook at 330 degrees f for 30 minutes.
Cool the cake down, slice and serve.
Nutrition: calories 231, fat 13, fiber 2, carbs 11, protein 5

133. Chocolate ramekins

Preparation time: 10 minutes
Cooking time: 20 minutes
Servings: 4
Ingredients:
2 cups cream cheese, soft
3 tablespoons sugar
4 eggs, whisked
1 teaspoon vanilla extract
½ cup heavy cream
2 cups white chocolate, melted
Directions:
In a bowl combine the cream cheese with the sugar and the other ingredients, whisk well, divide into 4 ramekins, put them in the air fryer's basket and cook at 370 degrees f for 20 minutes.
Serve cold.
Nutrition: calories 261, fat 12, fiber 6, carbs 12, protein 6

134. Grapes cake

Preparation time: 10 minutes
Cooking time: 25 minutes
Servings: 8
Ingredients:
1 cup coconut flour
1 teaspoon baking powder
¾ teaspoon almond extract
¾ cup sugar
Cooking spray

1 cup heavy cream
2 cup grapes, halved
1 egg, whisked
Directions:
In a bowl, combine the flour with the baking powder and the other ingredients except the cooking spray and whisk well.
Grease a cake pan with cooking spray, pour the cake batter inside, spread, introduce the pan in the air fryer and cook at 330 degrees f for 25 minutes.
Cool the cake down, slice and serve.
Nutrition: calories 214, fat 9, fiber 3, carbs 14, protein 8

135. Carrots bread
Preparation time: 10 minutes
Cooking time: 40 minutes
Servings: 6
Ingredients:
2 cups carrots, peeled and grated
1 cup sugar
3 eggs, whisked
2 cups white flour
1 tablespoon baking soda
1 cup almond milk
Directions:
In a bowl, combine the carrots with the sugar and the other ingredients, whisk well, pour this into a lined loaf pan, introduce the pan in the air fryer and cook at 340 degrees f for 40 minutes.
Cool the bread down, slice and serve.
Nutrition: calories 200, fat 5, fiber 3, carbs 13, protein 7

136. Pear pudding
Preparation time: 10 minutes
Cooking time: 20 minutes
Servings: 6
Ingredients:
3 tablespoons sugar
½ cup butter, melted
2 eggs, whisked
2 pears, peeled and chopped
1/3 cup almond milk
½ cup heavy cream
Directions:
In a bowl, combine the butter with the sugar and the other ingredients, whisk well and pour into a pudding pan.

Introduce the pan in the air fryer and cook at 340 degrees f for 20 minutes. Cool the pudding down, divide into bowls and serve.
Nutrition: calories 211, fat 4, fiber 6, carbs 14, protein 6

137. Lime cake
Preparation time: 10 minutes
Cooking time: 30 minutes
Servings: 4
Ingredients:
1 egg, whisked
2 tablespoons sugar
2 tablespoons butter, melted
½ cup almond milk
2 tablespoons lime juice
1 tablespoon lime zest, grated
1 cup heavy cream
½ teaspoon baking powder
Directions:
In a bowl, combine the egg with the sugar, butter and the other ingredients, whisk well and transfer to a cake pan lined with parchment paper.
Put the pan in your air fryer and cook at 320 degrees f for 30 minutes.
Serve the cake cold.
Nutrition: calories 213, fat 5, fiber 5, carbs 15, protein 6

138. Pear stew
Preparation time: 10 minutes
Cooking time: 20 minutes
Servings: 4
Ingredients:
2 teaspoons cinnamon powder
4 pears, cored and cut into wedges
1 cup water
2 tablespoons sugar
Directions:
In your air fryer's pan, combine the pears with the water and the other ingredients, cook at 300 degrees f for 20 minutes, divide into cups and serve cold.
Nutrition: calories 200, fat 3, fiber 4, carbs 16, protein 4

139. Avocado cream
Preparation time: 10 minutes
Cooking time: 10 minutes
Servings: 4

Ingredients:

2 avocados, peeled, pitted and mashed

2 cups heavy cream

2 tablespoons sugar

1 tablespoon lemon juice

Directions:

In a blender, combine the avocados with the cream and the other ingredients, pulse well, divide into 4 ramekins, introduce them in the fryer and cook at 320 degrees f for 10 minutes.

Serve the cream really cold.

Nutrition: calories 171, fat 1, fiber 4, carbs 8, protein 2

140. Apples and wine sauce

Preparation time: 10 minutes

Cooking time: 20 minutes

Servings: 4

Ingredients:

3 apples, cored and cut intro wedges

1 teaspoon nutmeg, ground

1 cup red wine

½ cup sugar

Directions:

In your air fryer's pan, combine the apples with the nutmeg and the other ingredients, toss and cook at 340 degrees f for 20 minutes.

Divide into bowls and serve.

Nutrition: calories 200, fat 1, fiber 4, carbs 12, protein 3

141. Mandarin cream

Preparation time: 10 minutes

Cooking time: 15 minutes

Servings: 4

Ingredients:

2 cups heavy cream

2 mandarins, peeled and chopped

1 teaspoon vanilla extract

2 tablespoons sugar

Directions:

In a bowl, combine the cream with the mandarins and the other ingredients, whisk, transfer to 4 ramekins, put them in the air fryer's basket and cook at 300 degrees f for 15 minutes.

Whisk the cream, divide it into cups and serve.

Nutrition: calories 200, fat 3, fiber 4, carbs 11, protein 3

142. Avocado cake

Preparation time: 10 minutes
Cooking time: 30 minutes
Servings: 4
Ingredients:
2 avocados, peeled, pitted and mashed
1 cup almond flour
2 teaspoons baking powder
1 cup sugar
1 cup butter, melted
3 tablespoons maple syrup
4 eggs, whisked
Directions:
In a bowl, combine the avocados with the flour and the other ingredients, whisk, pour this into a lined cake pan, introduce the pan in the fryer and cook at 340 degrees f for 30 minutes.
Leave the cake to cool down, slice and serve.
Nutrition: calories 213, fat 3, fiber 6, carbs 15, protein 4

143. Egg pudding

Preparation time: 10 minutes
Cooking time: 25 minutes
Serving: 6
Ingredients:
4 eggs, whisked
1 cup almond milk
½ cup heavy cream
¾ cup sugar
1 teaspoon cinnamon powder
½ teaspoon ginger powder
Directions:
In a bowl, combine the eggs with the almond milk and the other ingredients, whisk, pour into a pudding mould, put it in the air fryer and cook at 340 degrees f for 25 minutes.
Serve the pudding cold.
Nutrition: calories 200, fat 4, fiber 6, carbs 15, protein 4

144. Quinoa pudding

Preparation time: 10 minutes
Cooking time: 20 minutes
Servings: 6
Ingredients:
2 cups almond milk

1 teaspoon vanilla extract

1 teaspoon nutmeg, ground

1 cup quinoa

½ cup sugar

Directions:

In your air fryer's pan, combine the almond milk with the quinoa and the other ingredients, whisk, and cook at 320 degrees f for 20 minutes.

Divide into bowls and serve.

Nutrition: calories 161, fat 3, fiber 5, carbs 14, protein 4

145.Cake with cream and strawberries

Preparation time: 10 minutes

Cooking time: 15 minutes

Servings: 2

Ingredients:

1 pure butter puff pastry to stretch

500g strawberries (clean and without skin)

1 bowl of custard

3 tbsp icing sugar baked at 210°C in the air fryer

Direction:

Unroll the puff pastry and place it on the baking sheet. Prick the bottom with a fork and spread the custard. Arrange the strawberries in a circle and sprinkle with icing sugar.

Cook in a fryer setting a 210°C for 15 minutes.

Remove the cake from the fryer with the tongs and let cool.

When serving sprinkle with icing sugar

And why not, add some whipped cream.

Nutrition:

Calories 212.6

Fat 8.3 g

Carbohydrate 31.9 g

Sugars 17.4 g

Protein2.3 g

Cholesterol 21.4 mg

146.Caramelized Pineapple and Vanilla Ice Cream

Preparation time: 0-10 minutes

Cooking time: 15-30 minutes

Servings: 4

Ingredients:

4 slices Pineapple

20g Butter

50g Cane sugar

Ice cream/vanilla cream
Direction:
Heat the Air Fryer at 1500C for 5 minutes. Let it brown for 15-30 minutes.
Then, take it out and top with the cream.
Nutrition:
Calories 648
Fat 36.4g
Carbohydrates 73.2g
Sugar 61.6g
Protein 9.5g
Cholesterol 94mg

147. Apple Pie

Preparation time: 20-30 minutes
Cooking time: 45-60 minutes
Servings: 3
Ingredients:
600g Flour
350g Margarine
150g Sugar
2 Eggs
50g Breadcrumbs
3 Apples
75g Raisins
75g Sugar
1tsp Cinnamon
Direction:
Put the flour, sugar, eggs, and margarine nuts in the blender just outside the refrigerator.
Mix everything until you get a compact and quite flexible mixture. Let it rest in the refrigerator for at least 30 minutes.
Preheat the air fryer at 1500C for 5 minutes.
Spread 2/3 of the mass of broken dough in 3-4 mm thick covering the previously floured and floured tank and making the edges adhere well, which should be at least 2 cm.
Place the breadcrumbs, apple slices, sugar, raisins, and cinnamon in the bottom; cover everything with the remaining dough and make holes in the top to allow steam to escape.
Cook for 40 minutes and then turn off the lower resistance.
Cook for another 20 minutes only with the upper resistance on. Once it has cooled, put it on a plate and serve.
Nutrition:
Calories 411

Fat 19.38g
Total Carbohydrate 57.5g
Sugars 50g
Protein3.72g
Cholesterol0mg

Vegetarian Recipes

148. Parmesan Broccoli and Asparagus

Preparation Time: 20 minutes
Cooking Time: 15 minutes
Servings: 4
Ingredients:
½ lb. asparagus, trimmed
1 broccoli head, florets separated
Juice of 1 lime
3 tbsp. parmesan, grated
2 tbsp. olive oil
Salt and black pepper to taste.
Directions:
Take a bowl and mix the asparagus with the broccoli and all the other ingredients except the parmesan, toss, transfer to your air fryer's basket and cook at 400°F for 15 minutes
Divide between plates, sprinkle the parmesan on top and serve.
Nutrition: Calories: 172; Fat: 5g; Fiber: 2g; Carbs: 4g; Protein: 9g

149. Italian Asparagus

Preparation Time: 15 minutes
Cooking Time: 10 minutes
Servings: 4
Ingredients:
1 lb. asparagus, trimmed
2 cups cherry tomatoes; halved
2 cups mozzarella, shredded
½ cup balsamic vinegar
2 tbsp. olive oil
A pinch of salt and black pepper
Directions:
In a pan that fits your air fryer, mix the asparagus with the rest of the ingredients except the mozzarella and toss
Put the pan in the air fryer and cook at 400°F for 10 minutes. Divide between plates and serve
Nutrition: Calories: 200; Fat: 6g; Fiber: 2g; Carbs: 3g; Protein: 6g

150. Spinach Cheese Pie

Preparation Time: 10 minutes
Cooking Time: 20 minutes
Servings: 4
Ingredients:
1 cup frozen chopped spinach, drained

¼ cup heavy whipping cream.
1 cup shredded sharp Cheddar cheese.
¼ cup diced yellow onion
6 large eggs.
Directions:
Take a medium bowl, whisk eggs and add cream. Add remaining ingredients to bowl.
Pour into a 6-inch round baking dish. Place into the air fryer basket. Adjust the temperature to 320 Degrees F and set the timer for 20 minutes
Eggs will be firm and slightly browned when cooked. Serve immediately.
Nutrition: Calories: 288; Protein: 18.0g; Fiber: 1.3g; Fat: 20.0g; Carbs: 3.9g

151. Garlic Tomatoes

Preparation Time: 5 minutes
Cooking Time: 15 minutes
Servings: 4
Ingredients:
1 lb. cherry tomatoes; halved
6 garlic cloves; minced
1 tbsp. olive oil
1 tbsp. dill; chopped.
1 tbsp. balsamic vinegar
Salt and black pepper to taste.
Directions:
In a pan that fits the air fryer, combine all the ingredients, toss gently.
Put the pan in the air fryer and cook at 380°F for 15 minutes
Divide between plates and serve.
Nutrition: Calories: 121; Fat: 3g; Fiber: 2g; Carbs: 4g; Protein: 6g

152. Zucchini and Olives

Preparation Time: 5 minutes
Cooking Time: 12 minutes
Servings: 4
Ingredients:
4 zucchinis; sliced
2 tbsp. olive oil
1 cup kalamata olives, pitted
2 tbsp. lime juice
2 tsp. balsamic vinegar
Salt and black pepper to taste.
Directions:
In a pan that fits your air fryer, mix the olives with all the other ingredients, toss, introduce in the fryer and cook at 390°F for 12 minutes

Divide the mix between plates and serve.
Nutrition: Calories: 150; Fat: 4g; Fiber: 2g; Carbs: 4g; Protein: 5g

153. Bacon Asparagus

Preparation Time: 5 minutes
Cooking Time: 10 minutes
Servings: 4
Ingredients:
2 lb. asparagus, trimmed
4 bacon slices, cooked and crumbled
1 cup cheddar cheese, shredded
4 garlic cloves; minced
2 tbsp. olive oil
Directions:
Take a bowl and mix the asparagus with the other ingredients except the bacon, toss and put in your air fryer's basket
Cook at 400°F for 10 minutes, divide between plates, sprinkle the bacon on top and serve.
Nutrition: Calories: 172; Fat: 6g; Fiber: 2g; Carbs: 5g; Protein: 8g

154. Broccoli and Almonds

Preparation Time: 5 minutes
Cooking Time: 12 minutes
Servings: 4
Ingredients:
1 lb. broccoli florets
½ cup almonds; chopped
3 garlic cloves; minced
1 tbsp. chives; chopped
2 tbsp. red vinegar
3 tbsp. coconut oil; melted
A pinch of salt and black pepper
Directions:
Take a bowl and mix the broccoli with the garlic, salt, pepper, vinegar and the oil and toss.
Put the broccoli in your air fryer's basket and cook at 380°F for 12 minutes
Divide between plates and serve with almonds and chives sprinkled on top.
Nutrition: Calories: 180; Fat: 4g; Fiber: 2g; Carbs: 4g; Protein: 6g

155. Turmeric Cabbage

Preparation Time: 5 minutes
Cooking Time: 15 minutes
Servings: 4

Ingredients:

1 green cabbage head, shredded

¼ cup ghee; melted

1 tbsp. dill; chopped.

2 tsp. turmeric powder

Directions:

In a pan that fits your air fryer, mix the cabbage with the rest of the ingredients except the dill, toss, put the pan in the fryer and cook at 370°F for 15 minutes

Divide everything between plates and serve with dill sprinkled on top.

Nutrition: Calories: 173; Fat: 5g; Fiber: 3g; Carbs: 6g; Protein: 7g

156. Parmesan Artichokes

Preparation Time: 10 minutes

Cooking Time: 10 minutes

Servings: 4

Ingredients:

¼ cup blanched finely ground almond flour.

2 medium artichokes, trimmed and quartered, center removed

1 large egg, beaten

½ cup grated vegetarian Parmesan cheese.

2 tbsp. coconut oil

½ tsp. crushed red pepper flakes.

Directions:

Take a large bowl, toss artichokes in coconut oil and then dip each piece into the egg.

Mix the Parmesan and almond flour in a large bowl. Add artichoke pieces and toss to cover as completely as possible, sprinkle with pepper flakes. Place into the air fryer basket

Adjust the temperature to 400 Degrees F and set the timer for 10 minutes. Toss the basket two times during cooking. Serve warm.

Nutrition: Calories: 189; Protein: 7.9g; Fiber: 4.2g; Fat: 13.5g; Carbs: 10.0g

157. Roasted Broccoli Salad

Preparation Time: 5 minutes

Cooking Time: 10 minutes

Servings: 2

Ingredients:

3 cups fresh broccoli florets.

½ medium lemon.

¼ cup sliced almonds.

2 tbsp. salted butter; melted.

Directions:

Place broccoli into a 6-inch round baking dish. Pour butter over broccoli. Add almonds and toss. Place dish into the air fryer basket

Adjust the temperature to 380 Degrees F and set the timer for 7 minutes. Stir halfway through the cooking time. When timer beeps, zest lemon onto broccoli and squeeze juice into pan. Toss. Serve warm.

Nutrition: Calories: 215; Protein: 6.4g; Fiber: 5.0g; Fat: 16.3g; Carbs: 12.1g

158. Protein Doughnut Holes

Preparation Time: 10 minutes

Cooking Time: 20 minutes

Servings: 12 holes

Ingredients:

½ cup blanched finely ground almond flour.

1 large egg.

½ cup granular erythritol.

½ cup low-carb vanilla protein powder

½ tsp. baking powder.

5 tbsp. unsalted butter; melted.

½ tsp. vanilla extract.

Directions:

Mix all ingredients in a large bowl. Place into the freezer for 20 minutes.

Wet your hands with water and roll the dough into twelve balls

Cut a piece of parchment to fit your air fryer basket. Working in batches as necessary, place doughnut holes into the air fryer basket on top of parchment

Adjust the temperature to 380 Degrees F and set the timer for 6 minutes. Flip doughnut holes halfway through the cooking time. Let cool completely before serving.

Nutrition: Calories: 221; Protein: 19.8g; Fiber: 1.7g; Fat: 14.3g; Carbs: 23.2g

159. Kale and Bell Peppers

Preparation Time: 5 minutes

Cooking Time: 10 minutes

Servings: 4

Ingredients:

1 ½ cups avocado, peeled, pitted and cubed

2 cups kale, torn

¼ cup olive oil

1 cup red bell pepper; sliced

1 tbsp. white vinegar

2 tbsp. lime juice

1 tbsp. mustard

A pinch of salt and black pepper

Directions:

In a pan that fits the air fryer, combine the kale with salt, pepper, avocado and half of the oil, toss.

Put in your air fryer and cook at 360°F for 10 minutes

In a bowl, combine the kale mix with the rest of the ingredients, toss and serve.

Nutrition: Calories: 131; Fat: 3g; Fiber: 2g; Carbs: 4g; Protein: 5g

160. Chocolate Chip Pan Cookie

Preparation Time: 10 minutes

Cooking Time: 7 minutes

Servings: 4

Ingredients:

½ cup blanched finely ground almond flour.

1 large egg.

¼ cup powdered erythritol

2 tbsp. unsalted butter; softened.

2 tbsp. low-carb, sugar-free chocolate chips

½ tsp. unflavored gelatin

½ tsp. baking powder.

½ tsp. vanilla extract.

Directions:

Take a large bowl, mix almond flour and erythritol. Stir in butter, egg and gelatin until combined.

Stir in baking powder and vanilla and then fold in chocolate chips

Pour batter into 6-inch round baking pan. Place pan into the air fryer basket.

Adjust the temperature to 300 Degrees F and set the timer for 7 minutes

When fully cooked, the top will be golden brown and a toothpick inserted in center will come out clean. Let cool at least 10 minutes.

Nutrition: Calories: 188; Protein: 5.6g; Fiber: 2.0g; Fat: 15.7g; Carbs: 16.8g

161. Roasted Asparagus

Preparation Time: 15 minutes

Cooking Time: 10 minutes

Servings: 4

Ingredients:

1 lb. asparagus, trimmed

1 tbsp. sweet paprika

3 tbsp. olive oil

A pinch of salt and black pepper

Directions:

Take a bowl and mix the asparagus with the rest of the ingredients and toss

Put the asparagus in your air fryer's basket and cook at 400°F for 10 minutes.

Divide between plates and serve

Nutrition: Calories: 200; Fat: 5g; Fiber: 2g; Carbs: 4g; Protein: 6g

162. Portobello Mini Pizzas

Preparation Time: 5 minutes
Cooking Time: 15 minutes
Servings: 2
Ingredients:
2 large portobello mushrooms
2 leaves fresh basil; chopped
⅔ cup shredded mozzarella cheese
4 grape tomatoes, sliced
1 tbsp. balsamic vinegar
2 tbsp. unsalted butter; melted.
½ tsp. garlic powder.
Directions:
Scoop out the inside of the mushrooms, leaving just the caps. Brush each cap with butter and sprinkle with garlic powder.
Fill each cap with mozzarella and sliced tomatoes. Place each mini pizza into a 6-inch round baking pan. Place pan into the air fryer basket.
Adjust the temperature to 380 Degrees F and set the timer for 10 minutes
Carefully remove the pizzas from the fryer basket and garnish with basil and a drizzle of vinegar.
Nutrition: Calories: 244; Protein: 10.4g; Fiber: 1.4g; Fat: 18.5g; Carbs: 6.8g

163. Frying Potatoes

Preparation time: 5 minutes
Cooking time: 40 minutes
Servings: 4
Ingredients:
5 to 6 medium potatoes
Olive oil in a spray bottle if possible
Mill salt
Freshly ground pepper
 Direction:
Wash the potatoes well and dry them.
Brush with a little oil on both sides if not with the oil
Crush some ground salt and pepper on top.
Place the potatoes in the fryer basket
Set the cooking at 190°C for 40 minutes, in the middle of cooking turn the potatoes for even cooking on both sides.
At the end of cooking, remove the potatoes from the basket, cut them in half and slightly scrape the melting potato inside and add only a little butter, and enjoy!
Nutrition:
Calories 365

Fat 17g
Carbohydrates 48g
Sugars 0.3g
Protein 4g
Cholesterol 0mg

164. Avocado Fries

Preparation time: 5 minutes
Cooking time: 10 minutes
Serving: 1
Ingredients:
1 egg
1 ripe avocado
½ tsp salt
½ cup of panko breadcrumbs
Direction:
Preheat the air fryer to 400°F (200°C) for 5 minutes.
Remove the avocado pit and cut into fries. In a small bowl, whisk the egg with the salt.
Enter the breadcrumbs on a plate.
Dip the quarters in the egg mixture, then in the breadcrumbs.
Put them in the fryer. Cook for 8-10 minutes.
Turn halfway through cooking.
Nutrition:
Calories 390
Fat 32g
Carbohydrates 24g
Sugars 3g
Protein 4g
Cholesterol 0mg

165. Crispy French Fries

Preparation time: 5 minutes; Cooking time: 10 minutes; Serve: 2
Ingredients:
2 medium sweet potatoes
2 tsp olive oil
½ tsp salt
½ tsp garlic powder
¼ tsp paprika
Black pepper
Direction:
Preheat the hot air fryer to 400°F (200°C)
Spray the basket with a little oil.

Cut the sweet potatoes into potato chips about 1 cm wide.
Add oil, salt, garlic powder, pepper and paprika.
Cook for 8 minutes, without overloading the basket.
Repeat 2 or 3 times, as necessary.
Nutrition:
Calories 240
Fat 9g
Carbohydrates 36g
Sugars 1g
Protein 3g
Cholesterol 0mg

166. Frying Potatoes with Butter
Preparation time: 5 minutes
Cooking time: 10 minutes
Servings: 2
Ingredients:
2 Russet potatoes
Butter
Fresh parsley (optional)
Direction:
Spray the basket with a little oil.
Open your potatoes along.
Make some holes with a fork.
Add the butter and parsley.
Transfer to the basket. If your air fryer to a temperature of 198°C (390°F).
Cook for 30 to 40 minutes.
Try about 30 minutes. Bon Appetite!
Nutrition:
Calories 365
Fat 17g
Carbohydrates 48g
Sugars 0.3g
Protein 4g
Cholesterol 0mg

167. Homemade French Fries
Preparation time: 5 minutes
Cooking time: 10 minutes
Servings: 2
Ingredients:
2.5 lb. sliced and sliced potato chips
1 tbsp olive oil

Salt and pepper to taste
1 tsp salt to season or paprika
Direction:
Put the fries in a bowl with very cold water.
Let it soak for at least 30 minutes.
Drain completely. Add the oil. Shake
Put them in the fryer bowl. Cook for 15 to 25 minutes. Set to 380°F (193°C).
Set the time according to your preferences or the power of your fryer to 23 minutes.
Nutrition:
Calories 118
Fat 7g
Carbohydrates 27
Sugars 1g
Protein 2
Cholesterol 0mg

Brunch Recipes

168. Radish Hash Browns

Preparation Time: 10 minutes
Cooking Time: 13 minutes
Servings: 4
Ingredients:
1 lb radishes, washed and cut off roots
1 tbsp olive oil
1/2 tsp paprika
1/2 tsp onion powder
1/2 tsp garlic powder
1 medium onion
1/4 tsp pepper
3/4 tsp sea salt
Directions:
Slice onion and radishes using a mandolin slicer.
Add sliced onion and radishes in a large mixing bowl and toss with olive oil.
Transfer onion and radish slices in air fryer basket and cook at 360 F for 8 minutes. Shake basket twice.
Return onion and radish slices in a mixing bowl and toss with seasonings.
Again, cook onion and radish slices in air fryer basket for 5 minutes at 400 F. Shake basket halfway through.
Serve and enjoy.
Nutrition:
Calories 62
Fat 3.7 g
Carbohydrates 7.1 g
Sugar 3.5 g
Protein 1.2 g
Cholesterol 0 mg

169. Vegetable Egg Cups

Preparation Time:10 minutes
Cooking Time:20 minutes
Servings:4
Ingredients:
4 eggs
1 tbsp cilantro, chopped
4 tbsp half and half
1 cup cheddar cheese, shredded
1 cup vegetables, diced
Pepper
Salt

Directions:

Spray four ramekins with cooking spray and set aside.

In a mixing bowl, whisk eggs with cilantro, half and half, vegetables, 1/2 cup cheese, pepper, and salt.

Pour egg mixture into the four ramekins.

Place ramekins in air fryer basket and cook at 300 F for 12 minutes.

Top with remaining 1/2 cup cheese and cook for 2 minutes more at 400 F.

Serve and enjoy.

Nutrition:

Calories 194

Fat 11.5 g

Carbohydrates 6 g

Sugar 0.5 g

Protein 13 g

Cholesterol 190 mg

170.Spinach Frittata

Preparation Time: 5 minutes

Cooking Time: 8 minutes

Servings: 1

Ingredients:

3 eggs

1 cup spinach, chopped

1 small onion, minced

2 tbsp mozzarella cheese, grated

Pepper

Salt

Directions:

Preheat the air fryer to 350 F.

Spray air fryer pan with cooking spray.

In a bowl, whisk eggs with remaining ingredients until well combined.

Pour egg mixture into the prepared pan and place pan in the air fryer basket.

Cook frittata for 8 minutes or until set.

Serve and enjoy.

Nutrition:

Calories 384

Fat 23.3 g

Carbohydrates 10.7 g

Sugar 4.1 g

Protein 34.3 g

Cholesterol 521 mg

171. Omelette Frittata

Preparation Time: 10 minutes
Cooking Time: 6 minutes
Servings: 2
Ingredients:
3 eggs, lightly beaten
2 tbsp cheddar cheese, shredded
2 tbsp heavy cream
2 mushrooms, sliced
1/4 small onion, chopped
1/4 bell pepper, diced
Pepper
Salt
Directions:
In a bowl, whisk eggs with cream, vegetables, pepper, and salt.
Preheat the air fryer to 400 F.
Pour egg mixture into the air fryer pan. Place pan in air fryer basket and cook for 5 minutes.
Add shredded cheese on top of the frittata and cook for 1 minute more.
Serve and enjoy.
Nutrition:
Calories 160
Fat 10 g
Carbohydrates 4 g
Sugar 2 g
Protein 12 g
Cholesterol 255 mg

172. Cheese Soufflés

Preparation Time: 10 minutes
Cooking Time: 6 minutes
Servings: 8
Ingredients:
6 large eggs, separated
3/4 cup heavy cream
1/4 tsp cayenne pepper
1/2 tsp xanthan gum
1/2 tsp pepper
1/4 tsp cream of tartar
2 tbsp chives, chopped
2 cups cheddar cheese, shredded
1 tsp salt
Directions:

Preheat the air fryer to 325 F.

Spray eight ramekins with cooking spray. Set aside.

In a bowl, whisk together almond flour, cayenne pepper, pepper, salt, and xanthan gum.

Slowly add heavy cream and mix to combine.

Whisk in egg yolks, chives, and cheese until well combined.

In a large bowl, add egg whites and cream of tartar and beat until stiff peaks form.

Fold egg white mixture into the almond flour mixture until combined.

Pour mixture into the prepared ramekins. Divide ramekins in batches.

Place the first batch of ramekins into the air fryer basket.

Cook soufflé for 20 minutes.

Serve and enjoy.

Nutrition:

Calories 210

Fat 16 g

Carbohydrates 1 g

Sugar 0.5 g

Protein 12 g

Cholesterol 185 mg

173. Simple Egg Soufflé

Preparation Time: 5 minutes

Cooking Time: 8 minutes

Servings: 2

Ingredients:

2 eggs

1/4 tsp chili pepper

2 tbsp heavy cream

1/4 tsp pepper

1 tbsp parsley, chopped

Salt

Directions:

In a bowl, whisk eggs with remaining gradients.

Spray two ramekins with cooking spray.

Pour egg mixture into the prepared ramekins and place into the air fryer basket.

Cook soufflé at 390 F for 8 minutes.

Serve and enjoy.

Nutrition:

Calories 116

Fat 10 g

Carbohydrates 1.1 g

Sugar 0.4 g

Protein 6 g
Cholesterol 184 mg

174. Vegetable Egg Soufflé

Preparation Time: 10 minutes
Cooking Time: 20 minutes
Servings: 4
Ingredients:
4 large eggs
1 tsp onion powder
1 tsp garlic powder
1 tsp red pepper, crushed
1/2 cup broccoli florets, chopped
1/2 cup mushrooms, chopped
Directions:
Spray four ramekins with cooking spray and set aside.
In a bowl, whisk eggs with onion powder, garlic powder, and red pepper.
Add mushrooms and broccoli and stir well.
Pour egg mixture into the prepared ramekins and place ramekins into the air fryer basket.
Cook at 350 F for 15 minutes. Make sure souffle is cooked if souffle is not cooked then cook for 5 minutes more.
Serve and enjoy.
Nutrition:
Calories 91
Fat 5.1 g
Carbohydrates 4.7 g
Sugar 2.6 g
Protein 7.4 g
Cholesterol 186 mg

175. Asparagus Frittata

Preparation Time: 10 minutes
Cooking Time: 10 minutes
Servings: 4
Ingredients:
6 eggs
3 mushrooms, sliced
10 asparagus, chopped
1/4 cup half and half
2 tsp butter, melted
1 cup mozzarella cheese, shredded
1 tsp pepper

1 tsp salt
Directions:
Toss mushrooms and asparagus with melted butter and add into the air fryer basket.
Cook mushrooms and asparagus at 350 F for 5 minutes. Shake basket twice.
Meanwhile, in a bowl, whisk together eggs, half and half, pepper, and salt.
Transfer cook mushrooms and asparagus into the air fryer baking dish.
Pour egg mixture over mushrooms and asparagus.
Place dish in the air fryer and cook at 350 F for 5 minutes or until eggs are set.
Slice and serve.
Nutrition:
Calories 211
Fat 13 g
Carbohydrates 4 g
Sugar 1 g
Protein 16 g
Cholesterol 272 mg

176. Spicy Cauliflower Rice

Preparation Time: 10 minutes
Cooking Time: 22 minutes
Servings: 2
Ingredients:
1 cauliflower head, cut into florets
1/2 tsp cumin
1/2 tsp chili powder
6 onion spring, chopped
2 jalapenos, chopped
4 tbsp olive oil
1 zucchini, trimmed and cut into cubes
1/2 tsp paprika
1/2 tsp garlic powder
1/2 tsp cayenne pepper
1/2 tsp pepper
1/2 tsp salt
Directions:
Preheat the air fryer to 370 F.
Add cauliflower florets into the food processor and process until it looks like rice.
Transfer cauliflower rice into the air fryer baking pan and drizzle with half oil.
Place pan in the air fryer and cook for 12 minutes, stir halfway through.
Heat remaining oil in a small pan over medium heat.
Add zucchini and cook for 5-8 minutes.

Add onion and jalapenos and cook for 5 minutes.

Add spices and stir well. Set aside.

Add cauliflower rice in the zucchini mixture and stir well.

Serve and enjoy.

Nutrition:

Calories 254

Fat 28 g

Carbohydrates 12.3 g

Sugar 5 g

Protein 4.3 g

Cholesterol 0 mg

177. Broccoli Stuffed Peppers

Preparation Time: 10 minutes

Cooking Time: 40 minutes

Servings: 2

Ingredients:

4 eggs

1/2 cup cheddar cheese, grated

2 bell peppers, cut in half and remove seeds

1/2 tsp garlic powder

1 tsp dried thyme

1/4 cup feta cheese, crumbled

1/2 cup broccoli, cooked

1/4 tsp pepper

1/2 tsp salt

Directions:

Preheat the air fryer to 325 F.

Stuff feta and broccoli into the bell peppers halved.

Beat egg in a bowl with seasoning and pour egg mixture into the pepper halved over feta and broccoli.

Place bell pepper halved into the air fryer basket and cook for 35-40 minutes.

Top with grated cheddar cheese and cook until cheese melted.

Serve and enjoy.

Nutrition:

Calories 340

Fat 22 g

Carbohydrates 12 g

Sugar 8.2 g

Protein 22 g

Cholesterol 374 mg

178. Zucchini Muffins

Preparation Time: 10 minutes
Cooking Time: 20 minutes
Servings: 8
Ingredients:
6 eggs
4 drops stevia
1/4 cup Swerve
1/3 cup coconut oil, melted
1 cup zucchini, grated
3/4 cup coconut flour
1/4 tsp ground nutmeg
1 tsp ground cinnamon
1/2 tsp baking soda
Directions:
Preheat the air fryer to 325 F.
Add all ingredients except zucchini in a bowl and mix well.
Add zucchini and stir well.
Pour batter into the silicone muffin molds and place into the air fryer basket.
Cook muffins for 20 minutes.
Serve and enjoy.
Nutrition:
Calories 136
Fat 12 g
Carbohydrates 1 g
Sugar 0.6 g
Protein 4 g
Cholesterol 123 mg

179. Jalapeno Breakfast Muffins

Preparation Time: 10 minutes
Cooking Time: 15 minutes
Servings: 8
Ingredients:
5 eggs
1/3 cup coconut oil, melted
2 tsp baking powder
3 tbsp erythritol
3 tbsp jalapenos, sliced
1/4 cup unsweetened coconut milk
2/3 cup coconut flour
3/4 tsp sea salt
Directions:

Preheat the air fryer to 325 F.

In a large bowl, stir together coconut flour, baking powder, erythritol, and sea salt.

Stir in eggs, jalapenos, coconut milk, and coconut oil until well combined.

Pour batter into the silicone muffin molds and place into the air fryer basket.

Cook muffins for 15 minutes.

Serve and enjoy.

Nutrition:

Calories 125

Fat 12 g

Carbohydrates 7 g

Sugar 6 g

Protein 3 g

Cholesterol 102 mg

180. Zucchini Noodles

Preparation Time: 10 minutes

Cooking Time: 44 minutes

Servings: 3

Ingredients:

1 egg

1/2 cup parmesan cheese, grated

1/2 cup feta cheese, crumbled

1 tbsp thyme

1 garlic clove, chopped

1 onion, chopped

2 medium zucchinis, trimmed and spiralized

2 tbsp olive oil

1 cup mozzarella cheese, grated

1/2 tsp pepper

1/2 tsp salt

Directions:

Preheat the air fryer to 350 F.

Add spiralized zucchini and salt in a colander and set aside for 10 minutes.

Wash zucchini noodles and pat dry with a paper towel.

Heat oil in a pan over medium heat.

Add garlic and onion and sauté for 3-4 minutes.

Add zucchini noodles and cook for 4-5 minutes or until softened.

Add zucchini mixture into the air fryer baking pan. Add egg, thyme, cheeses. Mix well and season.

Place pan in the air fryer and cook for 30-35 minutes.

Serve and enjoy.

Nutrition:

Calories 435
Fat 29 g
Carbohydrates 10.4 g
Sugar 5 g
Protein 25 g
Cholesterol 120 mg

181. Mushroom Frittata

Preparation Time: 10 minutes
Cooking Time: 13 minutes
Servings: 1
Ingredients:
1 cup egg whites
1 cup spinach, chopped
2 mushrooms, sliced
2 tbsp parmesan cheese, grated
Salt
Directions:
Spray pan with cooking spray and heat over medium heat.
Add mushrooms and sauté for 2-3 minutes. Add spinach and cook for 1-2 minutes or until wilted.
Transfer mushroom spinach mixture into the air fryer pan.
Whisk egg whites in a mixing bowl until frothy. Season with a pinch of salt.
Pour egg white mixture into the spinach and mushroom mixture and sprinkle with parmesan cheese.
Place pan in air fryer basket and cook frittata at 350 F for 8 minutes.
Slice and serve.
Nutrition:
Calories 176
Fat 3 g
Carbohydrates 4 g
Sugar 2.5 g
Protein 31 g
Cholesterol 8 mg

182. Egg Muffins

Preparation Time: 10 minutes
Cooking Time: 15 minutes
Servings: 12
Ingredients:
9 eggs
1/2 cup onion, sliced
1 tbsp olive oil

8 oz ground sausage
1/4 cup coconut milk
1/2 tsp oregano
1 1/2 cups spinach
3/4 cup bell peppers, chopped
Pepper
Salt
Directions:
Preheat the air fryer to 325 F.
Add ground sausage in a pan and sauté over medium heat for 5 minutes.
Add olive oil, oregano, bell pepper, and onion and sauté until onion is translucent.
Add spinach to the pan and cook for 30 seconds.
Remove pan from heat and set aside.
In a mixing bowl, whisk together eggs, coconut milk, pepper, and salt until well beaten.
Add sausage and vegetable mixture into the egg mixture and mix well.
Pour egg mixture into the silicone muffin molds and place into the air fryer basket. (Cook in batches)
Cook muffins for 15 minutes.
Serve and enjoy.
Nutrition:
Calories 135
Fat 11 g
Carbohydrates 1.5 g
Sugar 1 g
Protein 8 g
Cholesterol 140 mg

183. Potato Omelet

Preparation time: 15 minutes
Cooking time: 20 minutes
Servings: 4
Ingredients:
1 ½ potatoes; cubed
1 yellow onion; chopped.
2 tsp. olive oil
2 eggs
1/2 tsp. thyme; dried
1 green bell pepper; chopped
Salt and black pepper to the taste
Directions:

Heat up your air fryer at 350 degrees F; add oil, heat it up, add onion, bell pepper, salt and pepper; stir and cook for 5 minutes.

Add potatoes, thyme and eggs, stir, cover and cook at 360 °F, for 20 minutes.

Divide among plates and serve for breakfast.

Nutrition:

Calories: 241; Fat: 4; Fiber: 7; Carbs: 12; Protein: 7

184.Veggie Mix

Preparation time: 10 Minutes

Cooking time: 25 minutes

Servings: 6

Ingredients:

1 yellow onion; sliced

1 red bell pepper; chopped.

1 gold potato; chopped.

2 tbsp. olive oil

8 eggs

2 tbsp. mustard

3 cups milk

8 oz. brie; trimmed and cubed

12 oz. sourdough bread; cubed

4 oz. parmesan; grated

Salt and black pepper to the taste

Directions:

Heat up your air fryer at 350 degrees F; add oil, onion, potato and bell pepper and cook for 5 minutes.

In a bowl; mix eggs with milk, salt, pepper and mustard and whisk well.

Add bread and brie to your air fryer; Add the vegetables and seasoning mixture.

Add the rest of the bread and parmesan; toss just a little bit and cook for 20 minutes.

Divide among plates and serve for breakfast.

Nutrition:

Calories: 231; Fat: 5; Fiber: 10; Carbs: 20; Protein: 12

185.Special Corn Flakes Casserole

Preparation time: 10 Minutes

Cooking time: 8minutes

Servings: 5

Ingredients:

1/3 cup milk

4 tbsp. cream cheese; whipped

1/4 tsp. nutmeg; ground

1/4 cup blueberries

1 ½ cups corn flakes; crumbled
3 tsp. sugar
2 eggs; whisked
5 bread slices
Directions:
In a bowl; mix eggs with sugar, nutmeg and milk and whisk well.
In another bowl; mix cream cheese with blueberries and whisk well.
Put corn flakes in a third bowl.
Spread blueberry mix on each bread slice; then dip in eggs mix and dredge in corn flakes at the end.
Place bread in your air fryer's basket; heat up at 400 °F and bake for 8 minutes.
Divide among plates and serve for breakfast.
Nutrition:
Calories: 300; Fat: 5; Fiber: 7; Carbs: 16; Protein: 4

186. Broccoli Quiches

Preparation time: 10 Minutes
Cooking time: 20 minutes
Servings: 2
Ingredients:
1 broccoli head; florets separated and steamed
1 tomato; chopped.
1 tsp. thyme; chopped
1 carrots; chopped and steamed
2 oz. cheddar cheese; grated
2 oz. milk
1 tsp. parsley; chopped
2 eggs
Salt and black pepper to the taste
Directions:
In a bowl; mix eggs with milk, parsley, thyme, salt and pepper and whisk well.
Put broccoli, carrots and tomato in your air fryer.
Add eggs mix on top, spread cheddar cheese; cover and cook at 350 °F, for 20 minutes. Divide among plates and serve for breakfast.
Nutrition:
Calories: 214; Fat: 4; Fiber: 7; Carbs: 12; Protein: 3

187. Spinach Parcels

Preparation time: 10 Minutes
Cooking time: 4 minutes
Servings: 2
Ingredients:
1 lb. baby spinach leaves; roughly chopped

4 sheets filo pastry

1/2 lb. ricotta cheese

2 tbsp. pine nuts

1 eggs; whisked

Zest from 1 lemon; grated

Greek yogurt for serving

Salt and black pepper to the taste

Directions:

In a bowl; mix spinach with cheese, egg, lemon zest, salt, pepper and pine nuts and stir.

Arrange filo sheets on a working surface, divide spinach mix; fold diagonally to shape your parcels and place them in your preheated air fryer at 400 degrees F. Bake parcels for 4 minutes; divide them on plates and serve them with Greek yogurt on the side.

Nutrition:

Calories: 182; Fat: 4; Fiber: 8; Carbs: 9; Protein: 5

The Best Recipes Ever

188. Turkey Rolls

Preparation Time: 20 minutes

Cooking Time: 40 minutes

Servings: 3

Ingredients

1 pound turkey breast fillet

1 garlic clove, crushed

1½ teaspoons ground cumin

1 teaspoon ground cinnamon

½ teaspoon red chili powder

Salt, to taste

2 tablespoons olive oil

3 tablespoons fresh parsley, finely chopped

1 small red onion, finely chopped

Directions

Place the turkey fillet on a cutting board.

Carefully, cut horizontally along the length about 1/3 of way from the top, stopping about ¼-inch from the edge.

Open this part to have a long piece of fillet.

In a bowl, mix together the garlic, spices, and oil.

In a small cup, reserve about 1 tablespoon of oil mixture.

In the remaining oil mixture, add the parsley, and onion and mix well.

Set the temperature of Air Fryer to 355 degrees F. Grease an Air Fryer basket.

Coat the open side of fillet with onion mixture.

Roll the fillet tightly from the short side.

With a kitchen string, tie the roll at 1-1½-inch intervals.

Coat the outer side of roll with the reserved oil mixture.

Arrange roll into the prepared Air Fryer basket.

Air Fry for about 40 minutes.

Remove from Air Fryer and place the turkey roll onto a cutting board for about 5-10 minutes before slicing.

With a sharp knife, cut the turkey roll into desired size slices and serve.

Nutrition:

Calories: 239

Carbohydrate: 3.2g

Protein: 37.5g

Fat: 8.2g

Sugar: 0.9g

Sodium: 46mg

189. Turkey Meatloaf

Preparation Time: 20 minutes

Cooking Time: 20 minutes
Servings: 4
Ingredients
1 pound ground turkey
1 cup kale leaves, trimmed and finely chopped
1 cup onion, chopped
1 (4-ounces) can chopped green chilies
2 garlic cloves, minced
1 egg, beaten
½ cup fresh breadcrumbs
1 cup Monterey Jack cheese, grated
¼ cup salsa verde
3 tablespoons chopped fresh cilantro
1 teaspoon red chili powder
½ teaspoon ground cumin
½ teaspoon dried oregano, crushed
Salt and ground black pepper, as required
Directions
In a deep bowl, put all the ingredients and with your hands, mix until well combined.
Divide the turkey mixture into 4 equal-sized portions and shape each into a mini loaf.
Set the temperature of air fryer to 400 degrees F. Grease an air fryer basket.
Arrange loaves into the prepared air fryer basket.
Air fry for about 20 minutes.
Remove from air fryer and place the loaves onto plates for about 5 minutes before serving.
Serve warm.
Nutrition:
Calories: 435
Carbohydrate: 18.1g
Protein: 42.2g
Fat: 23.1g
Sugar: 3.6g
Sodium: 641mg

190. Buttered Duck Breasts

Preparation Time: 15 minutes
Cooking Time: 22 minutes
Servings: 4
Ingredients
2 (12-ounces) duck breasts
Salt and ground black pepper, as required

3 tablespoons unsalted butter, melted

½ teaspoon dried thyme, crushed

¼ teaspoon star anise powder

Directions

With a sharp knife, score the fat of duck breasts several times.

Season the duck breasts generously with salt and black pepper.

Set the temperature of Air Fryer to 390 degrees F. Grease an Air Fryer basket.

Arrange duck breasts into the prepared Air Fryer basket.

Air Fry for about 10 minutes.

Remove duck breasts from the basket and coat with melted butter and sprinkle with thyme and star anise powder.

Place duck breasts into the Air Fryer basket for the second time.

Air Fry for about 12 more minutes.

Remove from Air Fryer and place the duck breasts onto a cutting board for about 5-10 minutes before slicing.

Using a sharp knife, cut each duck breast into desired size slices and serve.

Nutrition:

Calories: 296

Carbohydrate: 0.1g

Protein: 37.5g

Fat: 15.5g

Sugar: 0g

Sodium: 100mg

191. Beer Coated Duck Breast

Preparation Time: 15 minutes

Cooking Time: 20 minutes

Servings: 2 servings

Ingredients

1 tablespoon olive oil

1 teaspoon mustard

1 tablespoon fresh thyme, chopped

1 cup beer

Salt and ground black pepper, as required

1 (10½-ounces) duck breast

6 cherry tomatoes

1 tablespoon balsamic vinegar

Directions

In a bowl, mix together the oil, mustard, thyme, beer, salt, and black pepper.

Add the duck breast and generously coat with marinade.

Cover and refrigerate for about 4 hours.

Set the temperature of Air Fryer to 390 degrees F.

With a piece of foil, cover the duck breast and arrange into an Air Fryer basket.

Air Fry for about 15 minutes.

Remove the foil from breast.

Now, set the temperature of Air Fryer to 355 degrees F. Grease the Air Fryer basket.

Place duck breast and tomatoes into the prepared Air Fryer basket.

Air Fry for about 5 minutes.

Remove from Air Fryer and place the duck breast onto a cutting board for about 5 minutes before slicing.

With a sharp knife, cut the duck breast into desired size slices and transfer onto serving plates.

Drizzle with vinegar and serve alongside the cherry tomatoes.

Nutrition

Calories: 332

Carbohydrate: 9.2g

Protein: 34.6g

Fat: 13.7g

Sugar: 2.5g

Sodium: 88mg

192. Duck Breast with Figs

Prep Time: 20 minutes

Cooking Time: 45 minutes

Servings: 2

Ingredients

2 cups fresh pomegranate juice

2 tablespoons lemon juice

3 tablespoons brown sugar

1 pound boneless duck breast

6 fresh figs, halved

1 teaspoon olive oil

Salt and ground black pepper, as required

1 tablespoon fresh thyme, chopped

Directions

In a medium saucepan, add the pomegranate juice, lemon juice, and brown sugar over medium heat and bring to a boil.

Now, lower the heat to low and cook for about 25 minutes until the mixture becomes thick.

Remove the pan from heat and let it cool slightly.

Set the temperature of Air Fryer to 400 degrees F. Grease an Air Fryer basket.

Score the fat of duck breasts several times using a sharp knife.

Sprinkle the duck breast with salt and black pepper.

Arrange duck breast into the prepared Air Fryer basket, skin side up.

Air Fry for about 14 minutes, flipping once halfway through.

Remove from Air Fryer and place the duck breast onto a cutting board for about 5-10 minutes.

Meanwhile, in a bowl, add the figs, oil, salt, and black pepper and toss to coat well.

Once again, set the temperature of Air Fryer to 400 degrees F. Grease the Air Fryer basket.

Arrange figs into the prepared basket in a single layer.

Air Fry for about 5 minutes.

Using a sharp knife, cut the duck breast into desired size slices and transfer onto serving plates alongside the roasted figs.

Drizzle with warm pomegranate juice mixture and serve with the garnishing of fresh thyme.

Nutrition:

Calories: 669

Carbohydrate: 90g

Protein: 519g

Fat: 12.1g

Sugar: 74g

Sodium: 110mg

193. Herbed Duck Legs

Preparation Time: 10 minutes

Cooking Time: 30 minutes

Servings: 2

Ingredients

1 garlic clove, minced

½ tablespoon fresh thyme, chopped

½ tablespoon fresh parsley, chopped

1 teaspoon five spice powder

Salt and ground black pepper, as required

2 duck legs

Directions

Set the temperature of air fryer to 340 degrees F. Grease an air fryer basket.

In a bowl, mix together the garlic, herbs, five spice powder, salt, and black pepper.

Generously rub the duck legs with garlic mixture.

Arrange duck legs into the prepared air fryer basket.

Air fry for about 25 minutes and then 5 more minutes at 390 degrees F.

Remove from air fryer and place the duck legs onto the serving platter.

Serve hot.

Nutrition

Calories: 138

Carbohydrate: 1g

Protein: 25g
Fat: 4.5g
Sugar: 0g
Sodium: 82mg

194. Easy Rib Eye Steak

Preparation Time: 10 minutes
Cooking Time: 14 minutes
 Servings: 4
Ingredients
2 lbs. rib eye steak
1 tablespoon olive oil
1 tablespoon steak rub*
Directions
Set the temperature of air fryer to 400 degrees F. Grease an air fryer basket.
Coat the steak with oil and then, generously rub with steak rub.
Place steak into the prepared air fryer basket.
Air fry for about 14 minutes, flipping once halfway through.
Remove from air fryer and place the steak onto a cutting board for about 10 minutes before slicing.
Cut the steak into desired size slices and transfer onto serving plates.
Serve immediately.
Nutrition
Calories: 438
Carbohydrate: 0g
Protein: 26.88g
Fat: 35.8g
Sugar: 0g
Sodium: 157mg

195. Buttered Striploin Steak

Servings: 2
Prep Time: 10 minutes
Cooking Time: 12 minutes
Ingredients
2 (7-ounces) striploin steak
1½ tablespoons butter, softened
Salt and ground black pepper, as required
Directions
Coat each steak evenly with butter and then, season with salt and black pepper.
Set the temperature of air fryer to 392 degrees F. Grease an air fryer basket.
Arrange steaks into the prepared air fryer basket.
Air fry for about 8-12 minutes.

Remove from air fryer and transfer the steaks onto serving plates.
Serve hot.
Nutrition
Calories: 595
Carbohydrate: 0g
Protein: 58.1g
Fat: 37.6g
Sugar: 0g
Sodium: 452mg

196. Simple New York Strip Steak

Prep Time: 10 minutes
Cooking Time: 8 minutes
Servings: 2
Ingredients
1 (9½-ounces) New York strip steak
Kosher salt and ground black pepper, as required
1 teaspoon olive oil
Directions
Set the temperature of air fryer to 400 degrees F. Grease an air fryer basket.
Coat the steak with oil and then, generously season with salt and black pepper.
Place steak into the prepared air fryer basket.
Air fry for about 7-8 minutes or until desired doneness.
Remove from air fryer and place the steak onto a cutting board for about 10 minutes before slicing.
Cut the steak into desired size slices and transfer onto serving plates.
Serve immediately.
Nutrition:
Calories: 186
Carbohydrate: 0g
Protein: 30.2g
Fat: 7g
Sugar: 0g
Sodium: 177mg

197. Crispy Sirloin Steak

Preparation Time: 15 minutes
Cooking Time: 10 minutes
Servings: 2 servings
Ingredients
1 cup white flour
2 eggs
1 cup panko breadcrumbs

1 teaspoon garlic powder
1 teaspoon onion powder
Salt and ground black pepper, as required
2 (6-ounces) sirloin steaks, pounded
Directions
In a shallow bowl, place the flour.
Crack the eggs in a second bowl and beat well.
In a third bowl, mix together the panko and spices.
Coat each steak with the white flour, then dip into beaten eggs and finally, coat with panko mixture.
Set the temperature of air fryer to 360 degrees F. Grease an air fryer basket.
Arrange steaks into the prepared air fryer basket.
Air fry for about 10 minutes.
Remove from air fryer and transfer the steaks onto the serving plates.
Serve immediately.
Nutrition:
Calories: 561
Carbohydrate: 6.1g
Protein: 31.9g
Fat: 50.3g
Sugar: 0.6g
Sodium: 100mg

198. Spiced & Herbed Skirt Steak

Preparation Time: 15 minutes
Cooking Time: 10 minutes
 Servings: 4
Ingredients
3 garlic cloves, minced
1 cup fresh parsley leaves, finely chopped
3 tablespoons fresh oregano, finely chopped
3 tablespoons fresh mint leaves, finely chopped
1 tablespoon ground cumin
2 teaspoons smoked paprika
1 teaspoon cayenne pepper
1 teaspoon red pepper flakes, crushed
Salt and ground black pepper, as required
¾ cup olive oil
3 tablespoons red wine vinegar
2 (8-ounces) skirt steaks
Directions
In a bowl, mix together the garlic, herbs, spices, oil, and vinegar.
In a resealable bag, place ¼ cup of the herb mixture and steaks.

Seal the bag and shake to coat well.

Refrigerate for about 24 hours.

Reserve the remaining herb mixture in refrigerator.

Take out the steaks from fridge and place at room temperature for about 30 minutes.

Set the temperature of air fryer to 390 degrees F. Grease an air fryer basket.

Arrange steaks into the prepared air fryer basket.

Air fry for about 8-10 minutes.

Remove from air fryer and place the steaks onto a cutting board for about 10 minutes before slicing.

Cut each steak into desired size slices and transfer onto serving platter.

Top with reserved herb mixture and serve.

Nutrition:

Calories: 561

Carbohydrate: 6.1g

Protein: 31.9g

Fat: 50.3g

Sugar: 0.6g

Sodium: 100mg

199. Skirt Steak with Veggies

Servings: 4

Preparation Time: 15 minutes

Cooking Time: 6 minutes

Ingredients

¼ cup olive oil, divided

2 tablespoons soy sauce

2 tablespoons honey

1 (12-ounces) skirt steak, cut into thin strips

½ pound fresh mushrooms, quartered

6 ounces snow peas

1 onion, cut into half rings

Salt and ground black pepper, as required

Directions

In a bowl, mix together 2 tablespoons of oil, soy sauce, and honey.

Add the steak strips and generously coat with the oil mixture.

In another bowl, add the vegetables, remaining oil, salt, and black pepper. Toss to coat well.

Set the temperature of air fryer to 390 degrees F. Grease an air fryer basket.

Arrange steak strips and vegetables into the prepared air fryer basket.

Air fry for about 5-6 minutes or until desired doneness.

Remove from air fryer and place the steak onto a cutting board for about 10 minutes before slicing.

Cut each steak into desired size slices and transfer onto serving plates.
Serve immediately alongside the veggies.
Nutrition:
Calories: 360
Carbohydrate: 16.7g
Protein: 26.7g
Fat: 21.5g
Sugar: 12.6g
Sodium: 522mg

200. Steak with Bell Peppers

Servings: 4
Preparation Time: 20 minutes
Cooking Time: 22 minutes
Ingredients
1 teaspoon dried oregano, crushed
1 teaspoon onion powder
1 teaspoon garlic powder
1 teaspoon red chili powder
1 teaspoon paprika
Salt, to taste
1¼ pounds beef steak, cut into thin strips
2 green bell peppers, seeded and cubed
1 red bell pepper, seeded and cubed
1 red onion, sliced
2 tablespoons olive oil
Directions
In a large bowl, mix together the oregano and spices.
Add the beef strips, bell peppers, onion, and oil. Mix until well combined.
Set the temperature of air fryer to 390 degrees F. Grease an air fryer basket.
Arrange steak strips mixture into the prepared Air Fryer basket in 2 batches.
Air Fry for about 10-11 minutes or until done completely.
Remove from air fryer and transfer the steak mixture onto serving plates.
Serve immediately.
Nutrition:
Calories: 372
Carbohydrate: 11.2g
Protein: 44.6g
Fat: 16.3g
Sugar: 6.2g
Sodium: 143mg

201. Buttered Filet Mignon

Servings: 4 servings
Preparation Time: 10 minutes
Cooking Time: 14 minutes)
Ingredients
2 (6-ounces) filet mignon steaks
1 tablespoon butter, softened
Salt and ground black pepper, as required
Directions
Coat each steak evenly with butter and then, season with salt and black pepper.
Set the temperature of air fryer to 390 degrees F. Grease an air fryer basket.
Arrange steaks into the prepared air fryer basket.
Air fry for about 14 minutes, flipping once halfway through.
Remove from the air fryer and transfer onto serving plates.
Serve hot.
Nutrition:
Calories: 403
Carbohydrate: 0g
Protein: 48.7g
Fat: 22g
Sugar: 0g
Sodium: 228mg

202. Bacon Wrapped Filet Mignon

Servings: 2 servings
Preparation Time: 15 minutes
Cooking Time: 15 minutes
Ingredients
2 bacon slices
2 (6-ounces) filet mignon steaks
Salt and ground black pepper, as required
1 teaspoon avocado oil
Directions
Wrap 1 bacon slice around each mignon steak and secure with a toothpick.
Season the steak evenly with salt and black pepper.
Then, coat each steak with avocado oil.
Set the temperature of air fryer to 375 degrees F. Grease an air fryer basket.
Arrange steaks into the prepared air fryer basket.
Air fry for about 15 minutes, flipping once halfway through.
Remove from air fryer and transfer the steaks onto serving plates.
Serve hot.
Nutrition:
Calories: 512

Carbohydrate: 0.5g
Protein: 59.4g
Fat: 28.6g
Sugar: 0g
Sodium: 857mg

203. Crispy Salt and Pepper Tofu

Preparation Time: 5 Minutes
Cooking Time: 15 Minutes
Servings: 4
Ingredients:
¼ cup chickpea flour
¼ cup arrowroot (or cornstarch)
1 teaspoon sea salt
1 teaspoon granulated garlic
½ teaspoon freshly grated black pepper
1 (15-ounce) package tofu, firm or extra-firm
Cooking oil spray (sunflower, safflower, or refined coconut)
Asian Spicy Sweet Sauce, optional
Directions:
1.In a medium bowl, combine the flour, arrowroot, salt, garlic, and pepper. Stir well to combine.
2.Cut the tofu into cubes (no need to press—if it's a bit watery, that's fine!). Place the cubes into the flour mixture. Toss well to coat. Spray the tofu with oil and toss again. (The spray will help the coating better stick to the tofu.)
3.Spray the air fryer basket with the oil. Place the tofu in a single layer in the air fryer basket (you may have to do this in 2 batches, depending on the size of your appliance) and spray the tops with oil. Fry for 8 minutes. Remove the air fryer basket and spray again with oil. Toss gently or turn the pieces over. Spray with oil again and fry for another 7 minutes, or until golden-browned and very crisp.
4.Serve immediately, either plain or with the Asian Spicy Sweet Sauce.
Nutrition: Calories 148; Total fat: 5g; Saturated fat: 0g; Cholesterol: 0mg; Sodium: 473mg; Carbohydrates: 14g; Fiber: 1g; Protein: 11g

204. Crispy Indian Wrap

Preparation Time: 20 Minutes
Cook Time: 8 Minutes
Servings: 4
Ingredients:
Cilantro Chutney
2¾ cups diced potato, cooked until tender
2 teaspoons oil (coconut, sunflower, or safflower)

3 large garlic cloves, minced or pressed
1½ tablespoons fresh lime juice
1½ teaspoons cumin powder
1 teaspoon onion granules
1 teaspoon coriander powder
½ teaspoon sea salt
½ teaspoon turmeric
¼ teaspoon cayenne powder
4 large flour tortillas, preferably whole grain or sprouted
1 cup cooked garbanzo beans (canned are fine), rinsed and drained
½ cup finely chopped cabbage
¼ cup minced red onion or scallion
Cooking oil spray (sunflower, safflower, or refined coconut)
Directions:
1.Make the Cilantro Chutney and set aside.
2.In a large bowl, mash the potatoes well, using a potato masher or large fork. Add the oil, garlic, lime, cumin, onion, coriander, salt, turmeric, and cayenne. Stir very well, until thoroughly combined. Set aside.
3.Lay the tortillas out flat on the counter. In the middle of each, evenly distribute the potato filling. Add some of the garbanzo beans, cabbage, and red onion to each, on top of the potatoes.
4.Spray the air fryer basket with oil and set aside. Enclose the Indian wraps by folding the bottom of the tortillas up and over the filling, then folding the sides in—and finally rolling the bottom up to form, essentially, an enclosed burrito.
5.Place the wraps in the air fryer basket, seam side down. They can touch each other a little bit, but if they're too crowded, you'll need to cook them in batches. Fry for 5 minutes. Spray with oil again, flip over, and cook an additional 2 or 3 minutes, until nicely browned and crisp. Serve topped with the Cilantro Chutney.
I find that Ezekiel brand sprouted whole-grain tortillas usually break when you try to wrap them. So I always seek out Alvarado Street Bakery brand, since they're much less likely to break on me!
Nutrition: Calories: 288; Total fat: 7g; Saturated fat: 1g; Cholesterol: 0mg; Sodium: 821mg; Carbohydrates: 50g; Fiber: 5g; Protein: 9g

205. Easy Peasy Pizza
Preparation Time: 5 Minutes
Cooking Time: 9 Minutes
Servings: 1
Ingredients:
Cooking oil spray (coconut, sunflower, or safflower)
1 flour tortilla, preferably sprouted or whole grain
¼ cup vegan pizza or marinara sauce

⅓ cup grated vegan mozzarella cheese or Cheesy Sauce

Toppings of your choice

Directions:

1.Spray the air fryer basket with oil. Place the tortilla in the air fryer basket. If the tortilla is a little bigger than the base, no probs! Simply fold the edges up a bit to form a semblance of a "crust."

2.Pour the sauce in the center, and evenly distribute it around the tortilla "crust" (I like to use the back of a spoon for this purpose).

3.Sprinkle evenly with vegan cheese, and add your toppings. Bake for 9 minutes, or until nicely browned. Remove carefully, cut into four pieces, and enjoy.

For a gluten-free version, use a brown rice tortilla. Create a Mexican pizza with Cheesy Sauce and black beans—and then top with fresh tomatoes, cilantro, red onions, and a little Green Chili Sauce. You can even air-fry the tortilla by itself until crisp and browned, and then top with hummus, spinach, basil, Kalamata olives, and tomatoes for a Greek-inspired pizza. Get creative and have fun!

Nutrition: Calories: 210; Total fat: 6g; Saturated fat: 1g; Cholesterol: 0mg; Sodium: 700mg; Carbohydrates: 33g; Fiber: 2g; Protein: 5g

206. Eggplant Parmigiana

Preparation Time: 15 Minutes

Cooking Time: 40 Minutes

Servings: 4

Ingredients:

1 medium eggplant (about 1 pound), sliced into ½-inch-thick rounds

2 tablespoons tamari or shoyu

3 tablespoons nondairy milk, plain and unsweetened

1 cup chickpea flour (see Substitution Tip)

1 tablespoon dried basil

1 tablespoon dried oregano

2 teaspoons garlic granules

2 teaspoons onion granules

½ teaspoon sea salt

½ teaspoon freshly ground black pepper

Cooking oil spray (sunflower, safflower, or refined coconut)

Vegan marinara sauce (your choice)

Shredded vegan cheese (preferably mozzarella; see Ingredient Tip)

Directions:

1.Place the eggplant slices in a large bowl, and pour the tamari and milk over the top. Turn the pieces over to coat them as evenly as possible with the liquids. Set aside.

2.Make the coating: In a medium bowl, combine the flour, basil, oregano, garlic, onion, salt, and pepper and stir well. Set aside.

3.Spray the air fryer basket with oil and set aside.

4.Stir the eggplant slices again and transfer them to a plate (stacking is fine). Do not discard the liquid in the bowl.

5.Bread the eggplant by tossing an eggplant round in the flour mixture. Then, dip in the liquid again. Double up on the coating by placing the eggplant again in the flour mixture, making sure that all sides are nicely breaded. Place in the air fryer basket.

6.Repeat with enough eggplant rounds to make a (mostly) single layer in the air fryer basket. (You'll need to cook it in batches, so that you don't have too much overlap and it cooks perfectly.)

7.Spray the tops of the eggplant with enough oil so that you no longer see dry patches in the coating. Fry for 8 minutes. Remove the air fryer basket and spray the tops again. Turn each piece over, again taking care not to overlap the rounds too much. Spray the tops with oil, again making sure that no dry patches remain. Fry for another 8 minutes, or until nicely browned and crisp.

8.Repeat steps 5 to 7 one more time, or until all of the eggplant is crisp and browned.

9.Finally, place half of the eggplant in a 6-inch round, 2-inch deep baking pan and top with marinara sauce and a sprinkle of vegan cheese. Fry for 3 minutes, or until the sauce is hot and cheese is melted (be careful not to overcook, or the eggplant edges will burn). Serve immediately, plain or over pasta. Otherwise, you can store the eggplant in the fridge for several days and then make a fresh batch whenever the mood strikes by repeating this step!

If you're not into chickpea flour (or are dying to make this and don't have it on hand), feel free to try an equal amount of another type of flour. Some that might work well include brown rice flour, whole-wheat pastry, or regular unbleached white. I personally like the chickpea flour here because of its nutritional profile and hearty consistency, but you may prefer another variety, and that's okay!

I haven't found a whole-food substitute for vegan mozzarella that works quite as well in this dish; if you prefer not to use packaged vegan cheese, simply omit.
Nutrition: Calories: 217; Total fat: 9g; Saturated fat: 1g; Cholesterol: 0mg; Sodium: 903mg; Carbohydrates: 38g; Fiber: 10g; Protein: 9g

207. Luscious Lazy Lasagna

Preparation Time: 15 Minutes
Cooking Time: 15 Minutes
Servings: 4
Ingredients:
8 ounces lasagna noodles, preferably bean-based, but any kind will do
1 tablespoon extra-virgin olive oil
2 cups crumbled extra-firm tofu, drained and water squeezed out
2 cups loosely packed fresh spinach
2 tablespoons nutritional yeast

2 tablespoons fresh lemon juice

1 teaspoon onion granules

1 teaspoon sea salt

⅛ teaspoon freshly ground black pepper

4 large garlic cloves, minced or pressed

2 cups vegan pasta sauce, your choice

½ cup shredded vegan cheese (preferably mozzarella)

Directions:

1.Cook the noodles until a little firmer than al dente (they'll get a little softer after you air-fry them in the lasagna). Drain and set aside.

2.While the noodles are cooking, make the filling. In a large pan over medium-high heat, add the olive oil, tofu, and spinach. Stir-fry for a minute, then add the nutritional yeast, lemon juice, onion, salt, pepper, and garlic. Stir well and cook just until the spinach is nicely wilted. Remove from heat.

3.To make half a batch (one 6-inch round, 2-inch deep baking pan) of lasagna: Spread a thin layer of pasta sauce in the baking pan. Layer 2 or 3 lasagna noodles on top of the sauce. Top with a little more sauce and some of the tofu mixture. Place another 2 or 3 noodles on top, and add another layer of sauce and then another layer of tofu. Finish with a layer of noodles, and then a final layer of sauce. Sprinkle about half of the vegan cheese on top (omit if you prefer; see the Ingredient Tip from the Eggplant Parmigiana).

4.Place the pan in the air fryer and bake for 15 minutes, or until the noodles are browning around the edges and the cheese is melted. Cut and serve.

5.If making the entire recipe now, repeat steps 3 and 4 (see Cooking Tip).

Please note that you'll need to make this recipe in two batches. If you're serving four people all at once, you'll want to repeat steps 3 and 4 once your first batch is done. However, if you're only serving one or two people when you make this, you'll prepare a second lasagna for another day after cooking your first batch. In that case, layer up your second lasagna as outlined in step 3 and then store it in the fridge (covered) for up to 4 or 5 days, and air-fry it whenever you're ready for another fresh-from-the-"oven" batch.

Nutrition: Calories: 317; Total fat: 8g; Saturated fat: 1g; Cholesterol: 0mg; Sodium: 1203mg; Carbohydrates: 46g; Fiber: 4g; Protein: 20g

Conclusion

I hope this Air Fryer Cookbook helps you understand the dynamics and principles of this revolutionary kitchen appliance, why you should use it and how it's going to change your outlook on food preparation and healthy living. The next step is to get into the right frame of mind and decide that it's time to take charge of your eating habits by only putting the best organic and free range ingredients in your Air Fryer.

Even if you have never tried the Air Fryer before, I can promise you one thing, after the 30 days, you will be kicking yourself for having not discovered this sooner.

I hope it was able to inspire you to clean up your kitchen from all the useless appliances that clutter your countertop and start putting the Air Fryer to good use.

The Air Fryer is definitely a change in lifestyle that will make things much easier for you and your family. You'll discover increased energy, decreased hunger, a boosted metabolism and of course a LOT more free time!

Happy Air Frying!

Introduction (Vol.2)

Marketed as a healthier and clean way to consume your beloved fast food meals, air fryers have undergone a massive popularity rise. These are supposed to help reduce the fat content among common foods such as fish sticks, empanadas, chicken wings and fries. Yet just how good does an air fryer cook? The book will glance at the facts to decide if the Many air fryer brands don't need oil to work with the unit, but a few teaspoons can enhance the texture and taste of deep-fried eats. While air-fried food can be enjoyed with no oil, the air fryer's uniqueness is that it just requires such a small amount.

Just 40 calories are available per teaspoon of oil (120 calories per tablespoon). The little bit of fat you apply makes brown and caramelize all too tasty and extra crispy results. When relative to the amount of oil in deep-fried foods, the amount you'll see in the air fryer is practically nothing, leading to fewer calories when saturated fat than the usual fried food. Advantages of using an appliance actually outweigh the dangers.

We all enjoy the flavor of deep-fried food but not the calories or hassle of frying in too much grease. The Philips Air fryer was designed to overcome this problem as its innovative nature helps you to cook food with either one or two tablespoons of oil when frying and remove extra fat from the meal. This recipe book contains only a handful of the recipes you can prepare on your Philips Air fryer. The options are endless, from French fries to spring rolls and even soufflés!

Healthier, quicker, and more efficiently, the Air fryer lets you cook, roast, barbecue, and steam. We hope you love using the Air fryer like many others around the world do, and the recipes inside encourage you to prepare safe, well-balanced meals for you and your family.

Chapter 1: Air fryer – An Introduction

Counter-space in nearly every kitchen is a precious asset. And if you've got a lot of it, the new cookery gadgets are accessible to the crowd and fill up. But this kind of appliance is one you're going to want to make space to.

It is like an microwave in the way that it bakes and roasts, but the distinction is that the heating elements are only placed on top and are supported by a big, keen fan, resulting in food that is super crispy in no time – and, most importantly, with less oil than deep-fried counterparts. Air fryers usually heat up very quickly and, due to the combination of a centralized heat source and fan size and location, they cook food rapidly and accurately. The cleaning is another significant aspect of air frying. Many buckets and racks of air fryers are suitable for dishwashers. We recommend a decent dishwasher cleaner, Such as this one by Casabella, for those not safe in the dishwasher. It is going to get into all the nooks and crannies — and encourage air circulation! — Wild, without walking.

1.1 What are air fryers and how they work?

What was first conceived as an appliance in 2010, in Europe and Australia? Since it was invented by Japan and North America, it is now, one day, a regular occurrence in the Western kitchen.

The Japanese also use it to make fried prawns, & it is used by the UK and the Netherlands to fry chips. Americans use this to prepare chicken wings, and the Indians use it to make samosa.

What do you mean by an Air Fryer?

The aim of an air-fryer is to disperse hot air around the fried food. There is a hydraulic ventilator, which circulates hot air at high speed around the product. This makes crusted bread and fried rice—these frieze foods such as chicken, popcorn, pastries, and fish. The downside is that no oil or less oil is required to cook the meal. Most air-fryers have controls of time and temperature, which help to prepare food well in the correct procedure. Feed is put above in the basket and rests on a drip tray. There are several marks on the market. We claim that it will save about 80 percent of the oil as opposed to traditional ovens. Most fryers have buckets that are frequently shaken to ensure that cooking is finished. Most versions do not support the business with an agitator that churns the food continuously when fried. It is popular with people every day since it is an oil-less cooking process. Most people have the impression that this cooking process affects the flavor, texture, and presentation of the food. Yet the research by Professor Shaker M. Arafat reveals that the food of the air fryer is great in taste, scent, color, hardness, crispness, oiliness, and so on than the conventional French fries. The traditional oven requires additional olive oil during the cooking process. This severely affects the health of the consumers.

Comparison-Deep Fryer vs. Air Fryer: Deep Fryer and Air Fryer sound close, as both cook every day. A different type of cooking food is used in these appliances, but the flavor is similar to that of processed tasty and crispy food.

Comparison-deep-fryer-vs-air-fryer -1 In addition to the operation, there is a substantial difference in design, power, protection, maintenance, and much more between the deep-fryer and the air-fryer. Let's look at the key differences between these two different kitchen appliances: Five major differences between Air Fryers and Deep Fryers Five main differences between Air Fryers and Deep Fryers Features Size and Performance Safety Maintenance Expense Five advantages that make such appliance more attractive than a Deep Fryer: features There's a lot of overlap even While auto-shut-off is bi

Size and performance: These machines are somewhat different in terms of scale and capacity as air fryers are usually low in size relative to the deep fryer, meaning that a deep fryer will cook food in huge amounts relative to the air fryer.

If you are searching from time to time for a fryer to cook snacks or a small dinner, then air fryer is the better choice because it has less potential to cook food in a limited period of time. However, a deep fryer is favored in an immense amount for daily purposes and preparing meals, because it has an enormous power that is sufficient to serve the whole household.

Healthy

Oil is important for having the right amount of crispiness. Deep fryers use a huge volume of oil to have the same volume of crispness, and on the other hand, air fryers use very small quantities of oil to produce the same effects, i.e., delicious and crisp foods.

So, prefer air fryer over deep fryer because the food created is less fatty, which will definitely protect you away from the side effects of fatty foods like obesity, heart attacks, and much more.

Maintenance

Both gadgets are easy to repair, as the tray needs to be cleaned out, among other important components. Nevertheless, cleaning air fryer is much easier than deep fryers, because you don't have to scrape the oil until you clean the fryer. Moreover, relative to the deep fryers, the size of the air fryer is low, meaning less time is required to clean the air fryer.

Cost, The quality of such kitchen appliances is not substantially different, but air fryer is higher relative to deep fryer because it uses quick air technology to cook food and is more efficient in delivering nutritious and tasty fry food.

Five features that make an Air Fryer stand out rather than a deep fryer:

- Auto turns off mode-this mode is really a security-changing device. Secure yourself from the toxic diet consequences too
- Comparable space-More room in the kitchen
- , Health-reduces to a low chance of developing heart disease and other health issues.
- Simpler maintenance-effort put on the specification of Air Fryer to make them more maintenance-friendly.
- You may also like: Is an air fryer the only possible alternative to deep frying?

Cooking food is a nutritious and cost-effective choice by Air Fryer. A new kitchen appliance has reached the market and earned enormous acclaim from people. Air Fryer is a modern technology that has achieved immense attention with its many advantages. It's made cooking simple, safe, and cost-effective, making it the best cooking gadget so far. There are many reasons to use this potent cooking tool. Let's look at some of the key reasons to use it that will allow you to cook healthier food in a short time: This popular cooking device uses hot air ventilation, which cooks the ingredients from all angles without using oil. This basically allows you to prepare healthier food because no oil is used. So, use this gadget to have a nice, tasty dinner.

Air Fryer has different cooking options that allow you to cook various food items like frying, roasting, baking, and much more. You do not have to spend money on several appliances to cook various food items in one gadget, with all the cooking choices. So, get this popular gadget and cook all sorts of food quickly.

Cook tasty meals using the gadget. Each air fryer includes a Book of Recipes. Thus with the aid of this book, you can conveniently cook numerous delicious food items.

The amazing thing about this gadget is its ease of use. People who find it difficult to control phones, due to the complicated keys, will certainly procure this device. This gadget doesn't have complicated buttons, so any person can easily control it.

These are some of the reasons which explain what cooking delicious and safe food means. Aside from these, another big explanation for using this device for cooking is that it conveniently cooks food at the ideal temperature. Additionally, this device comes with all of the security options. So, get this popular but useful cooking gadget as soon as possible.

The air fryer is fundamentally a convection oven with amped-up countertops. The small room makes cooking much quicker—the unit's top features a heating mechanism and a fan. Heat air in a basket-style fryer flows down and around food. This speedy processing makes the food crisp, close to deep frying. Air fryers prepare frozen foods to taste deep-fried — think frozen French fries, chicken wings, and mozzarella sticks. They do a fine job, too, with identical scratch-made recipes. And best of all, air-fryers will bake as well. For a liquid batter, you cannot do anything (unless you freeze it first). You can't do it in huge amounts either, so be prepared to cook in batches if you're feeding a crowd.

Cost. Air fryers range from $100 and $300 on the expensive side of home appliances, based on size and functionality. Find the perfect Outdoor Air Fryer.

Space. The air fryer is no little gadget, bigger than a toaster. To house one, you would need to give up precious storage (or counter) room.

Expertise. Essentially, air-fryers are plug and click. Place your food in the bowl, set the temperature and time, and bam! You're here to eat.

Great flavor & feel. Although an air fryer will show you results much closer to deep-frying than will your oven, it's still not the same at the end of the day.

The point can be made that using less gasoline, and it creates safer food. Frozen French fries served in the air fryer yield between 4 and 6 grams of fat versus a staggering 17 grams per serving of their deep-fried equivalent.

This is a fairly cool machine at the end of the day. You cannot break that as you fry up things like French fries or chicken nuggets. The results are much better than frying on the microwave, and your kitchen stays cool. Although cooking other meats and vegetables perform an excellent job, the air fryer really shines at deep-frying fake. And if you usually don't eat deep-fried foods, the investment actually isn't worth it.

1.2 Is meal cooked by air safe?

Air fried food's flavor and feel are similar to the performance related to deep frying as juicy inside, crispy outside. You only have to utilize a very small volume of oil, however, if any (It depends on what you are preparing).

Air frying might be "certainly a better option opposed to deep-frying if you agree to use only 1-2 teaspoons of seasoning oil based on plants, and rather than anything else, you hang to veggies cooked by air," says Nutrition Manager Jaclyn London who is RD, CDN, MS, from Good Housekeeping. "Weight control, decreased risk of cardiovascular illness, and better long-term wellbeing as when we get older it is essential to every gadget that lets you and your family update your veggie game."

1.3 Inside this kind of appliance, what can you possibly cook?

These kinds of appliances are very quick, and may be utilize to warm frozen meals or prepare all kinds of fresh produce such as chicken, beef, salmon, vegetables and pork chops before you understand how they work. Some meats don't need additional oil as they are already so tasty: simply sprinkle meal with salt as well as the spices and herbs you want. You should stick to the dry toppings — fewer humidity contributes to more crisp results. Wait until the last few minutes of cooking, whether you choose to marinade meats with a honey or BBQ sauce. Light meat cuts, or foods containing minimal to no fat, need browning oil and crisping up. Until cooking, spray the pork chops and chicken breasts boneless with a little grease. Because of its low smoke level, canola oil or vegetable oil is generally preferred, which means air fryer can sustain the high temperature. Until air fried, vegetables must also be put in oil. we advise spraying the veggies with salt, but use far less than you're like to: that crisp, air cooked bits hold a great deal of taste. We enjoy broccoli florets frying milk, sprouts in Brussels, and halves of baby potatoes. They're so crusted out! Beets, sweet potatoes with butternut squash all appear to be getting more delicious, and peppers as well as green beans do not take much time. First up, ask that another appliance is on the market. Most toaster ovens, similar to the Breville Smart Oven Air and the Cuisinart TOA-65, similar to the Ninja Foodie, similar to pressure cookers also have air frying capabilities. When you desire to opt for such appliance, remember it for big, air fryer microwave ovens, these air fryers alone cost in price between $40 for smaller handheld models to $400 in size. Remember how many people you are catering for while looking for such an appliance (Air Fryer) as smallest sized air fryers with the capacity of 1.2-liters can be suitable for 1 to 2 individuals, whereas the medium size with the capacity of 3 to 4 liters can be suitable for 2 to 3 individuals and the biggest with the capacity of 6 or more liters can be suitable for 4 to 6 individuals. Rather than shelves we recommend air fryers including buckets as they prepare more equally.

1.4 Tips for using Air fryer

1. When frying, shake the basket once or twice while making smaller things such as burgers, chicken, and croquettes. That ensures the food is equally cooked.

2. Don't get the food pot overcrowded. This affects how well the air circulates around the meal, increases the time to cook, and results in sub-optimal results.

3. Oil sprays and misters are great choices for adding oil uniformly to food before cooking. They may also be used to spray the mesh cooking basket bottom to ensure the food does not stick.

4. 3 Minutes to preheat the air fryer. This is enough time to reach the desired temperature for the Air fryer.

5. Until scrubbing or putting in the dishwasher, soak the cooking basket in soapy water to remove any food particles which remain on the cooking basket after use.

6. When frying foods that are normally high in fat, such as chicken wings, often empty fat from the Air fryer's bottom while cooking, to prevent unnecessary smoke.

7. To prevent splattering and unnecessary smoke, pat food dry before cooking while frying foods that have been marinated or immersed in a sauce.

8. Coat in small batches for foods that require breading to ensure even application. To ensure it adheres, press the breading onto fruit. When breading is too hard, fragments may become airborne and create unnecessary smoke, or they may become stuck behind the exhaust filter.

9. You can prepare a range of prepackaged foods in the Air fryer. As a reference, the traditional oven temperature is lowered by 70 degrees, and the cooking time is halved. Food can vary by exact times and temperatures.

10. Trim to leave 1/2 inch space around the bottom edge of the bowl, when using parchment paper or foil.

11. Consumption of raw or undercooked foods, poultry, fish, shellfish, or eggs may increase your risk of foodborne disease.

Guide to times and temperatures

		Min-max amount (oz.)	Time (min.)	Temp. °F	Shake halfway	Extra information
Thin frozen fries		10-25	12-16	390	✓	
Thick frozen fries		10-25	12-20	390	✓	
Homemade fries		10-28	18-30	360	✓	Soak 30 min/dry/Tbsp of oil 1/2 Tbsp - 10oz 1 1/2 Tbsp - 28oz
Potato wedges		10-28	18-30	360	✓	Soak 30 min/dry/Tbsp of oil 1/2 Tbsp - 10oz 1 1/2 Tbsp - 28oz
Potato cubes		10-25	12-18	360	✓	Soak 30 min/dry/Tbsp of oil 1/2 Tbsp - 10oz 1 1/2 Tbsp - 28oz
Cheese sticks		4-16	8-10	360	✓	Use ovenbaked
Chicken nuggets		4-18	6-10	390	✓	Use ovenbaked
Fish sticks		4-16	6-10	390		Use ovenbaked
Steak		4-18	8-12	360		
Pork chops		4-18	10-14	360		
Hamburger		4-18	7-14	360		
Chicken wings		4-18	18-22	360		
Drumsticks		4-18	18-22	360		
Chicken breast		4-18	10-15	360		

1.5 Air fryer errors that you need to know beforehand

Error # 1: Do not preheat the air fryer for long.

A decent quality air fryer is heating up so easily that you may not know you need to pre-heat it. Yet often, I'll find an air fryer recipe that makes no mention of preheating, so I'm still dissatisfied with the outcome.

Instead, consider the following: Preheat the air fryer 10 minutes before cooking. For specifics, see the manual for your air fryer, but most models recommend 10 to 15 minutes of preheating — plenty of room to cook the ingredients. That will mean the meal is more crippled than steamed.

Error# 2: The air fryer didn't have enough space.

Often small kitchens and small appliances run into this problem: The air fryer was pulled deep into a table under a cabinet. But that's a concern since convection is what air fryers rely on to get crisp food — and convection requires sufficient space and airflow.

Instead, consider this: configure the air fryer, so it has at least 5 inches of space on both sides. Go ahead & tuck the air fryer into a back counter or cabinet corner for safety reasons, but when in operation — to get the best out of your machine — allow the air fryer 5 inches of room around. Ensure sure your air fryer is always on a healthy heat-resistant surface during use!

At most air-fryers, the basket is small. There is ample space to prepare easily for two servings of meat or fish, or four servings of a vegetable hand — but that is it. Stacking or squishing food closely together might be enticing to have as much food as possible cooked at once, but the effects will actually be misleading.

Instead, use this: Cook in batches for quicker, healthier air fryer food. Cooking using an air fryer is typically easier than baking or grilling. So please don't bother cooking all at once! Instead, due to convection, cooking smaller batches back to back provides easier and quicker cooking-again. That will make for improved airflow in each lot.

Error # 3: Oil is used too little (or too much!) The air fryer promises deep-fried food satisfaction without all the deep-frying oil, but it can be hard to calculate how much oil simple foods need — especially frozen foods prepared to imitate fried foods alone.

Remember this: Most dishes use one and a half teaspoons of the oil, using a tiny amount of oil (or just a spritz of non-stick spray) to crisp the product without it being soggy while frying frozen products — like French fries or nuggets of chicken ». Coat the food with at least half a teaspoon of oil per batch for fresh vegetables or large proteins such as chicken or steak to ensure the food is crisp and crispy when frying hot.

Error # 4: Very few vegetable cuttings.

Air fryers are fitted with a basket that allows air to flow around the food, but the basket holes are wide, ensuring that small bits will fall through the basket and burn easily. Instead, do this: keep veggies 1/4-inch long, so they don't slip over. The width of a thick-cut French fry is a just-about-perfect food width that doesn't slip through basketball cracks and yet cooks quickly. Hold sweet potatoes, carrots, and the like at least 1/4 inch long, so they stay in the dish.

Error # 5: Batters don't work well in air fryers.

Some of our favorite deep-fried foods have fluffy batters that don't work in the air fryer, because they don't get the instant fix from a hot oil vat. Wet bruised goods with thicker coatings have to be adapted to the air fryer (think: corn dogs or tempura).

Alternatively, taking this into account: using ingredients that create a dense paste, not a loose batter. If you are craving foods that normally have wet batters but need a coating instead of working in the air fryer, the use of air fryer-specific recipes can help. Using the air fryer, if in question, use a traditional three-stage breading technique (flour, egg dip, crispy coating).

Error# 6: Not enough Air Fryer cleaning.

You do not know that when you use it, the fry bucket absorbs dirt and oil as you just dump the frozen tots into the air fryer.

Alternatively, consider this: For good cooks, let the air fryer cool and then clean after each use. Then wash the basketful full of fresh soapy water after longer air-frying sessions. Hey, this is an extra step, but it should mean a higher quality end product

Working Science of an Air Fryer Primarily, there are three systems where air fryer functions are listed below: Fast Air Technology This technology is the first critical system from the operating of an air fryer. Compared to the usual ovens or skillet, the food has cooked at the dual cost.

The heat is distributed out of the cooking area, which is placed very close to your meals in this way. It allows effective cooking of your meals.

Likewise, there might also be an exhaust fan, which generates rapid hot air that goes into the fryer's room. For no energy waste, the meal has fried on both angles. In an air fryer, for example, you could cook crunchy chips in around 15 minutes, while the standard ovens take at least 1/2 hour to create crunchier chips.

The air inside the fridge will in no way dry your meals. The heat that comes up in the lightest and lowest section helps your meals cook easily at the optimum temperature.

The upcoming important component of the exhaust system is the exhaust system, which plays an important role in air fryer functioning. Once the food is prepared, you will know that with the meal scent help.

The emissions from the excess air of the air fryer strainers before letting it discharge is the reason you won't ever detect any odors in the kitchen or your house. So soon as there is ample hot air in the air fryer, the exhaust mechanism began operating automatically. The smoke and mist inside the fryer are done before discharging to the outside air.

Cooling cap: A refrigeration system over the fryer's engine provided internal temperature control. This fryer's Filters allow air to flow through them to ensure the appliance's Inner Regions will stay cold.

It comes from the machine's correct general cooling. Because of this, the hot meals should only be eaten after the stir-frying process has been finished.

How to use air fryer: Cooking and Temperature Modification

When adjusting a recipe using a suggested deep-frying or cooking temperature in a traditional oven, lower the air fryer temperature from twenty-five degrees (Fahrenheit) to produce comparable effects. This change is important because the moving air makes cooking heat more continuous and intense than traditional cooking methods.

Don't forget to get the air fryer preheated to 104. Like you can for every other cooking process, it normally takes less than five minutes earlier, filling the cooking bowl.

Mixing Ingredients with Water, Sparingly Foods that are naturally oilier, like meatballs, need not be chucked in the excess oil. For foods bruised or dredged in water, we recommend spraying the basket from the air fryer or standing with spray from the frying.

Place the beaten food in the basket or stand in one plate and give the food a light spray of cooking to cover the top. The little bit of oil is essential to food processing to make it golden-brown, crispy, and appealing.

Fill the Air Fryer Floured Shelf or Box, and place battered foods in one coat in an air fryer box or shelf. Many versions have racks that even though yours does, do not hesitate to raise it by two levels. You should place the air fryer basket at the top for items such as French fries or "roasted" vegetables. A bigger basket, though, would potentially take a longer cooking time, which will lead to food that is not as fresh as a basket with a smaller amount of food. Moreover, providing full baskets that shake every three to five minutes is a great idea to make sure the food is cooking even as many iterations will melt the timer once you start the box, particularly for this reason.

Check Again, when moving air allows the air-fryer cooking system to sustain a more steady temperature relative to other cooking methods, foods tend to cook faster in an air fryer after frying or frying in a traditional oven. In other words, if you are converting a recipe you know previously, and you want to have fried in an air fryer, then you would want to check the food about two-thirds of how to test doneness during the appropriate cooking period. Will those fish sticks say they'll end in 15 minutes? Check them once, in ten minutes. We all know why you are considering buying an air fryer, so here it is: yup, frozen French chips can be put in the air fryer, no oil required, and fried at 350 ° F for around 15 minutes, To get rid of the extra starch, fresh-cut fries have to be immersed in warm water for ten or more minutes (30 minutes is even better). Using a kitchen towel to clean, rinse, and empty chips and then place it in one or two tbsp.

, Fresh vegetable oil, then fried for about twenty minutes at 350 ° F for oxygen, shaking a few times while cooking. And in any case, don't forget to salt them when the cooking is done.

Chapter 2: Side Dishes

In this chapter, we will be presenting air fryer recipes of several side dishes. People prefer having side dishes on their table along with the regular dishes.

2.1. Skin Wedges of Crispy Potato

Active for 40 minutes and total for 1 hour 40 min serves: 4

Ingredients:

- Six medium-sized potatoes in russet color
- Two full spoons of canola oil
- Half spoon of black pepper
- Half spoon of salt

Instructions:

1. To purify potatoes wash under hot water. In water boil potatoes for forty minutes with salt, or tender before the fork. Chill in fridge absolutely (about 30 minutes).

2. The black pepper, paprika, canola oil and salt are mixed in a mixing pot. Split the chilled potatoes into one-fourth each as well as throw them gently in the oil and spice mixture. Air Fryer has to be preheated to the 390 ° Fahrenheit.

3. Remove half of the baked potatoes to the bowl and put the skin down, taking care not to get overcrowded. Cook for 13-15 minutes each pan, or until shiny, reddish-brown.

2.2. French Fries

ACTIVE: 10 MIN TOTAL: 1 HR 15 MIN SERVES: 4

Ingredients:

- 6 Medium-sized Peeled potatoes
- Two tablespoons of olive oil

Instructions:

1. Peel the potatoes and cut them into 3-inch slices to 1/2 inch. Soak the potatoes in water for thirty minutes, then rinse thoroughly with a paper towel, and pat dry.

1. Air fryer preheats to 360 ° F. Place the potatoes in a large tub, pour in the oil, and gently brush the potatoes. Add the potatoes to the boil and simmer for 30 minutes until they are crisp. Shake while cooking 2-3 times

2. Thicker cut potatoes cook longer, although thinner cut potatoes cook quicker.

2.3. Potato Croquettes

Active: 30 minutes total: 45 min serves: 4

Ingredients:

For the filling

- Two medium russet potatoes, peeled and cubed
- One egg yolk
- 1/2 cup of parmesan cheese, grated
- Two tablespoons of all-
- Two tablespoons of chives, finely chopped
- One pinch of salt
- One pinch of black pepper
- One pinch of nutmeg

For the breading

- Two tablespoons of vegetable oil
- 1 cup of all-purpose flour
- Two eggs, beaten
- 1/2 cup of breadcrumbs

Instructions:

1. Boil the salted water in the potato cubes for 15 minutes. Use a potato masher or ricer, rinse and finely mash in a large tub. Fully Good. The egg yolk, butter,

flour, and chives are added in. Cook with cinnamon, nutmeg, and pepper. Shape the potato filling in and set aside the size of golf balls.

2. Air fryer preheat to 390 ° F. Mix the oil than breadcrumbs, then whisk until the mixture is crumbly and loose. Place each ball of potatoes in the flour, then the eggs and then the breadcrumbs and roll into a funnel. Push the croquettes on paint and make sure it adheres. Place half of the croquettes in the cooking pot, cook for 7-8 minutes every pan, or until golden brown.

2.4. Potatoes au Gratin

Active: 10 minutes total: 25 min serves: 4

Ingredients:

- Three small russet potatoes,
- 1/4 cup washed milk
- 1/4 cup cream
- One tablespoon black pepper
- 1/2 cup Gruyère nutmeg
- 1/4 cup or semi-mature cheese, rubbed

Instructions:

1. Air fryer preheats to 390 ° F. Slice off the wafer-thin onions. Mix the milk and cream in a cup and season with salt, pepper, and nutmeg to taste. Cover slices of potato with the milk mixture.

2. Move the potato slices to a 6-inch baking pan, then dump over the potatoes the remainder of the cream mixture from the tub. In the cooking basket, position the baking pan and move the bowl into the air fryer. Heat the timer and bake the gratin for 15 minutes. The cheese is uniformly spread over potatoes. Set the timer again for 10 minutes, then bake the gratin until well browned.

2.5. Rosemary Russet Potato Chips

Active: 40 minutes total: 1 hr. 10 min serves: 2

Ingredients:

- Two small russet potatoes
- One teaspoon of olive oil
- One teaspoon of rosemary,
- One pinch of salt

Instructions:

1. Scrub the potatoes to purify under hot water. Split the potatoes lengthwise and cut them immediately into thin chips into a water-filled mixing cup. Soak the potatoes, changing the water several times, for 30 minutes.
Drain well with a paper towel, then pat absolutely dry.

2. Air fryer preheat to 330 ° F. Place the potatoes in a mixing bowl of olive oil. Place them in the basket and cook for 30 minutes or until golden brown, regularly rotating to ensure even cooking of the chips. Toss in a big bowl with rosemary and salt, when done and still dry.

Chapter 3: Air fryer recipes of Appetizers

This chapter will present air fryer recipes of appetizers.

3.1. Cheddar Bacon Croquettes

Active: 40 minutes total: 50 min serves: 6

Ingredients:

- 1 pound of sharp cheddar cheese,
- 1 pound of bacon, thinly cut, room temperature

For the breading

- Four spoons full of olive oil
- 1 cup of all-purpose flour
- Two eggs
- 1 cup of seasoned breadcrumbs

Instructions:

1. Break the cheddar cheese block into six pieces of similar thickness, around 1-inch x 1¾- inch each. Take 2 slices of bacon and wrap them around each slab of cheddar, with the cheese fully enclosed. Take off some extra fat. Place the bacon cheddar bits in the freezer to firm for 5 minutes. Freeze not.

2. Air fryer preheat to 390 ° F. Mix the oil than breadcrumbs, then whisk until the mixture is crumbly and loose. Place each block of cheddar in the flour, then put the eggs, then the breadcrumbs. Push the croquettes on paint and make sure it adheres. Place the croquettes in the basket and cook for 7-8 minutes or until they are golden brown.

Tip: Double coat the croquettes by dipping them into the egg a second time and then into the breadcrumbs to guarantee the cheese doesn't run dry.

3.2 Crispy Fried Spring Rolls

Active: 20 minutes total: 25 min serves: 4

Ingredients:

For the filling

- 4 oz. Cooked chicken breast, shredded
- One celery stalk, sliced

- One medium carrot, sliced
- 1/2 cup thin mushrooms, sliced
- 1/2 teaspoon ginger, finely chopped
- One teaspoon sugar
- One teaspoon chicken stock powder

For the spring roll wrappers
- One egg, beaten
- One teaspoon cornstarch
- Eight spring roll wrappers
- 1/2 tablespoon vegetable oil

Instructions:

1. Have the filling finished? Place the shredded chicken in a bowl & blend with the mushrooms, carrots, and celery. Attach the ground ginger, sugar, and chicken stock and mix uniformly.

2. Combine the cornstarch with the egg and combine to create a smooth paste; set aside. Place some filling on and roll it up on each spring roll wrapper, sealing the ends with the egg mixture.

3. Air fryer preheat to 390 ° F. Brush the spring rolls gently with oil before placing them in the kitchen tub. Fry in two lots, fry for 3-4 minutes each pan, or until golden brown. Serve with soy or mild chili sauce.

3.3 Feta Triangles

Active: 20 min total: 30 min serves: five

Ingredients:
- One egg yolk
- 4 ounces of feta cheese
- Two tablespoons of flat-leafed parsley, finely chopped
- One scallion, finely chopped
- Two sheets of frozen filo pastry, defrosted

- Two tablespoons of olive oil.

Instructions:

1. In a pot, smash the egg yolk and blend in the feta, parsley, and scallion; sauté with pepper to taste. Cut into three strips each layer of filo dough. Scoop a full feta combination teaspoon at the underside of a pastry sheet. Fold over the tip of the pastry to shape a rectangle, fold the strip in a zigzag fashion until the filling is rolled into a rectangle. Repeat before both of the filo and feta is used.

2. Air fryer preheat to 390 ° F. Brush the filo with a little oil and put three triangles in the basket for frying. Slide into the Air fryer basket and steam for 3 minutes. Change the temperature to 360 ° F, then cook until golden brown for 2 minutes. Repeat it with the remaining feta triangles.

3.4 Korean BBQ Satay

Active: 15 minutes total: 30 min serves: 4

Ingredients:

- one pound of boneless skinless chicken tender
- 1/2 cup of low sodium soy sauce
- 1/2 cup of pineapple juice
- 1/4 cup of sesame oil
- Four garlic cloves, sliced
- Four scallions, sliced
- 1 cup of fresh ginger, grated
- Two teaspoons of sesame seeds, toasted
- One tablespoon of black pepper

Instructions:

1. Skewer each tender chicken, flaking extra meat or fat. Add the remaining ingredients in a large mixing pot. Attach the skewered chicken to the tub, blend well and sealed, refrigerate for up to 24 hours.

2. Air fryer preheat to 390 ° F. Brush chicken with a paper towel, fully dry. Attach half skewers to the basket and cook for 5-7 minutes each batch.

3.5 Jerk Chicken Wings

Active: 15 minutes total: 45 min serves: 6

Ingredients:

- four pounds of chicken wings
- Two tablespoons of olive oil
- Two tablespoons of soy sauce
- Six cloves of garlic, finely chopped
- One habanero pepper, seeds and ribs cut, finely chopped
- One tablespoon of allspice
- One teaspoon of cinnamon
- One teaspoon of white pepper
- One teaspoon of salt
- Two tablespoons of brown sugar
- One tablespoon of fresh thyme, finely chopped
- One teaspoon of white pepper

Instructions:

1. Add all the ingredients in a mixing pot, completely coating the chicken with the seasonings and marinade. Switch to a 1-gallon jar, then refrigerate for up to 24 hours for 2 hours.
2. Air fryer preheat to 390 ° F. Cut the wings and remove all liquid from the bag. Fully dry Pat wings with a paper towel. Place half the wings in the basket and cook for 14-16 minutes every pan, shaking halfway through. Serve with dipping sauce or ranch dressing in blue cheese.

3.6 Moroccan Meatballs with Mint Yogurt

Active: 25 minutes total: 40 min serves: 4

Ingredients:

For the meatballs

- one pound of ground lamb
- 4 ounces of ground turkey
- 1 1/2 tablespoons of parsley, finely chopped
- One tablespoon basil, finely chopped
- One teaspoon of ground cumin
- One teaspoon of ground coriander
- One teaspoon of cayenne pepper
- One teaspoon of red chili paste
- Two garlic cloves, finely chopped
- 1/4 cup of olive oil
- One teaspoon of salt
- One egg of white

For the basil yog

Instructions:

1. Air fryer preheats to 390 ° F. Combine all ingredients for the meatballs in a large mixing pot, For smoothing the meatball out to the size of a golf ball, roll the meatballs between your hands in a circular motion. Place half the meatballs into the basket and cook for 6-8 minutes each pan.

2. When cooking the meatballs add all of the mint yogurt ingredients to a small mixing bowl and blend well. Garnish with the meatballs and fresh mint and olives.

3.7 Pigs in a Blanket

Active: fifteen min total: thirty min serves: four

Ingredients:

- 12-ounce cocktail franks
- 8-ounce crescent can of rolls

Instructions:

1. Remove from the box the cocktail franks, and drain; pat dry on paper towels. Cut the dough into triangular lines, around 1-inch x 1.5 inches. Roll the strips along with the franks, such that the ends are visible. Place it in the freezer to firm for 5 minutes

2. Air fryer preheat to 330 ° F. Take the franks from the fridge, then put half of them in the basket. Cook for 6-8 minutes every pan, or until golden brown.

3.8. Stuffed Garlic Mushrooms

Active: ten min total: twenty min serves: 4

Ingredients:

For the stuffing

- 12 button mushrooms
- One slice of white bread
- One garlic clove,
- One tablespoon of flat-leafed parsley, finely chopped
- black ground pepper to taste
- One tablespoon of olive oil

Instructions:

1. Air fryer preheats to 390 ° F. Grind the slices of bread into fine crumbs in a food processor, then blend to taste with the garlic, parsley, and pepper. Then add in the olive oil when completely mixed.

2. Cut off the stalks of the mushrooms and cover the caps with breadcrumbs. Pat crumbs into caps to ensure that loose crumbs are not sucked up onto the ventilator. Place the caps of the mushrooms in the cooking basket and slip them into the air fryer. Cook the champignons for 10 minutes, or until golden and crispy

3.9. Buffalo Cauliflower Bites

Ingredients:

- 1 cup of all-purpose flour
- One teaspoon of kosher salt
- One teaspoon of garlic powder
- One teaspoon of onion powder
- Two eggs
- 1/2 cup of whole milk
- 2 cups Panko breadcrumbs
- One large head of cauliflower, sliced into florets
- 1 1/2 cup of ranch dressing
- 1 cup of hot sauce
- Chopped parsley, for garnishing

Instructions:

1. In a small dish, mix the flour, salt, garlic powder, and onion. In a second cup, whisk the egg and milk together. Place the Breadcrumbs in a separate bowl.
2. Dip one flower of cauliflower into the flour mixture, then apply the mixture of eggs and then the breadcrumbs. Repeat before you bread all of the cauliflower.
3. Without overcrowding, add some of the cauliflower to the fry basket. Pick the Fry configuration (8 minutes to 400F degrees).
4. Halfway swirl the tub. When time is up, cut the cauliflower with caution. Cook another 2-3 minutes if the larger parts aren't fork-tender. Repeat until the entire cauliflower is baked.

5. Meanwhile, whisk together the ranch and hot sauce in a large saucepan. Heat to dry, over low altitude. Put the cauliflower into the warm sauce and eat right away. Garnish with peregrinate.

3.10. Cheddar Scallion Biscuits

Ingredients

- 2 cups of all-purpose flour
- Two tablespoons of baking powder
- 1/2 teaspoon salt
- 1/2 cup (4 ounces or eight tablespoons) cold unsalted butter, sliced into eight parts
- 1 cup shredded cheddar cheese
- 1/4 cup crumbled bacon
- One scallion, minced
- 1 cup cold strong whipping cream

Instructions

1. Add the baking powder, flour, and salt in a bowl, using a pastry knife to remove the butter or use the fingers until the paste is crumbly and looks like little pebbles.
2. Add the cheese, ham, scallion, and cream and stir until it is moistened and a dough forms.
3. Knead the dough gently on a finely floured surface, about 3-4 times. Roll the dough to a thickness of ¾.

4. Cut about nine biscuits (you would need to pick the scraps and roll them out again) using a two 1/2-inch diameter cookie cutter.

5. Without overcrowding, add some of the biscuits to the fry bowl. Choose the environment for the bake, increase the temperature to 350 degrees F, and change the time to 20 minutes or to a golden brown. Take off the biscuits gently until the time is over. Repeat until the biscuits are all baked.

Chapter 4: Scrumptious Air fryer Appetizers

This chapter will present some more palatable air fryer recipes that can be served as appetizers.

4.1. Cheesy Garlic & Herb Pull-Apart Bread

Ingredients

- 1 round loaf of sourdough bread
- Three cloves of garlic, minced
- Two tablespoons of finely chopped parsley
- Eight tablespoons of butter melted
- 1 cup of shredded cheese mix (cheddar, Monty jack, mozzarella, etc.)

Instructions

1. Split the bread into 1-inch slices; be careful not to split it all the way to the loaf's middle. Rotate, and repeat, 90 degrees.
2. Remove the sliced bread pieces and put them softly together with the shredded cheese.
3. Blend the garlic, parsley, and butter together in a little cup, then rub over the crust.
4. Place the fry configuration in your air fryer basket at 400 degrees F, minimize the time to ten minutes and bake until the cheese is melted and the surface is crispy and crisp.

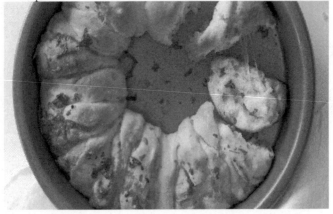

4.2 Sweet Potato Fries with Sriracha Mayonnaise

Ingredients

- One big sweet potato, sliced and cut into 1/4-inch long strips
- 1/4 cup cornstarch
- One teaspoon kosher salt

194

- One teaspoon garlic powder
- 1/2 teaspoon paprika
- Two tablespoons of olive oil
- 1/2 cup mayonnaise
- Two tablespoons sriracha
- Two teaspoons of lemon juice
- Chopped parsley, for garnish

Instructions

1. Apply the sweet potato strips to a broad zip-top plastic container. Fill the bag with the cornstarch, oil, garlic powder, and paprika.
2. Shake to paint the potatoes full.
3. Pour the oil into the bag and shake to paint.
4. Without overcrowding, add some of the fries to the fry tub.
5. Use the Fry setting (400F degrees) and change the time to 15 minutes or until the inside is tendered, and the outside is crispy.
6. To hit your ideal crispness, add an additional 5 minutes if needed. Halfway shake the tub. When time is up, cut the fries carefully. Repeat until they prepare all the fries.
7. Whisk the mayonnaise, sriracha, and lemon juice combined, when doing so.
8. Serve the fries with mayonnaise sriracha and chopped parsley immediately.

4.3 Mozzarella Cheese Balls

Ingredients

- 8 ounces mozzarella ciliegine (cherry-sized mozzarella balls), washed and patted dry
- 1/4 cup all-purpose flour
- 1/4 tablespoon kosher salt

195

- One egg
- 1/2 cup Panko breadcrumbs
- 1/4 cup grated Parmesan cheese
- Chopped parsley and marinara sauce, for serving

Instructions

1. In a dish, mix the flour and salt. Beat the egg gently in a second, shallow cup. Combine the breadcrumbs and cheese into a single, small dish.
2. Operating for one ball at a time, dredge in a mixture of flour, then milk, and breadcrumbs.
3. Place on a tray in a single plate. Freeze for 2 hours max.
4. Avoid overcrowding add a few balls to the fry bowl. Use the Setup Fry (400F degrees) and set the time to 6 minutes.
5. When time is up, apply with caution. Repeat until the balls are all fried.
6. Serve with parsley and marinara sauce right away.

4.4 Loaded Baked Potatoes

Ingredients

- 4 Small russet potatoes
- 1/2 cup sliced Mexican blend cheese
- Three strips of grilled bacon, diced
- Sour cream
- One teaspoon of minced chives

Instructions

1. Scrub the potatoes and poke the tines of a fork all over.
2. Place your air fryer in the basket and click the fry level to 400 degrees after Scaling up the time to 40 minutes.

3. Cook the potatoes until tender, with more or less time depending on the size you may require.
4. Cut, let sit at room temperature for about 5 minutes, then slice down the middle in half and scatter two teaspoons of cheese on top.
5. Place it back again in the air fryer for 1-2 minutes to melt.
6. Cut and finish with a dollop of sour cream, bacon diced, and chives sliced.
7.

4.5 Parmesan Zucchini Fries with Herb Dipping Sauce
<u>Ingredients</u>
- 2 Medium zucchini
- 1 cup panko
- 1 cup of Italian style bread crumbs
- 1 cup of finely ground parmesan cheese
- One egg + 2 tablespoons of water Salt and black pepper

For the dressing:
3/4 cup of Greek yogurt 1/4 cup of sour cream one tablespoon of hazelnut parsley one tablespoon of hazelnut chives one lemon juiced salt and pigment to fit

<u>Instructions</u>
1. Cut the zucchini in half lengthwise and after that into sticks no more than half-inch thick and four inches long.
2. Whisk the water and egg in a bowl and season with salt and pepper.
3. Mix the panko, bread crumbs, parmesan cheese & salt, and pepper in a shallow bowl.
4. Working in small amounts, dip the zucchini into the milk, then cover them in the breadcrumbs.
5. Put in the air fryer basket in a plate, click the fry setting at 400 degrees F, and reduce the cooking time to 10 minutes. Shake the bowl in half for

197

better preparation. After 10 minutes, test and add 1-2 minutes of extra cooking time if needed.

6. Remove gently, then season with kosher salt.
7. Repeat with remaining fried zucchini. When fried, chuck all the fries back into the air fryer to reheat for 2-3 minutes.
8. When the fries are heating up, mix the sauce together in a little cup, whisking sour cream, Greek yogurt, dill, parsley, chives, lemon juice, and salt and pepper together to compare.

4.6 Smoked Paprika and Parm Potato Wedges
Ingredients
- Two Yukon gold potatoes, sliced in 6 wedges each
- One tablespoon of olive oil (optional)
- 1/2 teaspoon of smoked paprika
- 1/4 teaspoon salt
- 1/4 cup of grated parmesan cheese

Instructions
1. Drain the potatoes and sliced into six wedges each. Put the wedges in a bowl and then drizzle with olive oil if necessary. Sprinkle over with salt and paprika.
2. Place the wedges in the basket of the air fryer and click the fry level to 400 degrees F. Shorten time to 20 minutes. After 10 minutes, the basket shake. Sprinkle the parmesan cheese thinly over the potatoes when the potatoes are tender, then cook for 2 minutes to brown the cheese

4.7 Roasted Chickpea Snacks

Ingredients

- Chickpeas 15-ounce
- One teaspoon olive oil
- 1/2 teaspoon lime juice
- Pinch cayenne pepper
- Pinch cumin

Instructions

1. Wash and rinse chickpeas and pat dry. Place them in a little bowl and apply the oil and lime juice to drizzle. Remove the salt, pepper, cumin, and mix to shake.
2. Add the chickpeas in the air fryer basket. At 400 degrees F, click the fry setting and raising the time to 15 minutes.
3. During cooking, shake the basket several times to ensure cooking is correct.
4. Around 15 minutes, check a chickpea to see if it's done-it's going to be fully dried and crisp with no moisture in the middle. Continue to cook as desired, until the chickpeas are dry and crunchy. Let them cool fully before being placed in a sealed container.

4.8 "Marinated" Artichoke Hearts

If one like jarred marinated artichokes and don't like all of the oil they are swimming in, you will love these. They're good warm or chilled.

Ingredients

- One tablespoon of lemon juice
- One tablespoon of olive oil
- One teaspoon of oregano
- 1/2 teaspoon of thyme
- Pinch of red pepper flakes
- Pinch of garlic powder
- Pepper to taste
- Some black pepper grinds
- 12 ounces of frozen artichoke heart

Instructions

1. Layer the lemon juice, olive oil, oregano, thyme, garlic powder, salt, and pepper in a small cup. Attach the artichokes, and throw the artichokes to paint.
2. Place the artichokes in the basket of the air fryer and set the temperature manually to 350 degrees F. Set the timer 5 minutes.
3. Serve dry or cool until chilled.

Chapter 5: Air fryer Breakfast recipes

Breakfast is a crucial meal of our daily routine. Having a healthy and delicious breakfast is a must to stay proactive all day. The chapter will provide breakfast recipes that can be made quickly through air fryer

5.1 Air Fryer Sausage Patties

Prep Time 2 minutes Total Time 10 minutes,

Air Fryer Sausage Patties, Breakfast Sausage Air Fryer Servings: 1 Calorie: 142 kcal **Ingredients**

- (Sausage links or patties)
- 1 Serving Breakfast Sausage (1.5 ounces/43 grams)

Blend with your favorite sauce.

Cut or shape the sausage into 1/4 "balls, and place it in the air fryer bowl.

Cook at 400 degrees for 8–10 minutes, turning on halfway.

Breakfast Cuisine: American

Boiled Eggs

Servings for: six eggs Calories: 78 kcal

Ingredients

- Six eggs
- Oil Spritz, on chickens, so they don't fall together.

Instructions

Put in the air fryer the wire rack or egg adapter that came with your air fryer or accessory kit.

Place all six eggs with string onto the shelf. When two eggs touch each other, they softly oil the eggs, as they stay together—Cook at 250 temperature for 18 to 20 minutes. Remove the eggs and put them in an ice-water pan.

Peel, cook, and eat your snack.

5.2 Air Fryer Breakfast Potatoes

<u>Breakfast</u>

Cuisine: American

Keyword: Air Fried Breakfast Potatoes, Servings: 4 Calories: 180 kcal

Ingredients

- 2-3 big potatoes can also use 1/2 bag of frozen diced potatoes to save time
- One onion, diced
- One red pepper, diced 1 tsp.
- Garlic paste with 1/2 tsp.
- One Teaspoon of paprika.
- One teaspoon water.
- And Spritz Your Favorite Oil

Instructions

Mix in a large bowl with all ingredients. (Simply spray the mixture until the correct quantity of oil is exceeded by using an oil mister.) Spritz the base of the air fryer basket to prevent damage, or using a filter.

Place the potatoes inside the air-fryer bowl.

Cook at 390 degrees for 15–20 minutes, stirring at frequent intervals.

5.3 Apple Baked by Air Fryer

In this world, your handmade apple granola or favorite cereal couldn't top this unbelievably sweet, sinuously delightful Apple Baked by Air Fryer.

This kind of recipe is the best possible way to turn pure and basic elements into totally indistinctive thing. These kinds of appliances are a blessing from above that makes it possible to receive fat, caramelized, and soft therapies, independent of the aim of weight loss.

All that you require is simply a shred of cinnamon and butter. This recipe for Apple baking is kind of American classic sure to add warmth to your style without crashing the bank with calories. Apple Baked by Air Fryer officially clocks under

150 calories (including Smart Carb variety carbohydrates), which carry the bakery flavor to a few of your preferred calorie-loaded baked goods. Why do you want apples to consider now? For a flex meal get up.

For two serving, per serving calories is 139, Register as one-half SmartCarb, one-half Power Oil, and one **Additional Ingredient:**

- One average Pear or Apple
- Two spoons Walnuts.
- Two tbsp. small raisins
- Dark margarine, one and half tsp. melted.
- 1/4 tsp. cinnamon.
- Nutmeg 1/4 cup water

Guidance:
• Heat the fryer to 350 ° Fahrenheit in advance.

Instructions:

Slice the pear or apple about the center in half, and spoon some flesh out.

Put the pear or apple in the saucepan (air fryer component) or in the base of the air fryer (after the attachment is removed).

Combine a small cup of margarine, sugar, nutmeg, raisins and walnut.

Put this mix into halve centers of apple or pear.

Put water inside the casserole.

Bake 20 more minutes.

5.4 Air Fryer Cinnamon Rolls

The tasty little cinnamon rolls will bake in just 10 minutes AND have an alternate grocery use store-bought bread dough as the basis. Of course, if you want to make the dough from scratch, then that's always good!

Time for preparation: 20 McCook Time: 9 minutes Total time: 29 servings: 8

Ingredients to be added

- One pound of frozen bread flour,

- One-fourth cup of cooled and melted butter
- Three-fourth cup of sugar (Brown)
- One and half spoon of cinnamon (Ground)
- Coat of cream cheese
- Smoothed 4 ounces of cream cheese
- 2 tbsp. Butter, smooth
- 1 1/4 cups of powdered sugar
- 1/2 tablespoon of vanilla directions. Now, allow the bread to spread in a thirteen-inch triangle of eleven inch on a gently floured surface. Place the rectangle in front of the thirteen-inch foot. Brush the molten butter across the bottom of the pastry, remaining   one-inch edge exposed farthest from you.

Instructions

Within a shallow pot, add the cinnamon and brown sugar. Sprinkle onto buttered bread the mixture uniformly and reveal the one-inch side. Enfold the bread into shape of log beginning at the bottom nearest to you. Enfold the bread firmly, making sure that it spreads uniformly, pushing out any pockets of air. Put pressure on the bread onto the wraps to tie it together until you reach the uncovered bottom of the dough.

Cut the log into eight pieces, slice the bread gently with a gesture to saw, so you don't flatten it. Flip the upside-down slices and cover them with a neat cloth. Now let wraps sit for sixty to eighty min in the moderately hot area of your kitchen.

Put the butter and cream cheese in an oven to make the coating. Soften the paste inside the oven for thirty sec at a moment, so it is fast to blend. Add the sugar in powdered form bit by bit, then mix to blend. Now add the whisk and vanilla extract till smoothness. Now keep it separately.

Once the wraps have grown, Heat the fryer in advance till 350 Fahrenheit.

Shift 4 of the wraps into fryer's bucket. Switch the wraps over fifteen-minute air-cook, and cook for another four minutes. Match with four remaining wraps.

Now, Let the wraps chill down for some time until the coating. Put a large coating of cream cheese over mild hot cinnamon wraps, causing a little of the coating to spill down the border of the wraps. Serve a little hot, and be delighted!

5.5 Cranberry Pecan Muffins (Gluten-Free) Air Fryer Recipe

An easy blender recipe for weekend brunch or breakfast that serves cranberry pecan muffins (gluten-free) every day. These muffins are fried in the air fryer and take about 15 minutes to bake Fast during the fall and winter months, and other baked goods contain Simple Cranberries.

We don't always need to limit cranberry baking to falling and winter months. Cookies and muffins containing fresh cranberries can be used at any time of year. If fresh cranberries are out of season, a frozen bag of cranberries is still available for collection.

To be honest, I've just used fresh cranberries a couple of times up to this year. I dove into the cranberry bog this year and made several muffins with fresh cranberries and a fast sandwich.

Sure, they were utterly irresistible— the well-baked cranberries adding a sweet tartness. If you need to chill in the afternoon, make a cup of tea and savor this gluten-free cranberry pecan muffins air fryer recipe.

For example, muffins are great for breakfast at every time of year. This is a recipe for a blender means you can cook up this dish in no time. Let's bake instead!

Prep Time: 15 minutes

Bake Time 10 minutes or less:

Total Time: 25-35 min.

Yield: 6-8 muffins

Cooking: Muffins

Ingredients

- 1/4 cup of cashew milk (or use whatever milk you prefer)
- Two big eggs

- 1/2 tsp. of vanilla essence.
- 1 1/2 cup Almond Flour
- 1/4 cup Monk fruit extract (or using your favorite sweetener)
- 1 tsp. baking powder.
- Cinnamon: 1/4 tsp.
- 1/8 tsp. Salt
- 1/2 cup fresh cranberries
- 1/4 cup chopped pecans

Instructions

Try adding the milk, eggs, and vanilla extract to the mixer and blend for 20-30 seconds together.

In the almond – mix for another 30-45 seconds, add the flour, sugar, baking powder, cinnamon, and salt until well mixed.

Remove the blender jar off the foundation and mix in 1/2 the fresh cranberries and pecans. Transfer the mixture to silicone muffin cups. Finish each of the muffins with some remaining fresh cranberries.

Place the muffins in the air-fryer basket and bake on 325-or for 12-15 minutes until the toothpick is clean.

Lift from the air fryer and cool on the wire rack.

Drizzle with a maple glaze where possible. The melted white chocolate is also drizzled over some of the muffins, bake in a preheated 325-degree oven for twenty-five to thirty minutes for Oven Baking, or until a toothpick comes out clean.

5.6 Air Fryer Strawberry Pop-Tarts

Maybe the best invention is still Air Fryer Baked Pop-Tarts of Raspberry! Almost all of you probably recall Pop-Tarts. Well, few of you could even eat or feed Pop-Tarts to your kids. We all have sentimental recollection from our early years, which include Pop-Tarts. Our moms often bought the cinnamon essence variety, for some excuse. We have nothing about cinnamon, but a kid's strawberry flavor tastes unusually great!

Total calories are 274 with fat equal to 14 grams along with carbs equal to 32 grams and protein equal to 3 grams. Handmade Pop-Tarts of Strawberry in air fryer is a fast and simple nutritious meal for cream cheese with low fat, stevia and Greek vanilla yogurt added sugar-free frosting. To adults a child-friendly meal is great as well!

Preparation Time is ten min and Total Time is twenty-five min top for the servings of six individuals, this meal has total of 274 kilo calories.

Ingredients

- Two cooled pie crusts
- One table spoon of cornstarch
- One-third cup of preserved strawberry with low sugar.
- Half cup of simple, non-fat Greek vanilla yogurt I used a cutting board made of bamboo.

Instructions:

Slice the two pie crusts into six rectangles, by using a pizza cutter or knife (From each pie crust three). Growing to surround the pop-tart will be fairly lengthy until you turn it around.

Place the cornstarch and preserves in a pot, then mix well.

Drop a spoonful of preserves onto the crust and put the preserves on the crust's top.

To save, fold the pop-tarts over each, using a fork to create horizontal and vertical lines around the sides and create sensations of each of the pop-tarts.

Now put the pop-tarts in Air Fryer. Sprinkle on grease. I want to use the olive oil.

Please bake at 375 Fahrenheit for at least ten min also you will to examine the pop-tarts for about eight min to make sure they're not too crisp to your liking.

Bring together stevia, Greek yogurt and cream cheese in a tub to make the frosting.

Enable the pop-tarts to chill down before removing the fryer. Well it is really crucial. Unless you don't let them cool off, then they could crack. Drop Pop-Tart from the fryer. Cover each with frosting. Sprinkle of sugar over the sprinkles.

Recommended baking two to three pop-tarts at single time in fryer. As you may pile them up, also they will separate finely until they've completely cooled up. Though not adding them to ensure delivery works best.

5.7 Peanut Butter and Jelly Air Fried Doughnuts

Look at those light, fluffy doughnuts, oozing jam, and dripping peanut butter glaze? New from the fryer! To air fryers, such beauties are a wonder.

Ingredients (6 Doughnuts):

- 1 1/4 cups of all-purpose flour
- 1/3 cup of sugar
- 1/2 teaspoon baking powder
- 1/2 teaspoon baking soda
- 3/4 teaspoon salt
- 1 Egg
- 1/2 cup buttermilk
- One teaspoon vanilla
- Two tablespoons of unsalted butter which should be melted and cooled
- One tablespoon melted butter to clean the tops

Filling: • 1/2 cup Blueberry or raspberry jelly (not preserved)

Instructions:

Build a well in the middle of the dry product, then spill the water. Mix with a fork, and finish mixing with a large spoon before the flour is added.

Turn the dough out into a well-floured sheet. Mind this would be very sticky at first. Perform the dough very slowly until it reaches a 3/4 "thickness and then pat it out, Using a 3 1/2 "knife to remove the dough circles and to wipe the melting butter. Try to Cut out 2 "pieces of parchment paper (doesn't need to be precise) and put each dough round on the board, then in the air fryer. Act in loads depending on how many you can fit inside your fryer. Fry at 350 degrees for 11 minutes, using a squeeze bottle or pastry container, each doughnut can fill with jelly.

Blueberry Lemon Muffins

Training Time: 5-8 minutes. Cook Hour: 10-12 min. Average time: 25-35 min. Cuisine: American

Ingredients:

- 2 1/2 cups of self-rising flour
- 1/2 cup of monk fruit (or using your choice sugar)
- 1/2 cup of milk
- 1/4 cup of avocado oil (any soft cooking oil)
- Two eggs
- 1 cup of blueberries
- One lemon zest
- One lemon juice
- 1 tsp. Vanilla
- Brown topping sugar (a little sprinkling on top of each muffin-less than a teaspoon) Direction Mix the self-growing flour and sugar. Set aside in a small bowl.
  Layer milk, sugar, lemon juice, bacon, and coffee in a small saucepan

Instructions:

Attach the flour mixture to the liquid mixture and stir in the blueberries until combined.

In silicone cupcake cups, spoon the batter, sprinkle 1/2 tsp. — brown sugar on top of each muffin;

Bake for 10 minutes at 320 degrees; check the muffins at 6 minutes to ensure that they do not cook too quickly. Place one toothpick in the center of a muffin, and it ends until the toothpick comes out clean and the muffins brown. No need to over-bake the muffins; once they are removed from the air fryer, they can carry on to cook for another minute or two.

Remove and make it new.

This dish can also be cooked on the oven for 12-15 minutes at 350 degrees.

Put all these in a plastic bag and refrigerate if you have extra muffins. They're going to live 4-5 days, new. When they are ready to eat, seal the muffin tightly in a paper
towel and cook for 10 seconds in the microwave. Serve with a big glass of milk, coffee, tea or hot cocoa,

5.9 Air Fryer French toast Soldiers

You will have to go with lots of troops, and two wonderful soft boiled eggs. They were good, and because of the egg factor and the kick of the carbs, that will leave you complete for hours and hours.

While this isn't everyone's cup of tea, the mixture of eggs and breakfast bread has always been a great one.

You drip the bread into an egg and then prepare it outside with a tasty coating of butter. So you do so, however much you want. And a good Berries seasoning!!!

This recipe (which is really simple to make) takes just a few minutes and makes the ideal breakfast to set you up for the day.

Prep Time 5 mins Cook Time 10 mins Total Time 15 mins Servings: 2

Ingredients:

- 4 Slices of Full Meal Bread
- 2 Broad Eggs
- 1/4 Cup Whole Milk
- 1/4 Cup Brown Sugar
- 1 Tbsp. Honey
- 1 Tsp. Cinnamon
- Nutmeg pinch
- Icing Sugar pinch

Instructions

Cut up the bread slices into troops. Any soldiers slice will make 4.

Put the remaining ingredients in a mixing bowl (except icing sugar), then blend properly.

Dip each soldier into the mixture to well cover the mixture and put it in the Air Fryer. Once you're done, you'll have 16 soldiers, and so everyone will be warm and soaked from the mix.

Put on 160c for 10 minutes, or until the toast is crispy and cool and not sticky anymore. By cooking, turn them over halfway so that both sides of the soldiers have a fair chance to cook equally.

Serve with some new berries and a swirl of icing sugar.

Chapter 6: Air fryer recipes of Lunches

In this chapter, we will present air fryer recipes of main course meals for lunches.

6.1 Chimichurri Steak

Active: fifteen minutes total: 35 minutes serves: 2

Ingredients:

For chimichurri

- One-pound skirt steak
- One cup parsley, finely chopped
- One-fourth cup of basil, finely chopped
- Two tea-spoon of oregano, finely chopped
- Three garlic cloves, finely chopped
- One tea-spoon of red pepper
- One tea-spoon of cumin
- One tea-spoon of cayenne pepper
- One tea-spoon of black pepper
- One-fourth cup of olive oil

Instructions:

1. Combine the Chimichurri ingredients into a mixing pot. Cut the steak into two 8-ounce portions, and add the chimichurri 1/4 cup to a re-sealable jar. Refrigerate after 24 hours for 2 hours. Switch from the fridge 30 minutes before cooking.
2. Air fryer preheat to 390 ° F. Pat dry steak with a towel made from rubber. Attach the steak to the pot, and prep for medium-rare for 8-10 minutes.
3. Garnish with 2 Chimichurri tablespoons on top and serve.

6.2 Roasted Heirloom Tomato with Baked Feta

Active: twenty minutes total: 35 minutes serves: 4

Ingredients:

For the tomato

- One heirloom tomato
- One 8-ounce block of feta cheese
- Half cup of red onions
- One tablespoon of olive oil
- One pinch of salt

For the basil pesto

- 1/2 cup of parsley, finely chopped
- 1/2 cup of parmesan cheese, rubbed
- Three tablespoons of pine nuts, toasted
- One garlic clove
- olive oil
- One pinch of salt

Instructions:

1. Make pesto. Attach the parsley, spinach, parmesan, garlic, toast pine nuts, and salt in a food processor.
2. Switch on the food processor, and apply the olive oil gradually. Store and refrigerate until ready to use, once all the olive oil is mixed into the pesto.
3. 2. Air fryer preheat to 390 ° F. Break the tomato and feta into thin slices, 1/2 inch long.
4. With a paper towel, dry the tomato. Place one spoonful of pesto on top of each slice of tomatoes and finish with the feta. Throw the red onions with one spoonful of olive oil and put them on top of the feta.
5. Place the tomatoes/feta in the basket and cook for 12-14 minutes or until the feta begins softening and browning. Finish off with a tablespoon of salt and an extra basil pesto spoonful.

6.3 Portabella Pepperoni Pizza

Active: 5 min total: 10 min serves: 1

Ingredients:

- One portabella mushroom cap,
- One spoonful of olive oil
- One spoonful of tomato sauce
- One spoonful of mozzarella, sliced
- Four slices of pepperoni
- One pinch of salt
- One pinch of Italian seasoning

Instructions:

1. Air fryer preheat to 330 °F. Drizzle olive oil on either side of the portabella, then season the portabella inside with salt and Italian seasonings. Print the tomato sauces around the mushroom uniformly, and then finish with the cheese.

2. Place the portabella in the basket and then slide into the air fryer. Take the cooking basket from the Air fryer after 1 minute, and put the pepperoni slices on top of the portabella pizza.

3. Cook for 3 to 5 minutes. Full with newly ground parmesan cheese and crushed red flakes.

6.4. Mushroom, Onion and Feta Frittata

Active: 15 minutes total: 25 minutes serves: 2

Ingredients:

- Three eggs
- Two cups of button mushrooms,
- Half red onion washed
- One table-spoon of olive oil
- Three table-spoons of feta cheese,

- One pinch of salt crumbled

Instructions:

1. Peel and cut half a red onion into slices 1/4 inches long. Clean mushrooms first; then cut into slices 1/4 inch long. Sweat the onions and mushrooms under a medium flame in a sauté pan with olive oil until tender. Remove from oil, and put to cool on a dry cooking towel.

2. Air fryer preheat to 330 ° F. Crack 3 eggs in a mixing bowl and whisk deeply and vigorously, then add a pinch of salt. Cover the top and bottom of a 6-ounce ramekin with a thin layer of pan mist. Pour the eggs into the ramekin, then the combination of the onions and mushrooms and then the cheese. Place the ramekin in the pot, and cook for 10 to 12 minutes in the air fryer. When you see a sticking knife in the middle, the frittata is finished, and the knife comes out clean.

6.5 Roasted Cornish Game Hen

Active for 15 min and total for 30 min serves: 4

Ingredients:

- One cornish hen (approx. Two pounds)
- Half cup of olive oil
- One-fourth teaspoon of crushed red pepper flakes
- One teaspoon of thyme
- One teaspoon of rosemary
- One-fourth teaspoon of salt
- One-fourth teaspoon of 1 lemon sugar zest

Instructions:

1. Place the Cornish hen upright on a cutting board and use a boning knife or a chef's knife with the back of the hen facing you to start cutting from the top of

the backbone to the bottom of the backbone, dividing into two slices. Break bone from the back.

Break the hen lengthwise, and slit the breastplate across. Take the hen's two pieces, and set them apart.

2. Combine all the ingredients for the marinade in a mixing bowl and feed the hens. Refrigerate up to 24 hours for 1 hour.

3. Air fryer preheat to 390 ° F. Cut the hens from the marinade, then remove any excess liquid with a strainer. Pat dry with a towel made from cotton. Attach the hens to the kitchen basket and cook for 14-16 minutes, or until the leg is at 165 ° F indoor.

6.6 Teriyaki Glazed Halibut Steak in Air fryer

Active for 30 min and total for 39 to 41 min, serving for 3

Ingredients:

For the marinade:

- One pound of halibut steak
- Two-third cup of soy sauce (low sodium)
- Half cup of mirin (Japanese cooking wine)
- One-fourth cup of sugar 2 cups of lime juice
- One-fourth cup of orange juice
- One-fourth teaspoon of crushed red pepper flakes
- One-fourth teaspoon of ginger powder
- One clove of garlic (smash)

Instructions:

1. Both ingredients for the teriyaki glaze/marinade are mixed in a saucepan.

2. Take to a boil, and halve, then cool.

3. When cooled, pour half of the glaze/marinade with the halibut into a resealable jar.

4. Chill for 30 minutes.

5. Air fryer preheat to 390 ° F.

6. In the Air, fryer put marinated halibut and cook for 9-11 minutes.

7. When done, sweep over the halibut steak a little of the residual glaze.

8. Serve over a white rice bed of chutney basil/mint.

6.7 Cajun Shrimp

At least active for five minutes and minutes in total are ten min with serving for two people.

Ingredients for the recipe

- Half pound of tiger shrimp (Sixteen to Twenty)
- One-fourth spoon of pepper (Cayenne)
- Half spoon of old bay seasoning
- One-fourth spoon of paprika (Smoked)
- One pinch of salt
- One spoon of olive oil

Instructions:

1. Fryers should be heated to 390 ° Fahrenheit beforehand. Mix all the ingredients in a bowl, brush the shrimp with the oil and the spices. Put the shrimp in the pan to bake for 5 minutes. Serve with rice.

6.8 Coconut Shrimp

<u>**Ingredients:**</u>

- One-fourth cup of cornstarch
- One table-spoon salt
- Two egg whites
- One cup of flaked sweetened coconut
- Half pound of raw shrimp, peeled, deveined, and patted dry cocktail sauce to serve in a small dish, mix cornstarch and salt together.

Instructions

1. Drop the egg whites into a second small cup. Remove the coconut to a single, shallow dish.
2. Start with one shrimp at a time, dredging in a combination of cornstarch, first egg whites, and then coconut.
3. Avoid overcrowding add ample shrimp to the fry basket.
4. Pick the shrimp configuration (15 minutes of 330F degrees). When time is up, cut the shrimp completely. Continue until the shrimp are all fried.
5. Serve the shrimp with cocktail sauce right away.

6.9 Caprese Stuffed Mushrooms

Ingredients:

- One to eight-ounce container baby Portobello mushrooms
- four ounces of fresh mozzarella
- Cherry tomatoes
- Two table-spoons of bread crumbs or panko
- Pesto sauce (homemade or bought)

Instructions:

New basil ingredients Pesto Sauce: one cup of basil packing leaves two small cloves of garlic, peeled and sliced three tablespoons of pine nuts one-third cup of extra virgin olive oil one-third cup of Parmigiano Reggiano, a touch of a Reggiano Use a small spoon to pick out the mushrooms inside for more space for filling.

Put the basil, garlic and pine nuts together in a food processor while making the pesto, and pulse until broken down. Scrape the sides down, and add the cheese. The olive oil from the top drizzle with the motor working until the pesto is smooth.

Spray with salt and set on aside.

Cub the mozzarella into one-inch pieces and put one slice in the center of each mushroom, then cover with half of a cherry tomato. Sprinkle the breadcrumbs with the mushrooms and put them in a single layer in the air fryer bowl. This will need to be done in two lots, depending on the number of mushrooms you like.

6.10 Fish and Chips
<u>Ingredients:</u>

- Take two potatoes (russet) should be peeled and cut into chunks
- Two table-spoon of vegetable oil
- One tea-spoon of kosher salt
- One-fourth cup of all-purpose flour
- One egg
- One table-spoon of water
- Three-fourth cup of Panko breadcrumbs
- One-fourth cup of Parmesan cheese (grated)
- One-pound of cod, sliced into thick fillet and dried out
- Chopped parsley, Tartar sauce and Malt vinegar for serving.

<u>Instructions:</u>

In a bigger bowl, mix together the oil, salt and potato chunks. Place some of the chunks to the fry bucket without overpopulating it. Select the Fry Setting (400 Fahrenheit degrees for twenty minutes). Shake the bucket halfway through. Once the timer stops, carefully remove the wedges. Repeat the steps of the whole process until all of the potato wedges are cooked properly. In 1 shallow bowl, add the all-purpose flour. In a 2nd shallow bowl, lightly beat together the egg and water. In a third less deep bowl, mix together the breadcrumbs and cheese. Work with one piece at a time, dip the cod in flour, then egg, then breadcrumbs. Put fish in the fry basket of air fryer without over piling. Press the Fish Setting (330F degrees for 15 minutes). Once the time is over, carefully remove and check for tenderness. Repeat all the steps of the whole process until all of the fish is ready. Serve hot immediately with potato wedges, tartar sauce, malt vinegar, and parsley Click the setting to cook at 400 degrees Fahrenheit. And cut the time to twelve minutes.

Remove a slice of fresh basil from the air fryer and finish with pesto sauce. Serve straight away.

6.11 Garlic Chipotle Fried Chicken

Ingredients:

- One fryer chicken, sliced
- Two garlic cloves
- Two canned chipotle peppers
- Two cups of buttermilk
- Half cup of lime juice
- Three tea-spoon of kosher salt
- Two eggs
- Two cups of all-purpose flour
- Two tea-spoon of black pepper
- Chopped cilantro, to present.

Instructions:

Put the chicken bits in two big zip-top plastic sachets. Mix the garlic, onions, buttermilk, lime juice, two tablespoon salt, and eggs together in a blender. Drop into plastic containers, fully covering bits of chicken. Seal and refrigerate for a total of 6 hours, up to 24 hours.

Whisk the rice, black pepper, and remaining one teaspoon of salt together in a small bowl until ready to prepare.

Drop pieces of chicken and let the mixture drain off excess buttermilk. Coat in flour, then put a few pieces without over-crowding in the fry bowl.

Pick the Chicken configuration (20 minutes of 400F degrees). Upon delivery, cut the chicken cautiously and check for an internal temperature of 165F degrees. Cook for 5-10 minutes, if the chicken isn't cooked. Repeat until all pieces of chicken cook.

Serve moist with chopped coriander.

6.12 Grilled Beef Fajitas
Ingredients:

- One-pound of steak
- One-fourth cup of vegetable oil
- One-fourth cup of soy sauce
- One-fourth cup of lime juice
- One garlic clove,
- Two tables-poon of sugar(brown)
- Two tea-spoon of chili powder
- One tea-spoon of black pepper mix together butter, soy sauce, lime juice, garlic, brown sugar, chili powder, cumin, and black pepper.
- 1/4 cup marinade reserve.

Instructions:

Pour the remainder into a large plastic zip-top bag. Stir beef into the marinade. Seal bag that squeezes as much air as possible. Massage once completely coated with blood. Refrigerate up to 24 hours and for at least 4 hours. When ready to eat, mix the reserved 1/4 cup marinade with bell peppers and onion.

Take meat off the marinade and pat off—place in basket fry. Pick the Meat (370F degrees) setting and change the time to 5 minutes. Flip then change the duration, depending on the thickness and required doneness, to 3-5 minutes. Remove the meat for 10 minutes and allow it to relax.

Remove from the marinade the ingredients, and add to the fry bowl. Set the temperature and time for 8-10 minutes to 370F degrees, or until the fork-tender.

Split meat into short strips. Serve with tomatoes, cilantro, tortillas, and sour cream.

6.13 Southwestern Stuffed Peppers
Ingredients:
- Two cups of cooked quinoa
- Four bell peppers (red, yellow or orange)
- One small yellow onion, finely diced
- Two garlic cloves, minced
- Half pound of ground beef or turkey
- One tea-spoon of ground cumin
- One tea-spoon of powder
- Half tea-spoon of garlic powder
- One cup of frozen or fresh corn kernels
- Half cup of shredded cheese (Mexican)
- Salt and pepper to taste and Sour cream, lime chunks and cilantro to eat

Instructions:
1. Prepare the quinoa kernels 1 1 1/2 cup Mexican blend shredded cheese Salt and pepper
2. Cut the stem from the peppers of the bell and detach from within the seeds and ribs, and set aside.
3. Drizzle 1/2 tablespoon of oil in a saute pan over medium heat and fry the onions and garlic until tender-about 5 minutes and move to a mixing bowl, blend in the ground beef or turkey, quinoa, corn and cumin, chili powder, garlic powder and season with salt and pepper to taste. Toss the shredded cheese in 1 cup, then break between the four bell peppers.

Cook in a saute pan when there is some remaining mixture and save for another day.

4. Place the loaded bell peppers in the air fryer basket and click the meat setting at 370 degrees F and set the tie at 160 degrees F for 25 minutes or until a thermometer is in the middle. With the remaining shredded cheese cut on the finish.

5. Place the cheese back in the air fryer for 1 minute to melt.

6. Serve with sour cream, sliced cilantro, and a slice of lime.

6.14 Nashville Hot Chicken Sandwiches

Ingredients:

- One Pound of skinless, boneless chicken thighs (about four)
- Two cups of buttermilk
- Half tea-spoon of cayenne pepper
- Half tea-spoon of chili powder
- Half tea-spoon of kosher salt
- Half tea-spoon of black pepper
- Half tea-spoon of garlic powder
- Half cup of all-purpose flour

Instructions:

For hot sauce: One cup of vegetable oil, two tea-spoon of chili powder, two tea-spoon of paprika, half tea-spoon of cumin, half tea-spoon of cayenne pepper and four wraps of brioche Coleslaw.

Whisk in the chicken to mix and then add. Marinate overnight or for a total of 1 hour.

Place the flour in a zip top sachet and separate it from the buttermilk. Attach the chicken to the starch, brush, and shake off the excess absolutely. Place

225

the fryer basket in the air, and press the fry button at 400 degrees F., decrease the time by 10 minutes before the internal temperature exceeds 165 F.

Let sit for about 5 minutes, while the hot sauce is being prepared.

Combine together the vegetable oil, chili powder, paprika, cumin, and cayenne pepper into a medium pot and carry it to a simmer. Remove from heat and then, right before eating, clean the chicken.

Serve the chicken on a brioche bun served with pickles and coleslaw.

6.15 Italian Baked Eggs

Ingredients:

- One to fifteen ounces of tomatoes can be smashed
- One small yellow onion,
- Two garlic cloves,
- Half tea-spoon of crushed red pepper flakes
- Salt and pepper to taste
- Four large eggs
- Two tea-spoons of parmesan
- Basil to garnish
- Toasted bread for serving

Instructions:

Half tablespoon of oil in a medium heat pot and saute the onion and garlic until tender, around five minutes. Put in the smashed tomatoes and boil. Season with the crushed red pepper, butter, and pepper flakes.

Ladle the sauce into 4-4 ounce ramekins until it is full 2/3 of the way. Place an egg carefully in the egg ramekin core, and position it in the air fryer. You may need to operate in batches, depending on the scale of the ramekins.

Click the fry setting at 400 degrees Fahrenheit and shorten the duration to 9 min, depending on how runny your yolks like. You want to fix the white completely before withdrawing the fryer from the cold.

226

Remove and season the egg with salt and pepper, then finish with half tablespoon of basil then cheese.
Serve on a toasted piece of bread.

Chapter 7: Air fryer Dinner Recipes

In this chapter, we will discuss air fryer dinner recipes.

7.1 Turkey Taco Sliders in air fryer

These little sliders have the taste of a taco, particularly if you have taco-friendly garnishes like guacamole, lettuce, tomatoes, or cilantro to top them.

Ingredients:

- One pound of ground turkey
- One taco seasoning pack (for one pound of meat)
- Half small yellow onion (diced)
- Half cup sliced cheddar cheese
- Eight slider buns
- Toppings as your need

Instructions:

Mix the onion, cheddar cheese, ground turkey and taco seasoning, in a small dish. Mix well with your fingertips, then break into eight even parts. Form each section into a 3-inch diameter patty – or suit your slider buns.

Put four patties into the air fryer basket and push the meat level to 370 degrees F. Shorten time to 10 minutes.

Now cook the remaining four patties in the same way, when the first set of four sliders are finished.

You are using your favorite toppings to serve on slider buns.

7.2 Mediterranean Chicken Wings with Olives

In an air fryer, chicken wings are a good occurrence-they cook quicker and stay plump and juicy. Wings cook easier when they are on one plate. When you cook more, you'll need to shake them more often or rearrange them for even cooking.

Ingredients

- One to Half pound of chicken wings
- One and half tea-spoon lemon juice

- One tea-spoon oregano
- Pinch of garlic powder
- Pinch of salt
- One-fourth to half cup of olive oil

Instructions:

Mix the chicken wings with the lemon juice, oregano, garlic powder, and salt in a bowl and combine to cover evenly.

Put the wings in the basket of the air fryer and press the chicken level to 400 degrees F. Reduce the duration for small wings to 15 minutes, and add another 5 to 10 minutes for bigger wings.

During the cooking time, shake the basket once or twice to ensure the heat and brown evenly. In the last five minutes, while cooking add the olives to steam them up.

The wings are finished until well browned, and the internal temperature exceeds 160 degrees or more. Serve hot and juicy.

7.3 Fried Avocado Tacos

Fried avocados have a pleasant crunch and a creamy richness, which makes meat in tacos a great substitute. This plays well for very understaffed avocados. They smooth out during frying.

Ingredients

- One avocado
- One egg
- Half cup panko bread crumbs
- Tortillas as your need
- Toppings as your need

Instructions:

Halve the avocado, cut the pit, and cut the flesh from the wrapper. Break the flesh of the avocado into eight equal wedges.

229

Throw the egg into a shallow bowl and gently beat it. Place the crumbs of the panko bread into another tub.

Dip the wedges of avocado into the egg to coat, then roll in the crumbs of toast. Sprinkle gently with salt until all of the wedges are powdered.

Place the wedges in a single layer inside the fryer. If they don't suit, put any away in a second batch to fry later. At 400 degrees F, click the fry setting and raising the time to 10 minutes. Turn the wedges or shake gently for even browning, around halfway through frying. The wedges are rendered when the surface is browned gently. Serve along with your favorite toppings on tortillas.

7.4 Tortilla Crusted Pork Loin Chops
Ingredients:

- Two 8-ounce of pork loin chops (Boneless)
- Half cup of buttermilk
- One tea-spoon of steak sauce, spicy sauce or Worcestershire sauce
- Half tea-spoon salt
- Half cup of flour
- One egg
- Half cup of tortilla chips (Broken)

Instructions:

Put the loin chops in a zip-top plastic sachet at least eight hours or up to twenty-four hours before frying. Attach the Worcestershire buttermilk sauce, then salt. Massage the container until the items are mixed. Seal the jar properly, and place it in the fridge. When cooked, remove the chops from the bag and dump the marinade. Pat fresh to the chops. Put the all-purpose flour in a bowl or a big plate, the egg in a shallow bowl and the chips smashed in a separate pot. Only break the potato. Dip each side of each chop in the flour, shake off the excess flour, and dip it into the egg to coat. Finally, place the chop with the broken tortilla chips in the bowl and press both sides onto the chips to cover. Place the seasoned chops in the air fryer bowl, then click the meat setting at 370 degrees F. and decrease the time to 15 minutes. Switch the chops about halfway through the cooking period to fry even further. The chops are finished when they are well browned, and, depending on the preferred doneness, the meat has reached about 140-160 degrees. Remove from the frying pan and wait 5 minutes before slicing or serving.

7.5 Mustard and Sage Fried Chicken Tenders
Ingredients:
- One table-spoon of mayonnaise
- One tea-spoon of mustard Dijon
- Half tea-spoon of dried sage
- Half cup of Panko bread crumbs
- One table-spoon of melted butter
- One strip of chicken breast

Instructions:
Mix mayonnaise, mustard, and sage in a shallow bowl.
In another tiny tub, add the bread crumbs and butter.
Stir to combine. Pat the paper towels on the chicken tenders warm. Brush the tenders gently with the mixture of mayonnaise, then coat with the crumbs of bread place the tenders in one single layer in the air fryer basket. Place the basket inside the air fryer.
And press 400 degrees button on the air fryer for cooking the chicken. And cut the time to eight minutes. Flip the tenders over after 4 minutes and start cooking until the coating has browned gently, and the chicken is cooked properly – it will reach 160 degrees on an instant-scan thermometer. You may need to add an extra 2-3 minutes, depending on the thickness of the tenders.

7.6 Grilled Scallion Cheese Sandwich

Bring the grilled cheese sandwich to the next point with the bacon mixed with the scallions. They are milder than most olives, and the green in the cheese looks pretty good.

Ingredients:

- Two table-spoon of melted butter
- Two slices of bread
- Two scallions, thinly sliced green pieces
- Three-fourth cup of rubbed medium cheddar cheese
- One table-spoon of rubbed parmesan cheese

Instructions:

Put half of the butter on one bread slice and put it in the air fryer basket side down. To the bread, add the cheddar cheese and scallions. The top slice of bread is gently buttered and placed onto the cheese and butterup the bread sides. Spray the bread with the parmesan on top.

Place the basket into the air fryer and set the temperature manually to 350 degrees F. Set the time for 5 minutes, turn over the sandwich, and cook for 1-2 minutes more.

When the cheese is completely melted inside, the sandwich is finished, and the bread is toasted to your liking.

Chapter 8: Air fryer Fish and Sea-food Recipes

We will be sharing dainty and palatable fish and sea-food recipes thereby adding variety to your healthy lifestyle.

8.1 Salmon with Lemon Dill Sauce & Asparagus

Ingredients:

- Two to six-ounce salmon filets
- Black pepper and Kosher salt
- Two tea-spoon avocado oil
- Half cup of Greek yogurt
- One table-spoon finely chopped dill
- One clove of garlic finely minced
- One lemon (Juiced)
- Pepper and salt to taste
- One bunch of asparagus

Instructions:

Half cup of Greek yogurt one tablespoon finely chopped dill one clove garlic, finely minced one lemon, juiced Salt and pepper to taste one bunch asparagus Cut a small round of butter paper and put it in the bottom of the air fryer and make sure the salmon is prevented from sticking to the air fryer. Sprinkle on the salmon fillets, kosher salt, and black pepper to taste and brush each with one teaspoon of avocado oil. Put in the basket of the air fryer and press the fish setting at 330 degrees, reduce the time to fifteen minutes for medium-rare, and twenty minutes for medium to well-done depending on the thickness of the fish. Once it is cooked, take out from the air fryer, place on a plate, and cover with foil to keep warm. Remove the piece of butter paper from the air fryer, then trim the ends of the asparagus, and put in the basket. Sprinkle the kosher salt and pepper to taste and if desired brush with a small amount of oil. Select the fry setting at 400 degrees F. and reduce the time to 8 minutes, cook the asparagus until it becomes tender as desired by you. If needed, cook for one to two additional minutes. While the asparagus is being cooked, make the sauce by mixing the Greek yogurt, dill, garlic, and lemon in a small serving bowl. Season with herbs and salt and pepper as per taste. Serve the salmon and asparagus along with the palatable sauce.

8.2 Bacon-Wrapped Shrimp

Active for 15 min and total for 35 min with the serving of four person

Ingredients:

- One pound of tiger shrimp, peeled and deveined,
- One pound of bacon thinly cut of room temperature

Instructions:

1. Take one slice of bacon & wrap it around the shrimp, starting at the head and finishing at the tail. Give the wrapped shrimp back to the fridge for 20 minutes.

2. Air fryer preheats to 390 ° F. Take the shrimp from the refrigerator and add half of them to the basket, cooking for 5-7 minutes on each pan. Drain before serving onto a paper towel.

8.3. Crab Croquettes

Active for 20 minutes and total of 35 min with serving of six persons

Ingredients:

For the filling

- One-pound crab meat
- Two egg whites pounded
- One tablespoon olive oil
- One-fourth cup of red onion, finely chopped
- One-fourth red bell pepper, finely chopped
- Two-pound of celery, finely chopped
- One-fourth tea-spoon of tarragon, finely chopped
- One-fourth tea-spoon of chives, finely chopped
- Half tea-spoon of parsley, finely chopped
- Half tea-spoon of cayenne pepper
- One-fourth cup of mayonnaise.

Instructions:

1. Add onions, peppers, celery and olive oil in a small saute pan over medium to high heat. Cook and sweat for about 4-5 minutes before translucent. Take off heat and set aside to cool.
2. Blend the panko breadcrumbs, olive oil & salt into a fine crumb in a food processor: placed panko paste, eggs, and flour aside in three different containers. In a wide mixing bowl, add remaining ingredients: crab meat, egg white, mayonnaise, sour cream, spices, and vegetables.
3. Air fryer preheats to 390 ° F. Mold crab mixture to golf balls size, roll each into flour, then into eggs and eventually into panko. Click the crumbs to stick to croquettes. Place croquettes in the bowl, prevent overcrowding—Cook for 8-10 minutes each pan, or until golden brown.

8.4 Salmon with Dill Sauce

Active for 15 min and total of 25 min with serving of two persons

Ingredients:

For the salmon

- Twelve ounces of salmon
- Two tea-spoon of olive oil
- One pinch of salt

For the dill sauce

- Half cup of Greek non-fat yogurt
- Half cup of sour cream
- One pinch of salt
- Two table-spoon dill, finely minced

Instructions:

1. Heat the fryer to 270 ° Fahrenheit beforehand. Split the salmon into two 6 ounce pieces and drizzle on each slice one tablespoon of olive oil. Finish with a squeeze of oil. Put the salmon in the pan and cook for 15-17 minutes.

2. Create sauce with dill. The pudding, sour cream, chopped dill, and salt are mixed in a mixing cup.

With the gravy, finish the fried salmon and garnish with an optional pinch of minced dill.

8.5 Cod Fish Nuggets

Active for15 minutes and total of 35 minutes with serving of four persons

Ingredients

- One-pound of cod for
- Two spoons full of olive oil
- One cup of all-purpose flour
- Two eggs, beaten
- Three-fourth cup of panko breadcrumbs
- One tea-spoon of salt

Instructions:

1. Heat the fryer to 390 ° Fahrenheit beforehand. Cut the cod into strips between one "by 2.5" in length. Blend together the panko breadcrumbs, olive oil, and salt into a fine crumb in a food processor: placed panko paste, eggs, and flour aside in three different containers.

2. Place each piece of cod in the flour, then add the eggs and then the sliced bread. Push the fish tightly onto the breadcrumbs to make sure they stay

with the food. Shake off the breadcrumbs of excess. Attach half of the cod nuggets to the cooking pot, cook for 8-10 minutes every pan, or until golden brown.

Chapter 9: Air fryer Meals and Snacks for kids

In this chapter, we will present air fryer recipes of meals and snacks for your kids.

9.1 Air fryer Egg-plant fries

Ingredients

- Two big eggs
- Half cup of Parmesan cheese (grated)
- Half cup of toasted wheat germ
- One tea-spoon of Italian seasoning
- Three-fourth tea-spoon garlic of salt
- One small eggplant (approximately One to One-fourth pound) Cooking spray one cup of meatless pasta sauce.

Instructions

Heat the fryer to 375 ° Fahrenheit beforehand. Whisk the eggs into a small cup. Mix the seasonings, milk and wheat germ into another small cup. Trim the eggplant ends; cut the eggplant into 1/2-inch- thick slices lengthwise. Lengthwise sliced into 1/2-in slices. Strips and stripes. Dip the eggplant in milk, then coat with a mixture of cheese.

In packets, place eggplant in an air-fryer basket in a single layer on a greased tray; spritz with cooking spray—Cook for 4-5 minutes before golden brown. Turn; spritz with spray to cook—Cook for 4- minutes before golden brown. Serve right away with pasta sauce.

Check Kitchen tip: In our research, we found that cook times vary drastically between air fryers models. As a result, we gave on suggested cook times longer than standard ranges. Start checking listed for the first time and change as needed. Nutrition Details 1 serving: 135 calories, 5 g of fat (2 g of saturated fat), 68 mg of cholesterol, 577 mg of sodium, 15 g of carbohydrate (6 g of starch, 4 g of fiber). Diabetic exchanges: one grain, one fat, one-half starch.

9.2 Air fryer Chicken Tenders
Ingredients:
- Half cup of panko bread crumbs
- Half cup of potato chips,
- Half cup of broken cheese crackers
- One-fourth cup of Parmesan cheese (grated)
- Two bacon strips, crumbled and fried
- Two tea-spoons of fresh chives
- One-fourth cup of butter (melted)
- One table-spoon sour cream
- One-pound of chicken tenderloins

Instructions:
Heat the fryer to 400 ° Fahrenheit beforehand. Combine the first six ingredients into a small dish. Whisk sugar, and sour cream in another small tub. Dip the chicken in a mixture of butter and then in a mixture of crumbs, patting to make the coating adhere.

In plenty, place chicken in an air-fryer basket in a single layer on a greased tray; spritz with cooking spray. Cook, 7-8 minutes on either leg, until the coating, is golden brown and the chicken is no longer white. Serve with whipped cream and chives in turn.

9.3 Air fried Ravioli
Ingredients
- One cup of bread crumbs (cooked)
- One-fourth cup of Parmesan cheese (shredded)
- Two tea-spoons of basil (dried)
- Half cup of flour (all-purpose)
- Two big eggs, slightly beaten

- One box (Nine ounces) of beef ravioli (frozen and thawed)
- Baking spray
- Minced basil fresh (optional)
- One cup of marinara sauce (hot)

Instructions:

Heat the fryer to the 350° Fahrenheit beforehand. Parmesan cheese, basil and bread crumbs should be mixed together in a small dish. Place the eggs and flour in clean, shallow cups. Dip ravioli to coat the two sides in flour; shake off the waste. Dip in the shells, then in a paste of crumbs, tap lightly to help adhere to the coating.

In containers, place ravioli inside a greased air-fryer basket in a single layer; spritz with a spray for frying. Cook for three to four min, before golden brown. Turn it and spritz with spray to cook. Cook for three to four min, before golden brown. Instantly spray with extra Parmesan cheese and basil if required. Must serve it moist with a sauce made of marinara.

Check Kitchen tip: You may cook this dish in an electric skillet, on the stovetop or in deep fryer if you don't have an air fryer.

Nutritional Info: One piece is forty calories, one gram of fat, six milligram of cholesterol, six grams of carbohydrate, 117 milligram of sodium (one gram of fiber, one gram of starch) and two grams of protein.

9.4 Country Chicken Tenders

Active for 15 min and total 35 min with serving of four persons

Ingredients:

- One pound of chicken tender
- Three eggs,

- Half cup of seasoned breadcrumbs
- Half cup of all-purpose salt
- One and Half tea-spoon of salt
- One tea-spoon of black pepper
- Two tea-spoon of olive oil

Instructions:

Heat the fryer to 330 ° Fahrenheit beforehand. The breadcrumbs, eggs, and flour are set aside in three different containers. Season salt and pepper to the breadcrumbs. Mix the breadcrumbs with olive oil, then blend well. Put the chicken in the flour, then dip in the eggs and eventually cover the breadcrumbs with them. Push to ensure the chicken is safely and properly coated with the breadcrumbs.

Shake off some extra breading before bringing in the basket for frying. Cook half of the chicken tenders at once, cooking for 10 minutes a batch or until

golden brown

9.5 Grilled Cheese in air fryer

Active for 10 min and total of 15 min with serving for two person

Ingredients:

- Four slices
- Half cup of sharp cheddar cheese
- One-fourth cup of butter (melted)

Instructions:

Heat the fryer to 360° Fahrenheit beforehand. Layer the butter and cheese in different cups. Brush the butter over the four slices of bread on each side. Place the cheese on 2 of 4 bread slices. Bring the grilled cheese together and add to the bowl for preparation. Cook for four to five min, or until the cheese has melted golden brown.

9.6 Mini Cheeseburger Sliders

Active for 5 min and total of 15 min with serving of two persons.

Ingredients:

- Eight ounces of ground beef
- Two slices of cheddar cheese
- Two black pepper salt dinner rolls

Instructions:

Heat the fryer to 390° Fahrenheit beforehand. Divide the ground beef into two 4-ounce patties and apply salt and pepper to season. Attach the burgers to the pot, then cook for 10 minutes.

Remove from the Air fryer, cover the burgers with the cheese, and return to the Air fryer to cook for another minute.

9.7 Air fryer Taquitos

Ingredients

- Two big eggs
- Half cup of bread crumbs (dried)
- Three table-spoon of taco seasoning
- One pound of lean ground beef (90 percent lean)
- Ten corn tortillas (six inches), hot Cooking spray salsa and guacamole (optional)

Instructions

Heat the fryer to 350° Fahrenheit beforehand. Combine the taco seasoning, bacon and chocolate crumbs in a large dish. Attach the beef; blend well but gently. One-fourth cup spoon beef mixture in the center of each tortilla. Roll up tightly with toothpicks and be safe. In packets, place taquitos in air-fryer basket in a single layer on a greased tray; spritz with cooking mist.

Cook for six minutes; turn and cook for 6-7 minutes before the meat is cooked through, and the taquitos are golden brown and crispy. Throw out toothpicks before eating. Serve together with salsa and guacamole if needed.

Chapter 10: Vegetarian Heart-healthy Air fryer Recipes

More than half of heart-related deaths currently impact people below the age of 65 years, as per the AHA (American Heart Association) as well as the WHO (World Health Organization), whereas more than seventeen million people are dying every year because of heart disease. This is a shocking amount when someone realizes that eating healthy, exercising more and quitting smoking would avert eighty percent of such early deaths.

A vegetarian diet does not include cholesterol, a key factor and source of cardiovascular disease is reduced in saturated fat, that raises the risk of heart attack and stroke; and provides a variety of cardio-protective nutrients and antioxidants all without compromising on taste!

As the ADA (American Dietetic Association) has reported, an adequately vegetarian diet can aid in the prevention and treatment of these conditions, and others:

- Cardiac disease
- Cancer
- Stroke
- Alzheimer's
- High blood pressure
- Arthritis
- Diabetes
- Obesity

Using Fast Air Design, the Philips Air-fryer cooks, roasts and bakes meals wi th up to Eighty percent to hundred percent lesser oil, within half time, despite sacrificing on texture and taste! By rotating warm air all over the meal via an electrical fast speed fan, hardly any oil is needed whereas the meal stays completely pristine!

This nutritious baking option, paired with a varied vegetarian diet, will lead to weight loss and wellness, and also keep your heart safe and strong!

Following A Vegetarian Diet Saves Environment

Animal farming is the major cause of deforestation, water loss and environmental contamination, and accounts for even more greenhouse gas emissions than that of the whole transport sector.

It is a key cause of rain forest degradation, extinction of species, loss of habitat, sea-dead zones and degradation of the topsoil. The large proportion of the seed and green vegetable crops worldwide are animal feed. We may serve ten billion humans if we could use this land to produce food for straight human usage.

Each year human beings slaughter more than Sixty billion ground animals and near three trillion fish for meal. This is not only entirely needless, yet it involves often barbaric procedures like castration or dehorning despite anesthetics.

You're not only consuming a diet that's healthier for the health by consuming a vegetarian diet or reducing the meat intake, but it also means you're making a

245

strong ethical point. You remove support from industries that damage animals by withdrawing animal products from your diet. Choosing to back up the development of cruel food ensures you're not only eating with your hands but your conscience too.

10.1. Raw Broccoli

Ingredients

- One box of Nuggets Fry's Chicken-Style (Chia Chicken-Style or Fry's Rice Protein)
- One broccoli head
- Four table-spoon of seeds (slightly toasted and mixed)
- Half cup of cranberries, raisin and goji berries mix
- One mini pruned tomato (halved and washed)
- One apple (cored and diced)
- Half cup of chickpeas (cooked)

For the Mayonnaise (Vegan) Dressing

- One to two table-spoon of chickpeas (cooked)
- Two and half tea-spoon white vinegar (balsamic)

Instructions:

Put the nuggets in the air fryer at 185 ° C for 8 minutes. Remove the bucket from the fryer and raise the temperature to 200 ° C and cook for another two mins. The nuggets will be white and crispy. Slice half of the nuggets.

Cut the stiff stalk at the end of the broccoli, and vigorously wash the broccoli stem. Cut into small bits of bite form.

Place in a tub. Attach the remaining ingredients, including the nuggets, and combine them.

Attach the chickpeas, sugar, lemon juice, mustard, xylitol, and seasoning to the container of a handheld blender to make vegan mayonnaise home produced. Fill in the avocado, if any. Blitz to smooth and dense.

10.2. Chicken Style Skewers with Peanut Satay

Ingredients

- One package Fry's Chicken-Style Strips For Peanut Satay
- Four tbsp. peanut butter
- Half tea-spoon of cumin powder
- Four table-spoon of soy sauce
- Two tea-spoon of lemon juice
- One tea-spoon of garlic powder
- Half tea-spoon of ginger powder
- One tea-spoon of turmeric
- One and half table-spoon of sugar

Instructions:

Plant-based milk or tea, as needed, Scallions (or green onions), cut, for garnish Crushed peanuts, for garnish Fresh coriander, for garnishing Stir in all materials. Add a little amount of milk or water from the plant to thin out the mixture if required.

At 185 ° C, air fried the chicken-style Strips in the Air fryer for 6 minutes. * Mix Chicken-Style Strips and sauce in a pan to ensure the strips are coated with the sauce. For better results, marinate in the refrigerator for one hour (or overnight). Thread the skewers with the Chicken-Style Strings. Attach the chicken-style strips to the air fryer, then reheat with air fry for 2-3 minutes.

Spray skewers with crushed peanuts, cilantro and sliced scallions also serve sideways with leftover sauce

With the blender's head still in the bottle, continue pouring the oil in a while, raising it up and down and sideways until the oil emulsifies with the other ingredients. Seasoning flavor and change.

Add the mayonnaise and blend well into the salad tub.

10.3. Vegetarian Platter with Tzatziki and Prawn Style Pieces Recipe

Ingredients

- One Box of Fry Battered Prawn-Style Pieces
- Raw vegetables variety of your choice, sliced (e.g., carrots, sweet peas, baby corn, radishes, turnips, asparagus, etc.)

For Tzatziki

- One cup of silk tofu,
- Half cup of cubed cucumber, seeded and diced
- One-fourth tea-spoon of fresh dill
- One table-spoon fresh lemon juice
- Half tsp. fresh lemon zest
- One clove of garlic (finely minced)
- Pepper and salt to taste

Instructions:

In a food processor or blender, put together the tofu, lemon juice, lemon zest, garlic, and salt and pepper until smooth.

Combine the cucumber and dill in a small bowl with the ingredients mixed together. Refrigerate, preferably overnight, for a few hours.

Throw the Prawn-Style Broken Bits into the Airfryer tub. Cook at 185 ° C for about 8 minutes, shaking halfway to ensure even cooking until golden brown. *
Sprinkle with za'atar spice on the tzatziki and serve with Prawn-Style Bits and raw vegetables.

10.4. Curry Style Samosas

Ingredients

- Half box of Fry's Korma Curry Parts (defrosted)
- One medium potato, boiled and then mashed
- One big onion, finely chopped
- Two green chilies, finely chopped
- Half tea-spoon of mustard seeds
- Four curry leaves
- Half tea-spoon of ginger, minced
- Half tea-spoon of garlic, minced
- Half tea-spoon of turmeric powder
- Half to three-fourth tea-spoon of chili powder
- One tea-spoon of coriander
- Half tea-spoon of cumin powder
- Two table-spoon of fresh coriander, chopped
- Half tea-spoon of coriander powder
- Half tea-spoon of cumin powder

Instructions:

Add mustard seeds and leaves of curry, and let splutter. Stir in the chopped ginger, garlic and onions, and sauté until translucent.

Connect the green chilies, Korma Curry Bits, and the remaining spices. Mix well, then cook on low heat for 10-15 minutes. Connect water where necessary.

Attach the mashed potatoes to the saucepan and blend well to combine the flavors. Fry on for a few more minutes.

Attach the chopped cilantro and whisk well again. Switch off the fan, and let it cool off.

Spoon the mixture into samosa pastry in equal parts. Samosas insert. Brush the samosas with a thin slice of butter. Arrange the samosas next to each other in the Air fryer and cook at 185 ° C for fifteen minutes or until golden brown in color. Serve hot with a dip of your choice!

10.5. Mini Mushroom Pizza with Salad and Polony Recipe

Ingredients

- Four slices of Fry's sliced Sausage or Polony (chopped into cubes, cut into one-cm thickly, thawed)
- Four big mushrooms (portabella) scooped and washed
- Half bell pepper green (diced)
- One table-spoon of olive oil
- Three table-spoon of cheese vegan (shredded)
- Four table-spoon of tomato puree
- Pepper and salt as desired
- One or two pinches of Italian seasoning (dried)

Instructions:

Stretch the sauce (tomato) uniformly onto the mushrooms and cheese (vegan) and sliced bell pepper on top.

Put the mushrooms in the basket at 185 ° C and apply inside the fryer.

Remove the baking pot from the fryer after two to three mins, and put the sliced Polony or Sausage onto the pizza.

Bake at the constant temp. for another five mins. Cover with vegan cheese.

Serve with fresh vegetables and some crispy salad!

10.6. Home-made Nachos

Ingredients

- Two Crispy Crumbed Schnitzels (fried)
- 200 tortilla chips (light salted)
- One tea-spoon paprika (smoked)
- One tea-spoon ground coriander
- Half tea-spoon ground cumin
- Salt as desired
- Black olives
- One black beans tin rinsed and washed
- One bell pepper (green)
- Two avocados (mashed)
- Half red onion (minced)
- Two garlic cloves (sliced thin)
- A little coriander fresh (finely squeezed)
- One lime (juiced)
- Salsa
- Lime chunks

Instructions:

Sprinkle with smoked paprika, coriander, cumin, and salt onto the tortilla chips. Dash some olive oil over the beans.

Place the chips in the fryer at 185 ° C for two to three mins, shaking halfway through.

Place the Schnitzels into the Air fryer side by side. At 185 ° C, air fried the Schnitzels for 8 minutes until golden. * Slice them into slices, about 1 cm long, until baked.

In a cup, add the lime juice, avocado, onion, cilantro and garlic to make the guacamole—season to water.

Slice the half olives, the bell pepper and if necessary, pit them.

In a pot, put the chips and add the Schnitzel strings, black beans, guacamole, green pepper, black olives, salsa, hot sauce and lime wedges for topping.

10.7. Air fried Country Roast with Butternut and Carrot Sage Mash

Ingredients

- Fry's Soy and Quinoa Country Roast, sliced 2 cm thick
- One medium butternut, peeled and cut
- 300 g carrots, peeled and diced into small pieces (or using baby carrots)
- Olive oil (optional)
- Two cloves garlic, crushed
- Six fresh sage leaves
- Zest from 1 lemon
- Salt and pepper, to taste

Instructions:

Process Defrost the Country Roast completely until frying and detach from cardboard sleeve and pan.

Break the country roast into strips 2 cm thick. Apply a little oil using brush on each side of the slices and place side by side in the Air fryer tub, carefully, with a slight distance in each slice. Do not congest the air fryer, but to ensure reasonable heating, do smaller parts at a time.

Fry the food at 190 ° C for about 10 minutes, before the slices crispy and crisp.

251

Fill a pot with boiling water to prepare the mash, and then steam or cook the carrots and butternut for about 15 minutes, until very tender.

Meanwhile, over medium heat, apply the olive oil to a deep skillet. Stir in garlic and sauté to light color. Attach the leaves of a sage. Fry the sage for about 30 seconds, until just crisp.

Remove the sage for the absorption of excess oil and put it on paper towels.

Place the butternut and carrots in a food processor. Puree, before clean.

Add two tablespoons of the sage oil, and pump to mix a few times. To try, apply the lemon zest, salt and pepper, and mix until mixed.

Crumble sage leaves, scatter on top of the curry, and serve with slices of Country Roast.

10.8. Buddha Bowl with Chicken style Burgers and Hummus

Ingredients

- 2 Fry's Chicken-Style Burgers
- Two large sweet potatoes washed and cut into wedges
- 1 tsp. of olive oil
- 11/2 tsp. of paprika
- 1/2 tsp. of black pepper
- 1/2 tsp. of salt
- 1/2 cup of brown rice
- 1 cup of water

For the Hummus

- One can of chickpeas (keep water/brine from the bowl)
- Two cloves of garlic smashed
- 2 tbsp. of almond milk
- Juice of half a lemon
- 2 tbsp. of tahini
- 3-4 tsp. of chili powder
- 1 tsp. of cumin powder

Instructions:

Prepare the rice according to directions in the box.

Stir the sweet potatoes with a little bit of butter, paprika, salt, and pepper.

Attach the sweet potato wedges to the bowl at Air fryer. Be vigilant not to overpopulate. Cook at 200 ° C for 15 minutes, or toss halfway, until golden brown. While cooking the sweet potatoes, get started at the hummus. In a food processor, add the chickpeas, ginger, almond milk, lemon, tahini, chili powder, cumin, salt, and pepper. Where required, add extra chickpea water to the mixture. Blend until rich and smooth.

Cook the chicken-style burgers at 185 ° C for 8 minutes. * Serve with sliced cucumber, onions, rocket, avocado, and fresh coriander for the chicken-style burger, rice, and hummus.

* Reduce the cooking time if defrosted by the Chicken-style Burgers.

10.9. No meatballs with Hassel back potatoes

Ingredients

- One box Asian Spiced Burgers, thawed and rubbed
- One onion, finely chopped
- Three sprigs of fresh rosemary stalks cut and finely chopped
- Two tea-spoon of mustard Dijon
- One to two tea-spoon of dried oregano
- Two green chilies, finely chopped
- Two table-spoon of chickpea flour (or all-purpose meal)
- Two to three table-spoon of water
- One can of tinned sliced tomatoes or your choice pasta sauce
- Half cup of tomato sauce.

Instructions:

For grated burgers, add onions, rosemary, mustard, oregano, green chilies, chickpea flour (or all-purpose flour), and water. Well, mix to create a batter that can be rolled into balls.

Shape the batter into small balls using your hands, then set aside in the fridge for 5 minutes.

Place the meatballs in the air fryer, then cook at 200 ° C for 8 minutes.

Move the meatballs to a small ovenproof plate, add the tinned tomatoes (or pasta sauce) and tomato sauce, and put the plate in the Air fryer bowl. Alternatively, make a tin foil "dish" and put the meatballs and tinned tomatoes in it.

Slide the platter onto the air fryer. To warm everything through, set the temperature to 170 ° C and the timer for 5 minutes.

Prepare potatoes. If the potatoes are large, slice them in half. Cut slits about 0.5-1 cm apart and 1 cm from the base into the potatoes.

Brush the potatoes gently with olive oil (optional), then cook at 200 ° C for 15 minutes in the air fryer.

Open the air fryer and brush with the oil again (if necessary), spray with the herbs and salt, and cook for another 15 minutes or until the potatoes are cooked through.

Serve the potatoes with the meatballs and garnish with fresh rosemary and a green salad.

10.10. Mexican stuffed capsicum with meat-free mince

Ingredients

- Half box of Fry's Meat Free Mince
- Four medium-sized bell peppers

253

- Half cup of rice, cooked
- Half medium onion, chopped
- Two clove garlic, chopped
- One tea-spoon of olive oil
- One and half cups of diced tomatoes
- One tea-spoon of Worcestershire sauce
- One tea-spoon of Italian herbs
- Pepper and Salt as desired
- A little of vegan cheese, shredded or using vegan mayonnaise

Instructions:

Wash the bell peppers, add cubes of vegan cheese. Cook these for 3 minutes in hot water. Let peppers off the water and drain back.

In olive oil (or water), stir in the onion and garlic in a skillet until white.

To the onion and garlic, add the Meat Free Mince, 1 1/2 cups of tinned tomatoes, Worcestershire sauce, basil, and salt and pepper. Fry until the meat-free mince is heated through for a few minutes. * Add the thin mixture to the cooked rice and half the sliced vegan cheeses.

Stir to blend.

Stuff the mixture into the peppers. Finish with tinned tomatoes leftover and vegan cheese.

Arrange peppers piled upright in the Air fryer tub. If rough, you would need to slice the lower portion of the peppers thinly to make them stay on the plate without it tilting. Fry the air around at 200 ° C for about 10 minutes. If you want to make the peppers smoother, then cook longer.

When vegan cheese is not used, instead of until baked, finish with vegan mayonnaise.

10.11. Grilled Fruit Skewers with chocolate dip

Ingredients

- One table-spoon Fry's Cacao Kasha
- Two tea-spoon of almond milk
- One tea-spoon of maple syrup
- A pinch of vanilla powder or one-eighth tsp. of vanilla extract
- One mango washed and dipped
- One peach washed and dipped
- One pineapple dipped
- One pear dipped
- A little amount of chili flakes or cayenne pepper
- One tea-spoon of maple syrup
- Half fresh lemon, juiced coconut flakes, for serving skewers

Instructions:

Bring them together to form a paste. Coat the paste over bits of sliced fruit. Arrange the bits of fruit on skewers. In the Air fryer, place skewers next to each other for 10 minutes, at 185 ° C, before they are grilled. When they are frying, add Kasha, the Cacao, almond milk, vanilla and maple syrup in a small pot to make the chocolate sauce. Blend in until smooth. Serve the chocolate sauce with the fruit skewers, the pomegranate seeds, and the coconut flakes.

10.12. Cashew Cream with Vanilla Coconut Fruit Pie Deconstructed Recipe

Ingredients

- Three table-spoon Chia Kasha and Fry's Coffee
- One cup of strawberries
- One cup of frozen blueberries
- Two table-spoon of coconut flakes (desiccated)
- One tea-spoon of coconut oil
- Two tea-spoon of maple syrup
- A vanilla pinch
- A cinnamon pinch

For the Cashew Cream

- One cup of unsalted raw cashew (immersed in water for two hours)
- Half cup of water
- Two table-spoon of maple syrup
- One tea-spoon of vanilla extract
- A pinch of salt
- Mint for garnishing (fresh)

Instructions:

Attach the soaked cashew, sugar, maple syrup, coffee, and salt to a blender. Blend on top until rich and smooth. Switch the taste buds and desired consistency accordingly. Switch to a lined jar in the refrigerator, and ice to thicken for a few hours. We are moving on to the Kasha mix. In a cup, add the kasha, maple syrup, coconut desiccated, coconut flakes, coconut oil, vanilla, and cinnamon. The texture should be somewhat crumbly and fine.

Place the diced apple and frozen blueberries into the Air fryer in a tiny ramekin. Pour the fruit over the Kasha mixture and then bake for 10 minutes, at 185 ° C. Serve the Apple, and Blueberry Pie deconstructed with a new mint and cashew butter.

Chapter 11: Air fryer Brunch Recipes

In this chapter, you will be please to find several yummy and easy to cook air fryer brunch recipes. Try them at home. Your partner and kids are definitely going to love them. Add some colors and taste to your healthy lifestyle

11.1. Frittata Air Fryer Recipe

Mushrooms, tomatoes, and chive pull out the big guns for the garden-fresh flavor to accompany soft egg white clouds that don't require any cheese help. If you don't trust us please try it. This kind of fryer will allow a beautiful healthy way to indulge all the taste of your greasy and fried treats in a reduced manner, and this Frittata is a best "eggs-ample" (besides the pun). Instead of thinking about the "forbidden" things, all your friends love, concoct a sweet, protein-packed, and savory meal that will start your day out so you can't risk something ex here.

The Air Fryer Frittata that you'll get at just 75 calories all day is definitely the greatest bang for your Strong dollar. (If you're ever a bit uncertain about what this entails in your life, just try it once, how flexible is our favorite thing about this frittata. Eat half if you are, and get a great lunch. But, if you're after a full meal, cover half with one's favorite low-fat cheese & present it with fresh fruit, and you've got a fantastic flex meal to yourself.

Serving for two person and calories per serving are 75.

Ingredients

- One cup white of egg
- Two cups of green.
- One-fourth cup of tomatoes (sliced)
- One-fourth cup of mushrooms (sliced)
- Two table-spoon of milk (skimmed)
- Fresh chives (chopped)

Try Black pepper: 320 ° Fahrenheit preheat Air Fryer.

Instructions:

Combine all these things together in a pot.

Bake for fifteen minutes or until frittata is cooked through. Switch to a greased frying pan or to the bottom of the air fryer (after removing the accessory).

11.2 Breakfast Puffed Egg Tarts Recipe

These tarts consist of tasty bacon, melted cheese and puff pastry. Purity resides in those beautiful, yet still plain tarts. This pastry bakes each and every egg inside, creating a beautiful nest. Let me show you how these tarts are suitable for every occasion. You can not only satisfy the brunch of your visitor and can also make the tastiest refreshment on coming game night.

At this moment, you should hopefully make some realizing how adaptable these tarts are. Are you ready?

Ingredients

- Flour (all-purpose)
- One sheet of puff pastry frozen (490 grams or half of 17.3-oz), thawed
- Three-fourth cup of cheese (Monterey Jack, Gruyere or Cheddar), shredded
- Four large eggs separated
- One table-spoon of chives or parsley fresh (optional)

Instructions

Unfold the sheet of pastry on a gently flour spread area. Split to four squares.

Place two squares with an air fryer inside the box, dividing them. Air-fry ten mins or till the pastry is crispy and soft and shiny.

To do an indentation use spoon (metal one), open the bucket and push down the mid the of every rectangle. Spray three table-spoon in each indentation (45 mL) of cheese and gently break an egg into each pastry middle.

For seven to eleven mins or till fried to the perfect consistency of the eggs in fryer. Move to a wired frame over butter paper and allow to chill for five mins. If needed, spray with one-half of the parsley.

Serve hot Repeat phases two through four with the remaining cake, cheese, eggs, and parsley squares.

For this recipe, the puff pastry surface will be around nine inches of square and in case the pastry comes in a cube or your sheets have a different dimension, trim or roll it as desired into a square of nine inches.

The air fryers are getting really hot, particularly when they are heated to the full temperature. Usage of oven mitts or pads when holding the pot, and also during the bucket opening or closing.

In a small cup, gently break the egg to make it easy to putting the egg on the pastry. This recipe provide four tarts.

11.3 Vegan Brunch Hash Browns Recipe

This hash brown recipe is almost oil-free, you can use only a bit of oil brush for this air fryer recycling. Learn how to make the breakfast hash browns easy and delight your kids. This is a healthier addition to a hash brown recipe or version of the skillets. As it was originally named, Hashed Brown Potatoes is popular breakfast food in both the UK and North America. Julienned pan-fried potatoes are simple to cook. There are several variations of this currently available across continents. You'll appear to miss the golden bite of hash brown bits in the middle of the massive Bratwurst set, different kinds of sausages, and the German Breakfast's cold cuts spread. But instead, I tried the hash browns and was shocked to hear how delicious the humble potato in its crispy, gooey shape can be!

You can have the hash browns for your breakfast with scrambled eggs and toast, or use it as a side in your Sunday Brunch! I prefer the skillet version – because the original English recipe includes butter and fried sweet potatoes – but you can't feel your tongue all the time. Another hash brown recipe is the leaner and safer version of the original one made with almost no oil in an air fryer. Want to make breakfast with Hash browns?

The most important thing we have to bear in mind is to remove her starch potato and get it as lean as possible. So begin by soaking the shredded potatoes in cold water and drain the water when it starts getting cloudy. Echo this sentence once again to get rid of the extra starch.

Spray a non-stick saucepan on the bottom of the pan with a cooking spray or rub a small amount of oil and apply the potatoes over medium heat. We're not going to be boiling and browning over petrol; this stage is just about removing the rawness of the potato.

For this hash-brown recipe, we'll use cornstarch or corn flour to contribute to the crispiness. Place over a plate and cool for 20 minutes. Combine this shredded potato with a little corn flour to the season, and dust. This will also get the hash-browns created. You can miss that and get meaningless shapes placed between your hands 'palms. Air fried is what you need to do next, so eat it with your breakfast or ketchup.

Prep time 15 mins Overall time 30 mins Breakfast Cuisine: English Serves: 8 parts

Ingredients

- Four large potatoes (finely rubbed and peeled)
- Two table-spoon of corn flour
- Salt for taste
- Pepper powder for taste
- Two tea-spoon chili flakes
- One tea-spoon of garlic powder (optional)
- One teaspoon of oil (optional)

Instructions:

In a non-stick oven, heat one tablespoon of vegetable oil and sauté the shredded potatoes until cooked for three to four mins. Chill it down then place the potatoes on a plate. Slice and lightly mix the corn flour, salt, pepper, garlic, and onion powder and chili flakes. Stretch over the pan, and hold tightly with your fingertips.

Refrigerate for twenty mins heat air fryer at 180 deg. Centigrade beforehand. Slice the now cooled potato and cut into equal parts with a knife Sprinkle the air fryer wire basket with little oil Put the hash-brown bits in the basket and fry at 180 deg. Centigrade for fifteen mins Replace the basket and rotate the hash-browns at six mins so that they are evenly fried Serve hot with ketchup.

11.4 Quick Air Fryer Omelets Recipe

This omelet is tasty and prepare in eight mins, filled with cheese and fresh vegetables made in the air fryer!

It is another simple Recipe from Air Fryer! Most of our families are prone to get rushed in early morning. The pause button gets pressed several times at the last moment, the kid's grab their backpacks, and morning meal is mostly a second thought, but now it's so fast and simple that no word to skip breakfast. You may prepare your omelet ingredients at early morning or you may prepare them previous night. Well, I like to prepare in previous night.

For example, Scoop up about two table-spoon each one of the other ingredients and one-fourth cup of fresh mushrooms for an omelet of two eggs. Lots of fryers are designed with cooking pots, even if they weren't yours, this (6"x3") pan works great. For me Garden Herb is most liked for eggs. It's well balanced, in an appropriate little box.

No balancing several seasoning cans, so at dawn who has time for it? Usually Mornings are too fast and too quick. There's not enough time to make the delicious, fulfilling meal that your family needs, between getting ready for your working day and training your children for kindergarten. This omelet is sweet, flavorful, and tasty with some green onion garnish over it. The favorite part is, making it takes just eight mins, basically.

Go ahead and go outside Start making lunches for the children while ticking down the timer. There isn't any need to take care of a skillet on the burner. This omelet, baked inside fryer and stuffed with cheese and fresh vegetables is tasty and prepare in eight mins!

Ingredients

- Two eggs
- One-fourth cup of milk
- Fresh meat
- Pinch of salt
- Vegetables, sliced (mushrooms, ham, green onions and red bell pepper)
- One table-spoon of Garden Herb
- One-fourth cup of cheese (mozzarella or cheddar), shredded

Instructions

Inside a medium pot, combine the milk and eggs until well mixed. Put a table-spoon of salt over the egg mix. Attach a combination of eggs to the vegetables. Put mixture of egg onto a well-polished (6"x3") frame. Put the pan in fryer's bucket. Bake at 350 deg. Fahrenheit for eight to ten mins.

Scatter the seasoning breakfast on eggs halfway through frying, then scatter over the end of the bacon. Using a small spatula to extract the omelet from the pan sides, and transfer it to a tray. Add optional additional green onions to garnish.

11.5 Quick Air Fryer Breakfast Hand-held Bag Recipe

The rest of the families enjoy breakfast meals. Although we have morning meal for mid-day meal or late-night more often, it is also a sure success when bacons, sausages, and pancakes are included!

These morning meal bags (hand-held) are perfect for both adults and children alike. These might be eaten together or on the go as well as family. These could be filled with simply anything you like: ham, eggs, tomatoes, bacon, bell peppers, onions, or cream cheese and strawberry jam; you might even head in the opposite direction!

As for the hand-held bag, we utilized pastry sheets. However, you may also use cooled pastry crust, or can create crust on your own. Plus, you may also slice into any kind of shapes you want, but I find that rectangles fit best!

All of this begins with pastry slices. Cut them into rectangles, and continue your nice breakfast! The pastries for breakfast can be loaded up with simply anything you like. Along with a cheese swirl, we enjoy pancakes and bacon or sausage. A kid can achieve this with great ease!

Ingredients

- Five eggs
- Half cup of ham
- Half cup of bacon (cooked)
- Half cup of cheddar cheese (cooked and sliced)

Instructions:

Prepare eggs as standard scrambled eggs. When frying, in egg mix add meat if needed. Using a cutting board to arrange the pastry (puff) sheets and slice the rectangles with a knife or cookie cutter to ensure they must be all identical, and they match well together. On each of the rectangles of pastry, Spoon desired combos of egg, beef, and cheese.

Place a triangle of pastry over the mixture, then press the boundaries with a sealing fork together. When you were looking for a glossy, smooth pastry, spray with spray oil, but this is always optional. Put the morning meal bags in the bucket with air-fryer and fry for eight to ten mins at 370 deg. Fahrenheit.

Examine carefully and test every two to three mins for the required doneness

11.6 Breakfast Filled Peppers Recipe

At the beginning of a day, air-fried filled peppers are the great wit reasonable carb diet. A juicy bell pepper full of eggs that you may eat it during work every day. Simple and yummy. However, this air fryer breakfast stuffed peppers will work with any model; it doesn't matter what kind of air fryer you have. Here's how you can make stuffed peppers for the ultimate air fryer snack.

Four eggs, one halved bell pepper (seeds removed) with olive oil one tea-spoon in it to demonstrate the variations I used for fifteen mins at a lower temperature of 330 deg. Fahrenheit. In two eggs extract seeds, use whatever color you like eggs. I like two within half bell pepper, olive oil, pepper and salt with a little dry

Sirach flakes is wonderful too for a little heat If you add a little precooked beef/meat mixture, the time is likely to change marginally but not much

Course Breakfast, Cuisine American preparation time five mins, cooking time thirteen mins total time eighteen mins.

Each pepper bell is crushed into half of two shells. Sprinkle on as needed with spices. Place these onto a trivet or straight inside your alternative air fryer. Open the air fryer lid (fixed to the machine (Ninja Foodi).

Switch on the air fryer, for thirteen mins at 390 deg. Fahrenheit kindly push the button mentioned as Air Crisper (time can marginally differ based on how good the egg is finished, so it was great for us).

If you like your less brown egg and bell pepper to have on the bottom, simply add one egg to the bell pepper with air fryer set at 330 deg. Fahrenheit for fifteen mins. (As for hardened egg).

11.7 Air Fryer Bread Recipe

We tried all manner of ways to bake bread if you're without an oven and this was one of our favorites. The crust is clean and crisp, and the interior is warm and airy. Total time two hours and twenty min (including rising and cooling times) Active for 15 min and one loaf provided.

Ingredients

- Two table-spoon of butter (cooled, unsalted), plus butter for pan
- One and half tea-spoon of dry active yeast
- One and half tea-spoon of sugar
- One and half tea-spoon of salt (kosher)
- Two and two-third cups of flour (all-purpose)

Instructions

Cook's Note: While weighing flour, we spoon it into a dry measuring cup and level it off the waste. (Scoop the flour straight from the small bottle, adding to the dry baked).

Appropriate equipment: six by three-inch circular oven and 3.5-quarters of salt

Add the flour, yeast, sugar, salt, and 1 cup warm water to a stand mixer fitted with the dough hook attached. Add half cup of flour at low speed at a time with the mixer, waiting for each mixture to be completely absorbed before going more. After all the flour is added, knead over medium speed for eight minutes.

Transfer the dough to the prepared casserole, cover, and let it rise for approximately one hour until doubled in size.

Fasten the dough casserole to a 3.5-quarter fryer and set at 380 deg. Fahrenheit. Bake until the bread is dark brown for about twenty mins, and the internal temperature is 200 deg. Fahrenheit. Let the pan cool off for five mins, then turn onto a rack to cool off completely.

Chapter 12: Air fryer Meat Recipes

In this chapter, we will be mentioning some finger licking good meat recipes that can be easily cooked using an air fryer.

12.1. Air fryer Beef Stuffed bell peppers

Ingredients

- Six green bell peppers
- One pound of ground beef (Lean)
- One table-spoon of olive oil
- One-fourth cup of green onion (Diced)
- One-fourth cup of parsley (Fresh)
- Half table-spoon of ground sage
- Half table-spoon of garlic salt
- One cup of rice (Cooked)
- One cup of marinara sauce to taste
- One-fourth cup of mozzarella cheese (Shredded)

Instructions

Heat up a medium sized skillet with the ground beef and cook until well finished. Drain the beef, and go back to the oven. Add green onion, olive oil, parsley, sage and salt. Mix it well.

Add marinara and rice to the fried, then mix properly. Take every pepper off the rim, and clean the seeds. Scoop the mixture into each of the peppers and place it in the air fryer jar. (I did four in the first round, two in the second) bake at 355 Fahrenheit for ten min, open carefully and add cheese. Cook for another five min or until the pepper is mildly soft and the cheese melts.

12.2. Air fried Beef Tacos

Such tacos are so moist and crispy that you will never resort to conventional tacos again.

These are close to doing Oven Baked Tacos; but, it will give them a much more crispy taste if you are using the air fryer. They looked more like tacos style restaurant.

Ingredients

- Twelve corn taco shells (Crispy Shells, Hard)
- One pound of ground turkey
- One pack of standard (gluten free optional)
- Taco Seasoning
- Lettuce (Shredded)
- Black beans drained and rinsed
- Mexican cheese (Sliced)
- Salsa, Tomatoes, Onions

Instructions

Add the turkey in a medium sized skillet. If required rinse, bring in the taco seasoning as indicated on the box. Build cooked meat, shell taco, salad, cheese and beans.

The tacos are added to the air fryer. It is safest to cover it with foil, then coat it with non-stick cooking spray. Note-Adding foil is optional if you do line the air fryer's basket and make sure it is not fully covered to allow the air to flow even.

Bake for four min on 355 Fahrenheit or 360 Fahrenheit until its crispy. (Some Air Fryers have 355 deg. Fahrenheit as an option and others only 350 or 360 deg. Fahrenheit) Notes: We love to top up our recipes with all our ingredients, and then toast them in the air fryer. However, if you choose you can add toppings afterwards. If you do this, apply the beef to the containers, heat them up at 355 deg. Fahrenheit for the four min and then scrape and finish with your preferred toppings.

Nutritional quantities differ according to ingredients and proportions used.

This is done from the supermarket of hard shells, which you then cook up in the air fryer to make them crispy.

12.3. Air Fried Steak and Asparagus Bundles

This recipe is keto-friendly, low carb and gluten-free. Asparagus and multicolor bell peppers are packed around soaked steaks. This delicious steak meal, cooked in an air fryer, is moments away.

These packes of steak and asparagus begin by marinating a steak on the flank. It can be marinated for as little as an hour and until overnight. This means you can do step one the night before and save some precious time for yourself.

Ingredients

- Two and half pounds of Flank steak (Sliced into six pieces)
- Black pepper or Kosher salt
- Half cup of Tamari sauce
- Two cloves of garlic (Crushed)

- One pound of asparagus (Trimmed)
- Three bell peppers (sliced thinly and seeded)
- One-fourth cup of vinegar (Balsamic)
- One-third cup of beef broth
- Two table-spoon butter (Unsalted)
- Olive oil spray

Instructions

Hint the steaks with pepper and salt. Put the steaks in a large zipper topped pack. Now in a sealed pot, add the garlic and tamari sauce. Brush the steaks, so that they are completely covered. Switch to the fridge and allow to soak for a duration of one hour till overnight. Once prepared to pile, separate steaks from marinade, then put them on a slicing tray or board. Break peppers and asparagus in equal measure, then place them in the middle of each steak piece.

Wrap the steak all over the potatoes, and tightly grasp the tooth. Heat the fryer up to get ready in advance. Place the packages in the air fryer container, based on the size of your air fryer working in the packets. Mist vegetables, by an olive oil mist. Bake for Five mins at 400 deg Fahrenheit. Eliminate the steak bundles and just let rest for five mins before slicing or serving. While steak lies in pan heat mid-sized sauce pan low heat butter, balsamic vinegar and broth. Stir and blend. Keep cooking till sauce is thickened and reduced by half. Season to salt and pepper. Until dining, put sauce onto stacks of steaks.

Chapter 13: Air fryer Desserts

Desserts are an essential part of our daily routine .In this chapter, we will present different air fryer recipes of palatable desserts that will ensure a healthy lifestyle.

13.1. Peanut Butter Marshmallow Fluff Turnovers Recipe

Should be active for 15 mins and total of 20 mins with serving for 4 persons

Ingredients:

- Four sheets of filo pastry,
- Four table-spoon of peanut butter (chunky)
- Four tea-spoon of marshmallow fluff
- Two ounces of sugar
- One drop of sea salt (melted)

Instructions:

Air fryer preheats to 360 ° Fahrenheit. Brush one slice of butter with filo. Place a second filo sheet on top of the first, and spray with oil. Repeat until all four sheets have been used. Break the layers of the filo into strips of 4 (3"x 12")

Place one tablespoon of peanut butter on the underside of a filo strip, and one teaspoon of marshmallow fluff. Fold the sheet tip over the filling to form a triangle and fold twice in a zigzag way until the filling is fully wrapped.

To close the ends of the turnover use a brush of butter. Place the turnovers in the kitchen basket and cook until golden brown and puffy for three to five mins. For a sweet and salty mix finish with a brush of sea salt.

13.2. Vanilla Soufflé Recipe

Should be active for 20 min and total for 1 hour 30 mins with serving for 4 persons

Ingredients

- One-fourth cup of flour (all-purpose)
- One-fourth cup of butter
- One cup of milk (whole)
- One-fourth cup of sugar
- Two tea-spoon of vanilla extract
- One vanilla bean
- Five whites of egg
- Four yolks of egg

- One ounce of sugar
- One tartar cream

Instructions:

1. Blend the butter and flour till a shape like paste is made. Warm the milk in a saucepan, then add the sugar. Place the bean on top and carry it to the boil. To the boiling milk, add butter and flour blend. Beat aggressively with a comb of wire to make sure there should be no bulges. Stir it for a few minutes before the mixture thickens. Take off the sun, remove the bean and let it chill in bath of ice for ten mins.

2. Take soufflé dishes or six ramekins (3-ounce) whilst the blend is cooling. Butter brush, and dust with a teaspoon of sugar. Vigorously whip the vanilla extract and yolks of egg in another mixing pot, then blend it with mixture of milk.

3. Now, whip the whites of egg, tartar sugar and milk separately until the egg whites develop medium-firm peaks Enfold the whites of egg into the base of the soufflé and spill over the dishes for baking purpose and clean the tops off.

4. Air fryer preheat till 330 ° Fahrenheit. In the cooking pot, put 2 or 3 dishes of soufflé, and cook each batch for 12 to 15 mins. Present with sugar in powdered form over the soufflé with the hand of chocolate sauce.

13.3. Strawberry and Nutella stuffed Wontons Recipe

Ingredients

- 12 Wonton wrappers
- One-fourth cup finely chopped
- One-fourth cup of strawberries
- Two table-spoon of Nutella
- One table-spoon of butter (melted)
- One-fourth cup of strong whipping cream
- Powdered sugar for dusting

Instructions:

Spread Nutella about half tea-spoon into the middle, then add a few chopped strawberries to the top. Paste the water to the bottom of the wrapping. Take one corner and fold it to form a triangle diagonally. Push down to the phone. Undo for wontons left over

Brush the fry basket with melted butter then add some wontons. Set the temperature and time within 5 mins to 350 F degrees. When time is up, cut the wontons gently using tongs. Cook for another one to three mins, if they're not golden enough and crispy enough. Repeat before they prepare all the wontons.

Alternatively, heat up the remaining one-fourth cup Nutella and heavy cream in a medium saucepan until thick and creamy, sometimes whisking.

Lightly brush with powdered sugar, then cut with sauce to eat wontons. Serve with dipping sauce leftover.

13.4. Mini Cheesecakes Recipe

<u>Ingredients</u>

- Half cup of graham cracker crumbs
- Two table-spoons butter (unsalted, melted)
- 12 ounces of cream cheese (full-fat, diluted)
- Two-third cup of granulated sugar
- One egg
- Half table-spoon of vanilla extract
- Whipped cream and fresh fruit

<u>Instructions:</u>

In a small bowl, blend with the crumbs and melted butter.

Push four six-ounce ramekins back onto the bottom.

Beat thoroughly the cream cheese and sugar in a large mixing cup until smooth and moist, around two to three mins. Pour in the egg and pour for another minute or before put in. Beat them in coffee.

Divide the batter among the ramekins and tightly seal in foil. Make pinholes to ventilate through the surface of the foil.

In the fry bucket position, two ramekins. The remaining two ramekins refrigerate. Set the temperature and time for 25 mins to 310 degrees, or until the tops become solid to the touch when shook with a gentle jiggle. Cover thoroughly with tongs. Continue on two ramekins left over.

Then refrigerate full for at least 4 hours, or overnight.

Serve with whipped fruit and milk.

13.5. Monkey Bread Recipe

Ingredients

- Two ounces of canned biscuits
- Two tea-spoons of unsalted butter
- One-fourth cup of milk
- One-fourth cup of brown sugar
- One-fourth cup of cane sugar
- Half tea-spoon of ground cinnamon

Instructions:

In a shallow saucepan, mix butter and milk and simmer over medium heat until the butter is melted and put away.

The palm sugar, cane sugar, and cinnamon blend together in a small pot.

Break the cookies into pieces, and roll them into circles. Dip the ball of dough into the combination of butter/milk and then roll in the sugar with cinnamon.

Then put the sugar-coated dough either in a mini pan (4 inches in diameter or 3 cup capacity) or in a 6-inch springform pan with a piece of rolled aluminum foil in the middle. Be sure to create an even single layer at the bottom and build up if necessary from there.

Place the cake mold in the air fryer basket and push the cake temperature to 320 degrees F. Set the time for thirty minutes, after 10 minutes, stop the air fryer and put a circle of aluminum foil very carefully on top of the cake pan to avoid burning of the monkey bread-please make sure the foil does not contact the top of the cooking item.

Put back in the air fryer and start frying for another 20 minutes at 320 degrees, the top is going to be really crispy, and you want to make sure the dough is fried through in the middle.

Let the cake pan cool off the basket for about 10-15 minutes before removing it. To eat: Place a plate over the cake pan and turn over easily, remove the cake pan, and eat moist.

13.6. Blueberry Turnovers Recipe

Ingredients

- Half cup of blueberries (fresh)
- One-fourth cup of white granulated sugar
- Two tea-spoon of cornstarch
- Half table-spoon of ground cinnamon (Zest)
- One lemon juice
- Package of puff pastry (17 oz.), thawed
- One egg plus one table-spoon of water for egg wash
- Half cup of sugar in rough.

Instructions:

The blueberries, butter, cornstarch, lemon juice, zest, and cinnamon are mixed in a medium dish.

Place onto the work surface on a sheet of puff pastry and cut into four even squares. Place one to two spoons full of blueberry filling in the middle of a square and fold into a rectangle, press down to close the edges. Continue with three squares left and a second layer of puff pastry.

Mix the egg wash and spray over the puff pastry, then cover the sides of the pastry again with the tines of the fork.

Cut a small slice on top of each pastry using a paring knife, and then dust in the raw with sugar.

Spray the air fryer with olive oil spray, then put two turnovers in the basket at a time, move the remaining turnovers to a tray and hold cooled. Click the bake/dessert position at 320 degrees and raising the time to 15 minutes or until a rich golden brown puff pastry is available.

Remove the cooked turnovers and repeat the process with the others, making sure that the basket is sprayed in between each pan.

Serve dry or at room temperature.

13.7. Oatmeal Chocolate Chip Cookies with Air Fryer

No need to preheat the oven for those delights of chocolate chips! Whip up a fresh batch of air fryer cookies for a ready in minutes treat.

This dish is given to us by Diane Neth, who belong to Menno (South Dakota). This dish provide us with around six dozen tiny cookies.

Ingredients

- One cup of butter
- Three-fourth cup of sugar
- Three-fourth cup of brown sugar (powdered)
- Two big eggs
- One tea-spoon of vanilla extract
- Three cups of oats (fast-cooking)
- One and half cup of flour (all-purpose)
- One box of vanilla (3.4 ounces) instant pudding mix
- One tea-spoon of baking soda
- One tea-spoon of salt
- Two cups of chocolate chips (semi-sweet)
- One cup of almonds (diced), optional

Instructions:

Step 1: Preheat the fryer Attach foil to the fryer pot.

Stage 2: Combine the dough with the sugar and butter in a big tub, until soft and fluffy—place in Coffee and Bacon. Combine the rice, dry pudding mixture, baking soda, salt and flour into a separate dish. Slowly start to add creamy mix to the dry mixture and blend properly. Cover in the nuts and chocolate chips.

Phase 3: Fried the Surface!

Shape dough into balls by tablespoon-full. Slightly flatten every ball with spoon back and put the balls of cookie dough two inches away from each other on the fryer bucket lined with foil. The cookies are fried by air for at least five to eight mints or till light brown. Move the cookies gently to wire frames to chill down. Continue with extra bread. Love a treat with a big glass full of milk or two!

13.8. Chocolate Soufflé Recipe

And if you've never tried making a soufflé, making every time is a really simple recipe – you'll be surprised how easy it's to create.

By using air, fryer one can make this simple chocolate soufflé for a perfect Valentine's Day dinner, for a celebration or for some other event.

The list of ingredients is short. Of course, along with a few ramekins, you would need milk, cheese, cocoa, vanilla extract, the usual flour, and sugar.

Training Time: ca. 15 minutes Cook Time: 14 minutes Total Time: 35-45 min Yield: 2 servings Category: Dessert Cuisine: American

Ingredients

- Three ounces of chocolate (semi-sweet, sliced)
- One-fourth cup of butter
- Two eggs (divided)
- Three tea-spoons of sugar
- Half tea-spoon of vanilla extract (pure)
- Two tea-spoons of flour (all-purpose)
- Sugar (Powdered) for garnishing
- Cream (whipped) for coating (optional)

Instructions:

When you talk of soufflé, you know you're going to need special tools, it might take a lot of time to make it, or it might be rough. Sure, don't worry, it's pretty easy, and it doesn't take as long as you'd imagine. Start by

(1) Rubbing butter in ramekins and coating with sugar;

(2) Melting chocolate and butter together and set aside;

(3) Beating the egg yolks and beating in vanilla and sugar;

(4) Mixing the chocolate-butter mixture with the egg yolks;

(5) Stirring in the flour and blending.

(6) Heat the air fryer beforehand and whip the egg whites to soft peaks to almost 'stand-alone; (7) gently fold one-third of the egg whites into the chocolate mixture until the whites and chocolate mixture are blended together.

Give it a shot, which isn't that hard now.

This is better than you should have imagined.

Here's the recipe you can hold for making chocolate soufflé simple for two Ingredients Butter and two 6-ounce sugar ramekins. (Milk the ramekins and then apply the sugar to the milk, tossing it in a ramekin and removing the excess.) let the chocolate and butter melt together in a double boiler – set aside.

In a different tub, the egg yolks were pounding vigorously. Attach the sugar and vanilla extract and beat well again. Drizzle with butter and cookies, and blend well.

Mix in the rice, until there are no lumps.

Then preheat the air fryer for 330F. Gently fold 1/3 of the whipped egg whites into the chocolate mixture, then fold gently in the remaining egg whites until the chocolate mixture is mixed with all the whites.

Move the batter cautiously over to the buttered ramekins, leaving around 1/2-inch above. Put the ramekins in the air fryer and air-fry for 14 min. The soufflés would have beautifully gotten up and brown on top. (Don't panic if the top becomes a little dark – you'll cover it with powdered sugar in the next step.) Garnish it with powdered sugar and serve immediately.

Present a very moist soufflé and bring on the whipped cream overlay.

Conclusion

The air fryer can be called as a cooking device that cooks using the convection process, by rotating heated air flowing all over the meal. The convection oven is a downsized variant. At high rpm, a rotating fan revolve the heated air all over the meal, frying the meal and creating a crispy coating by two kinds of browning reactions. Caramelization, and a reaction from Maillard.

Conventional frying techniques cause the Maillard aftermath by immersing the foods entirely in heated oil, that reaches much higher degree of temperature than hot water. This type of fryer also works by covering the required food inside a slim layer of oil whereas air flows heated to 392 ° F. In doing so the appliance will utilize seventy percent to eighty percent fewer oil rather than conventional deep-frying brown foods.

Air fried food's flavor and feel are similar to the performance related to deep frying as juicy inside, crispy outside. You only have to utilize a very small volume of oil, however, if any (It depends on what you are preparing).

These kinds of appliances are very quick, and may be utilize to warm frozen meals or prepare all kinds of fresh produce such as chicken, beef, salmon, vegetables and pork chops before you understand how they work. Some meats don't need additional oil as they are already so tasty: simply sprinkle meal with salt as well as the spices and herbs you want. You should stick to the dry toppings — fewer humidity contributes to more crisp results. Wait until the last few minutes of cooking, whether you choose to marinade meats with a honey or BBQ sauce.

Light meat cuts, or foods containing minimal to no fat, need browning oil and crisping up. Until cooking, spray the pork chops and chicken breasts boneless with a little grease. Because of its low smoke level, canola oil or vegetable oil is generally preferred, which means air fryer can sustain the high temperature. Until air fried, vegetables must also be put in oil. we advise spraying the veggies with salt, but use far less than you're like to: that crisp, air cooked bits hold a great deal of taste. We enjoy broccoli florets frying milk, sprouts in Brussels, and halves of baby potatoes.

So yeah, contrary to deep-frying, air drying is certainly a better option if you agree to use just 1-2 tablespoons of seasoning oil, and rather than anything else, you stick to air-frying vegetables. Any gadget that lets you and your family update your veggie game is key to weight loss, chronic disease risk reduction, and long-term health enhancement as we age. Remember how many people you are catering for while looking for such an appliance (Air Fryer) as smallest sized air fryers with the capacity of 1.2-liters can be suitable for 1 to 2 individuals, whereas the medium size with the capacity of 3 to 4 liters can be suitable for 2 to 3 individuals and the biggest with the capacity of 6 or more liters can be suitable for 4 to 6 individuals. Rather than shelves we recommend air fryers including buckets as they prepare more equally.

Printed in Great Britain
by Amazon

00158